Leadership Studies
GCD

D0377175

Values Shift: A Guide to Personal and Organizational Transformation

Typography and Page Layout: Nicholas J. Vitale

Editing: Elaine Brett
Proofreading: Catherine Linberg
Indexing: Elaine Brett

Resource Publications
A division of Wipf and Stock Publishers
199 W 8th Ave, Suite 3
Eugene, OR 97401

Values Shift
A Guide to Personal and Organizational Transformation
By Hall, Brian P.
Copyright©1994 by Hall, Brian P.
ISBN: 1-59752-690-8
Publication date 5/12/2006
Previously published by Twin Lights Publishing, 1994

Values Shift

A Guide to Personal
and Organizational Transformation

Brian P. Hall

Wipf & Stock
PUBLISHERS
Eugene, Oregon

Contents

Preface

This book is the result of almost 30 years of research into the relationship of values to human and organizational development. The work began in 1965 with my first overseas assignment, in Central America, with the Anglican Church of Canada. It was there that I met and was influenced by Paulo Freire, Ivan Illich, and Erich Fromm. Their main impact was to make me conscious of the dynamic relationship between language and cultural, societal, and institutional development. I suppose, more than anything, they forced me to rethink all my presuppositions about the nature of human development, which until that time had been predominantly psychoanalytical in nature.

My experience in Central America not only forced me to rethink my view of the world, but it also posed dynamic questions about the nature of human values. Are they really self-chosen, as I had always assumed, or are they imposed upon us by the institutions we live in and through?

I struggled to discover a viable definition of values that could be pinpointed in human behavior. Naturally I was influenced by the values clarification movement, so popular in the 1960s. This resulted in three books titled *Value Clarification as Learning Process,* published by Paulist Press in 1973. The purpose of the book was to illustrate in a practical way the relationship between human development and values, particularly from an existential point of view.

After finishing my doctoral studies in 1969, I became preoccupied with the historical and developmental aspects of reality. I had grown up in Saint Albans, England, surrounded by the ruins of ancient Roman occupations and medieval cathedrals, and this had left me with memories and a consciousness of history that could not be ignored. New questions arose. Am I simply the product of a developmental history—the shadow of past generations, bound by the influence of culture and family ties?

Additionally, during this period I engaged in psychoanalytic training, half of which was done in Costa Rica in Spanish with a wonderful psychiatrist by the name of Alfredo Sotela. This experience heightened my awareness of languages, and of the fact that language is the repository of key words that I now call values—words that transcend language and occur in every person's meaning system, no matter what their cultural background is.

In 1976 I published another book called *The Development of Consciousness: A Confluent Theory of Values*. It reflected on a number of theories of human development, showing how the works of Maslow, Kohlberg, Erikson, and others coincided with the development of values and consciousness in the human being. As far as I am aware, this was the first time someone had tried to design a schema, no matter how inadequate, of how values can be specifically identified and related to the individual's stages of maturity.

As I reflect back on this period, I realize that it broke open a whole new perspective on what values really were. I was working with a cross-disciplinary team. But the person who influenced me most was Benjamin Tonna, a Maltese sociologist. We soon noticed that not only did certain values become priorities at different stages of maturity, but they also reflected various stages of faith development. This has now been well stated by James Fowler in a book titled *Stages of Faith*. Further, we realized that the values pointed to stages of leadership development in executives, and were reflected in the management design of different administrative frameworks.

With the help of Helen Thompson, Anthony D'Souza, and Benjamin Tonna, a series of publications resulted. *Developing Leadership by Stages* was published by Manohar in India in 1979. *God's Plans for Us* and *Leadership Through Values* were published in the U.S. in 1980, and *Shepherds and Lovers* in 1982.

At this juncture in the journey we had a lot of information and an interesting perspective on values and human development. The material we had developed was primarily an educational tool that gave people a fresh perspective, and often led to problem solving in counseling, in small administrative settings, and in educational curriculum design.

The problem was that we had gathered a great deal of information, but did not know how to make it practical. In 1979 I moved to Santa

Clara University as a professor in the Graduate Division of Counseling Psychology and Education. Two major changes occurred for me at this point: an increase in cross-disciplinary interaction, and the introduction of computer technology. Suddenly, the last 15 years of work took on an entirely new perspective.

My friend and research associate Benjamin Tonna was the critical link. As director for seven years of SEDOS, an international documentation center in Rome, Benjamin had written a book called *Gospel for the Cities.* He had carefully gathered comparative information on first- and third-world cities for some 20 years.

Together Tonna and I worked with various research associates in the United States and Europe—work that continues until the present time. Much of this book is based on that research. When we began our work, we felt that we were progressing and making important discoveries, but we still did not have a way to identify and measure values in a practical manner. What we have subsequently accomplished is to discover a way to assess and measure values in individuals, groups, and organizations.

We began to investigate the possibility of designing a computer program that would translate all the complexity of an individual's values into a profile that would give practical and concrete feedback. With the aid of Dr. Irving Yabroff, a computer engineer and programmer, we set about the task. After four years of research and considerable trial and error, we developed an instrument named the Hall-Tonna Inventory, which was originally published by Behaviordyne in Palo Alto, California.

The instrument is a questionnaire that documents and measures a given individual's values. Each question relates to a different value, so that an individual unfamiliar with the values is, in fact, documenting what his or her values are, and in what priority they are ordered. Between 1984 and 1987, reliability and validity studies were carried out to standardize the list of values. The studies were lead by Dr. Oren Harari at the University of San Francisco.

Once the individual's values were documented, we were then able develop profiles that provided almost unlimited information about the patterns that his or her specific values fell into. A significant contribution to the development of the instrumentation was made by Barbara Ledig, who for eight years continued to refine the instrumentation. We administered about 1,500 of these questionnaires to people in several different cultures, and from different class structures, professions, and disciplines.

We found that what we had was a method for examining the reality of human development, and that this methodology was, in turn, giving us new and often contradictory information. The instrument began to inform us of theoretical mistakes in our assumptions about the human condition. In other words, we had discovered a research method that was enabling us to discover new insights about human and organizational development.

The interest in organizational development came about when we wrote a computer program that compiled several individual profiles from a group of people to create a composite profile. What was amazing was that the group profile, termed the HT-Group, gave us information not previously available. A large international organization then invited us to attempt to do a similar analysis, not of individuals or a group, but of their central management documents. We did this by developing a scanning program that identified values in documents by analyzing the occurrence and repetition of key words. We again found ourselves confronted with new and unexpected information and insights.

In the final analysis, we discovered that after years of research about values, we were not dealing with value theory only, but with a system that tells us about the relationship between quality information and human and organizational development. Values are basically a quality information system that when understood tell about what drives human beings and organizations and causes them to be exceptional. It also informed us about the relationship between human, spiritual, and organizational development.

This book is about these research findings, and the results of using the new values technology to work with thousands of individuals and many organizations in the area of human and organizational development over the last ten years. A number of people have made important contributions, including Shirley McCune of MCREL Laboratories in Denver, John Kroening of Values Technology, Charles Joiner in Dayton, and my son, Martin Hall.

Part I of this book will examine what values are and how values shape consciousness. Part II will explore values and personal transformation in the context of leadership and organizational settings.

Part I

How Values Shape Consciousness

1

Values Shift

The core of culture is formed by values.
Geert Hofstede, *Cultures and Organizations*

Frederick came to me for mentoring, saying that he was very confused about his life and wanted to review his values. I had him fill out a values inventory, an instrument that analyzes a person's values and identifies the 12 to 15 core values that are most important in his or her life. Each of us has core values that give meaning to our lives, values that we feel are important in the workplace and that we need to survive on a daily basis.

In the first session I learned that he was an executive, superintendent of a medium-sized midwestern school system. He was 55 years of age, had been married for 27 years and had three children. His children were now adults who had all recently left home and started college. His wife had left him a year earlier and wanted a divorce. She was pursuing her own education by getting the degree and career she had always wanted.

"I have a doctoral degree," Frederick said. "I think she always blamed me because she couldn't finish her education when we got married. She had only one year left to complete her bachelor's degree, but child-rearing put an end to that. Besides, I was so busy in whatever school district I was working in that she was home-bound and didn't have much time for herself."

For the first 20 years of their marriage, everything had seemed okay at home and work. "But now I feel such a miserable failure at everything!" I asked him to explain what was going on at work. He suddenly got angry. "Are you serious? Kids carry guns to school. We've got drug problems, discipline problems, parent problems, more dropouts, and fewer students making it to college."

"How is it different now from how it was in the past?"

He looked at me sadly. "You know, years ago when there was a discipline problem, the kid was sent home. We were convinced that some kids were good learners and others weren't. And we are also more ethnically diverse now, not just black kids but Mexicans and Asians of all different language groups. At first I thought it was a challenge, but now I just can't handle it."

We talked for several sessions, and Frederick began to see that he had two issues: one was his personal foundation issue of loneliness and belonging, and the other involved what was going on at his job. In fact, his foundation issues of loss were weighing him down so much that he could not see any future for himself or for schools. All he could see was failure.

Slowly he began to separate out the pieces. One day he came to my office and said with a smile, "I have had a dream. Can my dreams be about my values?" I assured him that values energize us through the stories we tell, and that our stories sometimes manifest themselves as dreams. Here is Frederick's dream story.

The Healer

In my dream I was standing in a large church and a gentleman appeared before me. He called himself the Healer. He seemed to be Chinese, although I could not see his face clearly because it was dark.

"Sir," I said, "I have come for the black poison, which I understand you have."

"Yes, I do," replied the Healer. "But why do you want it? For it kills not only the body but also the soul!"

"Because," I replied, "I am divorced and have let my wife and children down, and I have failed miserably at my job. I am a failure as an educator."

The Healer smiled. "Here," he said, handing me the vial of black liquid. "You can take it, but only if you agree to one condition."

"Of course I will agree," I said. "What is the condition?"

He pointed out the window of the church, and I saw vast rolling hills and a mountain capped with snow in the distance. "Somewhere out there is the Saint. You must find him. Once you have done that, drink the black poison at your leisure." With that he disappeared.

Next I found myself with mules and servants trekking all over the mountains, going to little villages asking where I could find the Saint. The Saint apparently flew a little one-engine airplane and visited all the villages, healing people, fixing their houses, solving all sorts of problems, and then flying on just before I got to where he or she was supposed to be.

Finally, an old lady in a village halfway up the mountain I had seen from the church told me that the Saint had been missing for several weeks and that they were afraid the Saint's plane had crashed on the other side of the mountain. She told me to go over the mountain and find the Shepherd, because he was wise and would know where I could find what I was looking for. So off I went, marching into blizzards and snow.

Then one very foggy day as I was walking over the crest of a large slope, I heard some sheep bleating and there, sitting in front of an inviting fire, was the Shepherd, drinking coffee. He saw me and asked me to sit down. I sat down in front of him. He was very old and wore a fur-lined leather helmet that was molded to the top of his head as if it had grown there. It came down the side of his face, covering his ears and buttoning under his bearded chin.

"I'm looking for the Saint. Can you help me?" I asked.

"Maybe, when this darned weather clears." he replied. I nodded with thanks and took some of his coffee.

He began to talk. "Let me tell you about the Saint. He is a real good friend of mine." I told him I would like to hear about the Saint.

The Shepherd told me that the Saint's life had been very tragic. He had killed a child in a car accident, he had been married three times, and his children disapproved of him. He had been fired from most jobs that he had held.

I was very upset at what he was saying. Looking at the ground, I said, "Why do they call him the Saint if he failed in so many things?" When I looked up, the Shepherd had gone and I was left with the fire and dense fog as well.

Then the fog cleared. About a hundred yards away was the wreck of the Saint's airplane. There was a skeleton in the pilot's seat, and it had a leather hat on its head—the same one that the Shepherd had been wearing!

Values Shift

The dream signified an enormous emotional shift in Frederick. "Do you know what I learned?" he said. "I'm not a failure at all; I am a learner in

FIGURE 1-1. Frederick's Personal Values

When We Began	A Year Later
Work/Labor	Family/Belonging
Security	Belief/Philosophy
Family/Belonging	Sharing/Listening/Trust
Prestige/Image	Limitation/Acceptance
Social Affirmation	Limitation/Celebration

the very difficult school of life. And do you know what? I've got a lot to offer those kids and a lot of mistakes to draw on."

Frederick had begun to understand the paradox of success and failure—he saw that he was both the Saint and the Shepherd. I've now seen a similar shift in consciousness in the more than a hundred executives I have mentored. It is really a change in world view or mind set, or to put it another way, a paradigm shift. For Frederick, this shift came after a year of mentoring, at which point Frederick had a totally different attitude toward his work and everything he was doing. He was behaving differently because his changed view of reality had shifted his priorities.

I knew that this change had come about because of a shift in Frederick's values. To understand this shift, we first looked at his value priorities in his personal life—what was personally meaningful to him outside the work setting. Figure 1-1 illustrates his top five priority values when we began and a year later.

The definitions of these values are in Appendix A, but I think the meaning is self-evident. Looking at the first column, Frederick explained that this was how he had been up to the time he was divorced. Work always came before family. He did not feel safe when he was not working. The evenings were filled with board or parent meetings. He was very concerned about how others, particularly his constituents, saw him. Prestige—being politically correct, affirmed, and appreciated by school administrators and teachers—was very important to him.

The second column of Figure 1-1 describes his more recent behavior. Frederick explained it this way: "I see things differently. I feel really bad about the life I gave Julia, my former wife. Basically, my philosophy—the way I see things—has changed radically, both at home and at work. I now feel that relationships must come first; otherwise I'm no good to anyone. Accepting my limitations is recognizing that I had my priorities wrong for a long time, and celebrating them means I am doing things differently with my kids and the woman I plan to marry."

FIGURE 1-2. Frederick's Work-Related Values

When We Began	A Year Later
Education/Certification	Knowledge/Insight
Administration/Control	Service/Vocation
Efficiency/Planning	Sharing/Listening/Trust
Tradition	Interdependence
Independence	Synergy

We then began the second part of the mentoring process: designing the values he would be proud to see as part of his professional work environment—in his case, the administrative offices of the superintendent of schools. We made the assumption that his personal values were the foundation for what he does in the workplace—they don't disappear when he goes to work. Figure 1-2 summarizes Frederick's work-related values.

He explained that in the past Education as Certification had meant numbers: how many student absentee days he had in the district, whether the SAT scores went up or down, how many dropouts there were, and how many students went to prestigious colleges and universities. Things were done the way he had always done them (Administration/Control and Efficiency/Planning). Tradition to him implied the best schools and a classical education, and the proof of success was in the number of graduates who went to the "right" schools.

"I was a driven person," he said. "For the past ten years I had done this stuff without ever reflecting on the changing demographics and reality in my district. I didn't listen; I just did it." Finally, his style was to work independently, especially when it came to putting out fires. That was his responsibility, especially if it affected how he looked in public.

Column 2 shows how Frederick now views his values. He put it this way: "I just see things differently now, and I'm doing things differently than I did before. The bottom line is that I am recovering my vocation as a teacher, not only as a teacher, but as a *good* teacher, and that means being a learner. Although what I do as superintendent is administration, my real vocation is teaching. That's why I put Knowledge as Insight, rather than Education as numbers, as number one—not only for the students, but for me, too."

What really impressed me was that Frederick said that all the problems of the district, which had been a pain and overwhelming him a year ago, were now fun. "Why?" I asked.

FIGURE 1-3. The Values Shift Process

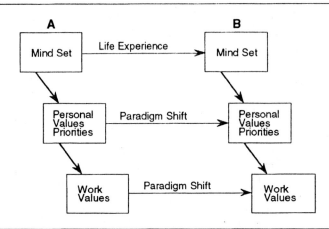

"Because before they were fires I had to put out. Now I talk to the students and ask why they carry guns—I feel their pain," he said. " I never appreciated Mexican-American kids; they were always lazy bums to me. Then I found out they knew more about family than I did.

"They complained about the food in the cafeteria. A year ago I would have yelled at them. This time I formed a committee of the kids and had them okay everything about the food on Wednesdays—financial planning, getting the menu, cleaning up, everything. They loved it. I loved it."

He told me that being interdependent and delegating through collaboration was the key to everything he did now. Synergy is having the group come up with answers. He noted that they did not always solve the problem, but at least now they were all in it together.

Values Shift, Mind Set, and Paradigm Shifts

What Frederick experienced with his values is beginning to happen to a lot of executives, and increasingly this shift in values is what is expected of leadership. Naturally, there is a great lag between what we expect and how people behave. Figure 1-3 illustrates what happens in a Values Shift like the one Frederick experienced.

In the boxes in column A we see that a particular world view was reflected in Frederick's personal values, and as the way he behaved with his family at home. At work this mind set becomes a different set of values. He was impersonal and basically very work-oriented in both places.

Then his life experience changes (column B). We might conclude that his wife got fed up and left him, so he changed his behavior. But that would be too simplistic, since his behavior, which is a result of his values, changed at work and home. We say that he had a paradigm shift: that is, he began to view the world—reality if you like—quite differently.

At a personal level, his mind set was different. Relationships were now a priority that gave quality to his life at home or at work. At home he was ready to build on past mistakes, to share and listen more; at work this was translated into a collaborative management style that is quite different and much more flexible and adaptable than before. He did not become this way because of therapy, skills training, or some phenomenal leadership program, but because of a shift in consciousness: a Values Shift. *Values Shift* is a study of this process and what causes this amazing transformation.

Values in Perspective

Frederick's experience anticipates the bigger picture of what is going on in organizations and society as a whole. His earlier experience was one of a fragmented reality in which work, home, and children were all separate. He ran his office in a clear, ordered, hierarchical manner, with everything in its place, everyone with an appropriate role and task. This is the mind set that sees the universe as a mechanical entity like a clock. The sixteenth century English physicist Isaac Newton was responsible for popularizing this view of human reality. Newtonian physics has dominated our way of thinking ever since. Margaret Wheatley (1992) puts it this way:

> It is interesting to note just how Newtonian most organizations are. The machine image of the spheres was captured by organizations in an emphasis on structure and parts. Responsibilities have been organized into functions. People have been organized into roles. Page after page of organizational charts depict the workings of a machine: the number of pieces, what fits where, who the big pieces are.
>
> This reduction into parts and the proliferation of separations has characterized not just organizations, but everything in the world during the past three hundred years. Knowledge was broken into disciplines and subjects, engineering became a prized science, and people were fragmented—counseled to use different parts of themselves in different settings. (p. 27)

This world view has been allowed society to organize and move forward, but it is effective only up to a certain point. This way of doing things does not adequately address the complexity of the new world into which Frederick was entering. His new view stressed a priority on relationships or connectedness as the central new way of doing things. This showed up in his value of Interdependence. But he also had a renewed emphasis on learning—celebrating one's limitations and being open to new ideas that do not fit the old paradigms.

The changes we are seeing in corporations today began with the three great revolutions: the French and American political revolutions at the end of the eighteenth century, and the Industrial Revolution in the nineteenth century. The Industrial Revolution—the revolution of technology that was built upon Newton's ideas—taught us efficiency, synchronization, centralization, and all we know about management and bureaucracy until the middle of the present century.

It also introduced a note of global optimism into our world view: it convinced us that all people could have wealth and power, that all problems of suffering and poverty could be solved by science. Out of this viewpoint grew our modern educational system and all its disciplines, from chemistry to medicine and the humanities, from sociology to psychology, all of which hardly existed before the nineteenth and early twentieth centuries.

The French and American political revolutions introduced the idea of individual freedom and the possibility of the value of independence and human dignity. These values gave us a new view of political science and humanity as a whole. In the United States, the first definitive position on women's rights was taken in 1848 under the leadership of Elizabeth Cady Stanton and Susan B. Anthony, who wrote and submitted in 1878 a proposed right-to-vote amendment to the Constitution, which finally passed generations later in 1921.

The new reality that anticipated the Values Shift we have been addressing came in the 1920s with Einstein's theory of relativity. Freud has also been an important influencer in this Values Shift. Of course there have been many important voices, but these two symbolize a paradigm shift in the way we view reality.

Einstein ushered in the "new" physics, which went far beyond his personal contribution about the relativity of time. Freud introduced a new in-depth notion about the human condition and a whole new psychology about the unconscious and about the uniqueness of the human being. We are now faced with a world that is based on a new and very different set of assumptions. Two of these important new assumptions have to do with connectedness and the uniqueness of individual human beings.

Connectedness.   In the late twentieth century, we see that all parts of our daily experience of living are connected to a larger whole. All atoms are connected to all other atoms. The physicist W. Heisenberger put it this way:

> The world thus appears as a complicated tissue of events, in which connections of different kinds alternate or overlap or combine and thereby determine the texture of the whole. (Capra, 1982, p. 81)

In the domain of communications we now have the possibility of everyone being connected through local and worldwide computer networks and electronic mail systems, fiber optics, and interactive television. Science originally addressed the world in terms of external events, where the key to discovery was the measurement of objective events such as a ray of light bending as it passed the sun. But the more physicists studied the so-called external reality, the more internal it became, so that the results observed by a scientist altered depending upon his or her point of view!

Our understanding of connectedness deepens when we look at the second assumption.

The Uniqueness of Individuals. In contemporary society, we believe that human beings are both unique and complex. This suggests that each person has something unique to contribute to society out of his or her own heritage. It is this assumption of human uniqueness that connects the disciplines of psychology and the social sciences to religion, allowing us to see this uniqueness as emerging from the internal universe of a human being, a vast unconscious realm. Jung (1963) saw this uniqueness as an expression of wholeness:

> My life is a story of the self-realization of the unconscious. Everything in my unconscious seeks outward manifestation, and the personality, too, desires to evolve out of its unconscious conditions and to experience itself as whole. (p. 3)

Building on the first assumption, we see that each person is a unique whole within the context of a global interconnectedness.

There are many implications for these two assumptions—not only in the worlds of science, computers, and electronic communication, but more significantly in spiritual development and the emergence of the new human being. The frontiers here are education, health, and organizational leadership. But we are way behind. We have investigated and become very disciplined in the measurement of material reality, but we have not made the same progress in the development of human beings. This is where values and values measurement comes in.

Values Assumptions

In the late 1960s, I was employed, as a part of a team, by the Anglican Church of Canada to conduct a social survey in Venezuela. The Anglican Church had a presence along the northern seaboard of Venezuela, consisting primarily of foreign nationals from Canada, the United States, and England. These people worked in and ran the oil industry, which was dominated by foreign interests. Our job was to gather data that was expected to show that it was a necessary and good thing for the Canadian church to initiate a new diocese in that region.

I met many thoughtful and knowledgeable executives who pointed out that, grateful as they were for the support of the church, the venture would surely be a disaster. It was their opinion, supported by strong trends in Venezuela at the time, that a revolution was imminent and that the result would be that the new ruling party would nationalize all foreign industry, sending 95 percent of all foreign personnel home. These executives believed that the new political powers would have Venezuelan management take over under the guidance of a few key foreign management consultants, whose job would be to ensure that the industry would continue to exist and be well managed in the future, but by Venezuelan citizens.

The message was clear. I sent a report back to Canada pointing out the folly of beginning any kind of mission in Venezuela, let alone a whole new diocese. Minimally it was suggested that they wait to see whether these revolutionary changes did in fact take place. After all, if all the foreign personnel were to leave, we would have no people to serve or begin a diocese with!

The team and I were immediately summoned to Toronto to address the church leaders. Fully expecting to be asked about our data and recommendations, I was surprised to discover that no one was a bit interested in what we had to say. We were fired! Within a few weeks, a new mission and new diocese were created and a brand-new bishop installed. Within six months there was a change in Venezuela and the whole venture fell apart. There was a scandal and the question arose: Why did no one listen to the Hall-Patten Report?

A year later I met Benjamin Tonna, a Maltese sociologist living in Rome. He ran a documentation center called SEDOS that collected information for people preparing to set up new missions, schools, and hospitals in foreign places. His research is documented in a book called *Gospel for the Cities: A Socio-Theology of Urban Ministry.*

I told him my story of the Venezuela project with some bitterness. I remember he moved his hand across his face, smiled, and said, "Brian, do you know what your problem is?"

A little embarrassed, I replied, "No, I don't think so."

He replied, "You think people make decisions based on the facts, but in fact they don't!" He went on to share several stories similar to my own. We concluded that *people make decisions from their predominant mind set, their own paradigm of reality, and the values that underlie them, even if the facts advise otherwise.*

We also saw that collecting quality information on people and groups would provide an invaluable resource—and what we meant by this was values information that would enable us to determine what criteria are used for decision making by organizations and their leadership. It was at that point in 1971 that we decided to construct a theory of values and to develop instruments for their measurement.

We also decided that our work would be based on four assumptions:

- That there is a universal set of values held by human beings (Chapter 2), and that these values transcend culture and gender. A list of these values would allow measurement and comparisons between various ethnic groups, men and women, or even sets of people in an organization (Chapter 4).

- That by studying the relationship of values to world views, that is, human mind sets, we would be able to see the relationship between values and human ethical, emotional, and spiritual development (Chapters 2, 5–10).

- That we would be able to develop methods for initiating permanent organizational change (Chapter 11 and Appendix C).

- That it would be necessary to develop instruments to measure the values, and that the instruments would need to be validated (Appendix B and Introduction).

Values Shift as Society in Transition

This book is about the results of our work. The actual process is documented in Appendix B and the Introduction. The point I want to make is that society as a whole is in a dramatic period of transition. Toffler (1990) calls this a "Power Shift" to the information age.

But this transition is not simply something that is going on outside in the world of education, politics, and business—it is really a shift that is internal to us humans. This inner connection is captured by our values, referred to in the next chapter as the Genesis Effect. What we are experiencing, all of us, is a Values Shift, often observed outside ourselves at first, but inevitably becoming internalized as a part of our own value systems.

An example of this process came from the Roman Catholic Church in the form of a council of bishops: Vatican II. Until the 1960s the Catholic Church was the largest, most efficient hierarchy the world had known. It was the ultimate mechanical Newtonian organizational system. Vatican II led by Pope John XXIII altered the mind set of the whole Catholic Church overnight. Since the fourth century the Mass had been celebrated by the priest, who stood in front of the altar with his back to the congregation—a very clear and intentional hierarchical structure. The council decreed that the priest should now stand behind the altar facing the people.

This simple symbolic but archetypal change altered the relationship of the church and its leadership to the people. Leadership was now collaborative and participative in a new relational arrangement. A shock wave went through the church—700 million members!

Placing a priority on relationship implied a different attitude toward other Christians and indeed non-Christian faiths, to say nothing of leadership style, gender, and sexuality. These issues are still very much alive in the Catholic Church 25 years later, because it is an organization in transition. But then so is the rest of society. The church was ahead of its time in experiencing a massive shift in its way of viewing the world—the Values Shift had begun. Since that time, practically all the leading institutions in society have began to deal with the same issues of human equality and emancipation.

In the United States, we have seen issues of human dignity and equality in the death of Martin Luther King and the fight for the rights of African-Americans, with similar movements for women, Hispanics, and Asians.

Globally, we see this transition occurring in the early 1990s in a massive reduction in global conflict, with peace discussions in the Middle East and even South Africa. With the fall of communism and the emancipation of the Eastern block, it as if a new republic is born every week! This transition is chaotic and often ugly with violence, but in reality a part of a global Values Shift away from the old mechanical and hierarchical order to one that demands increased freedom and human dignity.

When we look at these dramatic changes in terms of the practical implications, a study of values becomes a way for us not only to understand change, but also to manage and guide it. Because at the heart of the Values Shift is the idea that *values can be chosen consciously and measured, and can become a tool that allows us to choose a new set of futures, rather than live our lives under some other person's directive.*

Practical Applications

In the late 1970s I was asked to consult with a group called the Private Sector Initiative in the Northwestern United States. An over-reliance on government contracts and a decline in federally supported industry had caused massive unemployment in that part of the U.S.. The project had gathered representatives from all parts of public life—industrialists, bankers, university presidents, unions, and social agencies—to create an agency to deal with the problem. The agency was called PSI 84, because its target was to have 84 percent employment in the private sector by 1984.

When I first met with the PSI 84 board, it consisted of more than 30 people representing 30 different constituencies in the community.

FIGURE 1-4. An Organizational Values Shift

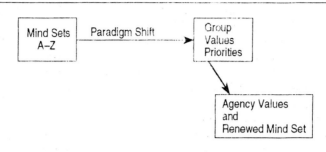

They had come to a consensus on an agenda of 300 programs, but they could come to no agreement on how to prioritize them! They were at a standstill. Every group had its own priorities and an infinite number of reasons why its agenda was superior to everyone else's. They asked me to help.

I took the whole group for a weekend retreat at a conference center in the San Juan Islands. We began after dinner at eight o'clock on a Friday evening. I divided the group up arbitrarily into six groups of five people each. After the introductions, I explained that underlying our various agendas were the values we held in common. I asked each group to study a list of values and their definitions—a list much like the one in Appendix A—and to come up with a list of five priority values that they felt were the most important for PSI 84 as a project and an agency.

Each group then shared publicly what values they had chosen and why. By noon on Saturday, they had a consensus of six values in order of priority. The two highest priorities were Human Dignity and Work/Labor. By three o'clock, they had prioritized their programs and set about the work of organizing the agency. We might diagram this process as shown in Figure 1-4.

The practical outcome was that the values instrumentation allowed a group of people with totally different mind sets and agendas to come to a rapid consensus through a common set of values. A discussion of values in a nonthreatening environment has a way of getting people to discuss their bottom-line concerns, about which there is usually very little disagreement.

Education and Values

Values measurement tools have now been developed that make a process such as the one just described even easier to accomplish. At the practical level, the instrumentation has been used to help school districts and teachers become clear about their personal values. They are then able to convert those values into a clear belief system about what education is and what learning methods need to be used in the local framework and culture. To be a practical tool in education, values work must be done within a collaborative framework in which administrators, students, parents, and teachers talk about their common values.

A recent program in Spain, entitled "Los Valores en La Ley Organica de Ordenacion General del Sistema Educativo: Un Analisis de Documentos a Traves de la Metodologia de Hall-Tonna"—a values analysis of Ministry of Education documents (Albizuri et al., 1993)—uncovered the central values system for all educational programs in Spain from the primary level up to professional education. This study has been used as a basis for local studies of the alignment of values and beliefs of administrative leadership, teachers, and parents and of methodologies for teaching.

Howard Gardner has demonstrated in books such as *Frames of Mind* (1985) and *The Unschooled Mind* (1991) that different children, especially those in differing ethnic groups, learn in different ways. He notes that we are faced with an interesting puzzle:

> Very young children who so readily master symbol systems like language and art forms like music, the same children who develop complex theories of universe or intricate theories of the mind, often experience the greatest difficulties upon entry in school.
>
> Somehow the natural, universal, or intuitive learning that takes place in one's home or immediate surroundings during the first years of life seems of an entirely different order from the school learning that is now required throughout the literate world. (1991, p. 2)

We are faced with a Values Shift—from a concept of school as mass production and a curriculum program with narrow teaching methods, to a system that recognizes the intricacy of differences in learning styles that flow from the mind set of parents and children, heavily influenced by their culture of origin. The Spanish project illustrates that although there is a generic set of values that any culture has, the belief system at the local level is unique and adds its own special character that must be taken into consideration.

Management and Values

Values measurement is an important tool for leadership and management development. In *Leadership Jazz*, Max DePree (1992) describes the impact of values on the leadership of organizations this way:

> Whether leaders articulate a personal philosophy or not, their behavior surely expresses a personal set of values and beliefs. This holds true in

businesses and hospitals and colleges and families. The way we build and hold our relationships, the physical settings we produce, the products and services our organizations provide, the way in which we communicate—all of these things reveal who we are. (pp. 5–6)

Management literature has recently been full of information about a major paradigm shift to a more collaborative form of leadership. Argyris (1990) calls this Model 2 (Model 1 is the Newtonian, mechanical model we spoke of earlier). Edgar Schein (1992) wrote about organizational culture as the key to enabling a values or paradigm shift.

I believe that cultures begin with leaders who impose their values and assumptions on a group. If that group is successful and the assumptions come to be taken for granted, we have then a culture that will define for later generations of members what kinds of leadership are acceptable. (p. 2)

The problem as Schein sees it is that assumptions from the past are now embedded in management leadership behavior so that it will perpetuate itself even when it becomes unproductive. For a Values Shift to occur, a different cultural expression, supported by leadership, is required.

Values measurement is very helpful in mentoring executives, as I did with Frederick in the case described at the beginning of this chapter. In the last several years my colleagues and I have worked with chief executives in several major industries in the fields of sales, health care, electronics, and banking, and we have found that getting the chief executive in touch with her or his personal values is a critical step in managing such a cultural shift.

But as both Schein and Argyris have pointed out, nothing really happens until the leaders' values and consequent assumptions about leadership and the organization become a shared reality of the management group and finally of the employees themselves.

The Personal Impact of a Values Shift

The concept of the Values Shift is a social phenomenon that affects us all at both a personal and societal level. We are in a major global transition that is naturally uncomfortable. It is a transition that is asking leadership in all areas of public and private life to reexamine its values:

- What values do I want to live my life by?
- What values would I be proud to see expressed in my family?
- What values am I proud to see exercised in my business through my administrative style, and how do I do that?
- What values are critical to an informed belief system in the schools so that our children in the future will form the kinds of values that

ensure human rights and equality, a peaceful solution to global conflicts, and careful nurturing of the planet, our island home?

Preview of the Book

Part I of the book through Chapter 6 looks at human behavior and consciousness and how they are reflected by the values we hold. Part II,
beginning with Chapter 7, looks at human transformation in terms of
leadership and organizational behavior. The emphasis is on the leader as
he or she is influenced by the system and is an influencer of it. In each
chapter I will share practical consultation cases or educational events
that relate to what was covered in that chapter.

The first priority of this book is to communicate an understanding of
values. Later books will spell out methods for using values in organizational consultation in more detail.

A number of people have asked me over the years why the concept of
values couldn't be a lot simpler, and why we need something so complicated that we need computers to measure it. My answer has been that
human beings are not simple—they are beautiful, full of depth, and very
complicated.

I invite you, the reader, to get involved so that your understanding of
values becomes a part of what you are about. This will give you a powerful advantage in all you do at home and at work.

2

Values and the Quality of Daily Life

> Virtue, then, being of two kinds, intellectual and moral, intellectual virtue in the main owes its birth and its growth to teaching (for which reason it requires experience and time), while moral virtue comes about as a result of habit.
>
> Aristotle, *The Nichomachean Ethics*

In 1968 in Costa Rica I began some work that led directly to my current understanding of the remarkable power of certain words—special kinds of words that my colleagues and I now call *values*. I was assigned to work in a small mission in Barrio Cuba, a barrio consisting of about 30,000 people. Most of them lived on only a few dollars a week, although the cost of living in Costa Rica at that time was about a third higher than in Canada or the United States. I began working in the barrio with a value-based model of community development that was inspired by the work of Paulo Freire.

19

Freire discovered that by teaching people to read and write through emotionally charged words in the language, they not only learned language skills, but they also became aware of the deeper meaning of words in the language. In Freire's terms they became "conscientized." What Freire was identifying was that certain words in the language are more central and powerful than others. Freire named the value behind this process "word," because it was a life-giving experience that made the learners more conscious of their own oppression, as well as their own power and potential. In a sense, all human beings are oppressed until they become aware of their own creative potential. Freire's point was that every person, no matter how illiterate, has something to give and say to the world.

My original task was simply to walk the barrio each day and talk to people, and to try to discover those words that are emotionally laden and habitually used in their language. One such word that kept repeating itself was *problema*, or "the problem." In Spanish this means something like "the dreadful, most difficult problem." The identified problem was that children were being prostituted as early as nine years of age in order to provide money for their family's survival. Some families had as many as twenty children, since more children meant more money. The result was rampant child abuse, abortion, and malnutrition.

Over a period of several months I gathered the people together into small groups in the barrio to discuss the *problema*. We wanted these group discussions in the barrio to have as the source of their motivation the power of certain words in the language. These words we later identified and named "values." After several months of discussion, the group concluded that the *problema* was child prostitution and too many pregnancies. We decided to hold public meetings to discuss these issues.

At one meeting there was a long period of silence, during which time I concluded that the venture was a failure. Then a woman stood up and said quietly, "When I am making love with a man, then at least I know that I am a woman." The group became silent for a few minutes. Finally a middle-aged man who was very much respected by the group stood up and spoke: "The barrio is not home to us so much as it is a place where we have to live, and when I, too, touch a woman, then at least it is something to be a human being."

We were able at that point to identify those two experiences with one term that had to do with being human: *self-worth*. This later became one of 125 values on a comprehensive list that Benjamin Tonna and I were to develop in the following 12 years. Self-worth is defined as follows:

> **106.** *Self-Worth:* The knowledge that when those one respects and esteems really know him/her, they will affirm that he/she is worthy of that respect.

The group came alive as a result of that experience. The meetings were now charged with energy. Whenever I think of the word *self-worth*, I think not just of a word in the dictionary or the definition given here, but of a series of images and experiences I had with those people over the months we spent together. The group converged so much around that word and what it meant that in the following months they initiated a family orientation clinic that is still in operation there today.

We had discovered in this simple word the experience of a value critical in the lives of those people. The creation and development of a simple list of words occupied our research for the next 12 years—words in the written and spoken language that carry special meanings that make people "conscious" or "aware." These are what we call values.

Values As the Source of Personal Transformation

The questions we want to explore in this book are these: *What is it that we need to know to transform a person into an exceptional human being? What is it we need to know to build a better society?* Personal transformation is intricately connected to organizational transformation, because people are able to change when they get positive reinforcement from the primary institutions in their lives—their families, their schools, and their work environments.

The quality of a business organization and its management style—the company's culture—is a product of its founders, its leadership, and the quality and maturity of the people who work there, and this is true of other groups as well. In fact it is my experience that, whether an organization is healthy or unhealthy, its culture is an extension of the leadership that founded it.

It is the thesis of this book that the critical factor in the transformation of people and organizations is their *values*. It is important to define what we mean by values. *Values are the ideals that give significance to our lives, that are reflected through the priorities that we choose, and that we act on consistently and repeatedly.* The years of research that led to the writing of this book showed us that values are identifiable and measurable, that they are designated by special code words in the spoken and written language, and that they are experienced through our feelings and imagination.

Since values are our primary source of knowledge about what is important to individuals and society, it follows that the priorities we choose to live our lives by are related to our understanding of reality. Yet at the same time there is enormous confusion about exactly what values are. This chapter will clarify what we mean by values, how they point to some basic assumptions about reality, and why they are so important to human transformation.

Virtues and Human Excellence

When we talk about human values, we are at some level assuming something about the quality of a person's life, and about human excellence. What does it mean to be a person of excellence? This is is a very old question. Socrates and Aristotle discussed it at length in the third and fourth centuries B.C., nearly 2500 years ago. Aristotle asked, What does it mean to be a virtuous person? Indeed what is virtue? In Aristotle's own words:

> Virtue, then, being of two kinds, intellectual and moral, intellectual virtue in the main owes its birth and its growth to teaching (for which reason it requires experience and time), while moral virtue comes about as a result of habit. (*The Nichomachean Ethics* II:1)

Values that affect the moral quality of a person are understood traditionally as *virtues*. For Aristotle and Socrates, virtues are the human qualities that make a person good. They include wisdom, understanding, temperance, and prudence. The virtues were seen as hierarchical—some virtues such as wisdom were thought to be superior to others.

Knowledge is the ordering of chaos, and we humans order things by categorizing and naming them. This process is at the very heart of language and communication. By naming objects such as tables and chairs and agreeing always to use the same name, we are able to talk about them. The knowledge explosion that accompanied the technological and scientific revolution of the nineteenth century had a lot to do with naming objects and describing the properties of those objects.[1]

At the heart of Aristotle's discussion of virtues is the question of what basic elements or qualities make up the good person. A named and ordered list of virtues such as wisdom, understanding, and prudence was developed. Each virtue could be seen as having its unique properties, which could be described in terms of feelings, behaviors, and skills.

The Hierarchy of Virtues

Aristotle's original list of virtues was short but for centuries remained the standard for what a good person is. The works of the Greek philosophers were well preserved in the Roman world, but were lost with the collapse of Rome in the fifth century. They were rediscovered by Arab scholars and were eventually made available to western civilization in the thirteenth century. The scholar who integrated Aristotle once again into the mainstream of western thought was Thomas Aquinas, who created a new, expanded list of virtues.

Like the Greeks, every culture and every religion has its own unique list of those human attributes that make up the virtuous person. These virtues are named and recognizable human behaviors that are expressed in everyday life as priorities. One of the most famous lists is from Paul in his first letter to the Corinthians, Chapter 13, in which he lists three priority virtues: "So faith, hope, and charity abide, these three; but the greatest of these is charity." In other words, the virtues were in reality a hierarchy of virtues.

When Thomas Aquinas was introduced to Aristotle, he adapted the ancient notion of virtues, listing the virtues of prudence, temperance, fortitude, and justice, but he added Paul's virtues of faith, hope, and charity as the highest priorities. This sevenfold system of virtues has had a great influence upon Christian morality and still does. But this is not unique to Christianity; every religion—Buddhism, Islam, and Judaism—all have their preferred list of virtues, what they consider to be most important. Although there is commonality among these priorities, there are also differences. Each culture in every society has its idea of what is virtuous. The more organized cultures have these ethical lists available in written form.

When the medieval theologians named their seven virtues and prioritized them, they were suggesting that these represented a superior form of moral behavior that should be universal for all human beings. It was believed that virtue was a divine right, and the aristocracy, bishops, and kings were naturally expected to inherit these virtues at birth. In *Macbeth* Shakespeare has Malcolm say of himself in relationship to the king:

> But I have none. The king-becoming graces—
> As justice, verity, temperance, stableness,
> Bounty, perseverance, mercy, lowliness,
> Devotion, patience, courage, fortitude . . . (act 4, scene 3)

This externally imposed system of virtues became the model to which all civilized persons should be formed through education. The virtues were supported by various systems of authority such as scripture. This external approach to excellence leaves very little room for the subjective element of personal choice.

Later writers expanded the list of virtues, and in the sixteenth and seventeenth centuries the virtues included an almost unlimited set of possibilities. For John Locke (1632–1704) virtues were culturally specific and were a list of attributes that a given society thought to be advantageous. For Aristotle the end to which virtue is directed is happiness, but for writers like Thomas Hobbes (1588–1679) and Baruch Spinoza (1632–1677), self-preservation determines virtuous conduct. Immanuel Kant (1724–1804) began to close the gap between an internal knowledge of virtue and virtue as an obligation to external societal norms.

But in this book we are speaking of values. Are values and virtues the same thing? The two are often confused, but they are distinct from one another.

A few pages back we defined values as *ideals that give significance to our lives, that are reflected through the priorities that we choose, and that we act on consistently and repeatedly.* We know that values are designated by special code words in the spoken and written language, and that they are experienced through our feelings and imagination.

Virtues, like values, are ideals expressed as priorities; they are named, and they can be described in behavioral terms. The difference is that virtues are a specific subset of values that are narrower in their intention and purpose. In our research we defined 125 distinct values. Seven, eight, or nine virtues would then be a specific few that a person, culture, or religion feels everyone should follow. In Aristotle's terms, these shorter lists of virtues are a prescription for an excellent life. Values, on the other hand, are the basic elements that stand behind *all* human behavior, and they are wider in scope.

Until the turn of twentieth century virtues were viewed as external norms to which civilized persons, particularly those of noble birth, conformed in their lives. It was the job of education to reinforce these norms in the uncivilized child by instruction and discipline. This approach came into modern times as character education, with the assumption that a given set of values needs to be formed in the child. Character education thought of values and virtues as being the same thing. These values were most often culturally specific. In the United States, for example, essential values would include honesty, democracy, liberty, and freedom, with the assumption that these are taught and reinforced by discipline.

A simple example of a modern list of virtues comes from corporate culture. Stephen R. Covey, in a book titled *The Seven Habits of Highly Effective People* (1990, p. 23), writes: "The seven habits of highly effective people embody many of the fundamental principles of human effectiveness. These habits are basic; they are primary. They represent the internalization of correct principles upon which enduring happiness and success are based." His discussion could be right out of Aristotle, but in fact it is a formula for leadership in the modern corporation and includes such virtues as being proactive and seeking understanding.

The sociologist Clyde Kluckholm (1951, p. 414) summarizes this transition from virtues to values: "All cultures have their *categorical* values, their 'musts' and 'must nots,' violations of which are attended by severe sanctions."

Recent Confusion About Values

Until recently values were seen primarily as a measurement used in the realm of economics. An object is assigned financial value, depending on the need for it in the marketplace. In the last 50 years there has been attention on human values. *Human values are the qualities that are evaluated high on an individual's list of priorities.* It is curious that in the economic arena values are measurable, but until recently a measurement standard has not been available for human values.

While the consideration of human virtues came from philosophers and religious thinkers, the concept of human values came from social psychologists and educators. Values became a public issue in U.S. education in the 1960s. It was a period of historical turmoil. National heroes like John and Robert Kennedy and Martin Luther King, Jr. were assassinated. The country was embroiled in a war that many believed to be morally wrong. Schools and communities faced dramatic increases in drug experimentation, and issues of race, sex, and human equality were beginning to emerge as critical concerns for everyone.

This caused confusion over what values were and were not that is still with us. The root of the confusion was that it was not clear whether values are personal subjective choices, or visible and objective standards imposed by an external system of authority.[2]

The Values Clarification Movement

In 1965 Louis Rath, Merrill Harmin, and Sidney Simon wrote a book titled *Values and Teaching.* This book ushered in a movement called the values clarification movement. In their book they defined values as those elements that show how a person has decided to use his life.

They make the point that they are interested not so much in the content of values and what values a child should or should not choose, but rather in the process of valuing itself. In this paraphrased passage, they suggest that there are seven criteria for how an individual forms and chooses a value:

1. *Choosing freely.* If a value is to guide one's life whether or not authority is watching, it must be a result of free choice.
2. *Choosing from among alternatives.* Obviously, there can be no choice if there are no alternatives from which to choose. It makes no sense, for example, to say that one values eating. One really has no choice in the matter.
3. *Choosing after thoughtful consideration of the consequences of each alternative.* For something to guide one's life intelligently and meaningfully, it must emerge from weighing and understanding the alternatives.
4. *Prizing and cherishing.* When we value something, we prize it, cherish it, esteem it, respect it, hold it dear. We are happy with our values.

5. *Affirming.* We are willing to publicly affirm our values. We may even be willing to champion them.

6. *Acting upon choices.* Values show up in aspects of our living. Nothing can be a value that does not give direction to actual living.

7. *Repeating.* When someone holds a value, it is very likely to reappear on a number of occasions in that person's life. It shows up in several different situations, at several different times. (pp. 28–29)

The authors said about these criteria: "A look at this process may make clear how we define a value. Unless something satisfies all seven of the criteria, . . . we do not call it a value. In other words, for a value to result, all of the seven requirements must apply. Collectively, they describe the process of valuing."

Their approach was a radical departure from the traditional works on virtues, because they see values as entirely personal and subjective, determined by what is important to the individual. They called attention to the fact that values are an empty concept if they are not related to the concrete behavior of the individual—in the way that person makes choices in the ongoing action of everyday life. The limitation of the approach is that we all need guidelines in our lives about what long-term priorities we choose. What they had to offer was a very positive contribution, but in departing so radically from the past, their followers tended to throw out any objective criteria for those values that a person needed to develop to achieve potential excellence in life.

Kohlberg and Moral Development

In the mid-1960s Lawrence Kohlberg began constructing a theory of moral development in which his purpose was to move beyond the traditional concept of virtues. He saw the schools as having an important role:

> The school, like the government, is an institution with a basic function of maintaining and transmitting some, but not all, of the consensual values of society. The most fundamental values of a society are termed *moral values*, and the major moral values, at least in our society, are the values of justice and truth. (1981, p. 295)

For Kohlberg and his associates, values clarification did not respond to the needs of our time, since for him the critical issue was not that of making subjective choices, but in knowing the difference between right and wrong. Kohlberg based his perspective on original research in which he demonstrated that ethical choices are developmental.

He distinguished between subjective values (as in the work of Rath, Harmin, and Simon) and what in the above quotation he called moral values. For Kohlberg, justice and truth are the highest virtues, as they were for Socrates and Aristotle, but his insight was that they only emerge in human behavior through a developmental process; they are values that we arrive at through the maturation process. Kohlberg described six stages of development to reach full maturity. To be able to choose justly, we must have reached the highest level of maturity. Following in the footsteps of Piaget, he noted that, just as our cognitive skills develop and are nurtured through childhood, so does our ability to choose right from wrong.

Abraham Maslow's Hierarchy of Values

In the early 1960s a psychologist named Abraham Maslow came up with a list of values that were both needs and motivators of human beings. His now-famous hierarchy of values was based on the idea that, before a person could look at the higher, more abstract values such as justice or peace, the basic values such as food and shelter, security, safety, and achievement and success had to be satisfied. In other words, justice is not going to be a primary concern for someone who has no food to eat and no roof over his head.

Maslow calls these primary needs D-cognition values because they are deficiencies that must be completed, and each accomplished value becomes the foundation for the higher values. The higher values he called B-cognition values, or "being" values. These are closer to the traditional idea of virtues, but they come from the domain of psychology rather than religion or moral education, and the list is more extensive than the traditional lists of virtues. Here is Maslow's list of "being" values from his well-known book *Toward a Psychology of Being* (1968).

1. **Wholeness** (unity, integration, tendency to oneness, interconnectedness, simplicity, organization, structure, dichotomy-transcendence, order)
2. **Perfection** (necessity, just-right-ness, just-so-ness, inevitability, suitability, justice, completeness, "oughtness")
3. **Completion** (ending, finality, justice, "it's finished," fulfillment, finis and telos, destiny, fate)
4. **Justice** (fairness, orderliness, lawfulness, "oughtness")
5. **Aliveness** (process, nondeadness, spontaneity, self-regulation, full-functioning)
6. **Richness** (differentiation, complexity, intricacy)
7. **Simplicity** (honesty, nakedness, essentiality, abstract, essential, skeletal structure)
8. **Beauty** (rightness, formal aliveness, simplicity, richness, wholeness, perfection, completion, uniqueness, honesty)

9. **Goodness** (rightness, desirability, oughtness, justice, benevolence, honesty)
10. **Uniqueness** (idiosyncrasy, individuality, noncomparability, novelty)
11. **Effortlessness** (ease, lack of strain, striving or difficulty, grace, perfect, beautiful functioning)
12. **Playfulness** (fun, joy, amusement, gaiety, humor, exuberance, effortlessness)
13. **Truth, honesty, reality** (nakedness, simplicity, richness, oughtness, beauty, pure, clean and unadulterated, completeness, essentiality)
14. **Self-sufficiency** (autonomy, independence, not-needing other-than-it-self-in-order-to-be-itself, self-determining, environment-transcendence, separateness, living by its own laws) (pp. 198–199)

Milton Rokeach's Terminal and Instrumental Values

In his work, Milton Rokeach differentiated between a value and a value system. A *value* for Rokeach is a belief and a specific mode of conduct and an end state of existence. A *value system* is an enduring organization of beliefs. He organized his list of values into two sets—terminal values and instrumental values. He defined *terminal values* as values that are ends in themselves. This is not unlike Aristotle's concept of happiness as the end to which virtue is directed. *Instrumental values* are the means that are used to achieve the terminal values. Figure 2-1 lists the 36 values that Rokeach defined—18 terminal values and 18 instrumental values. The words shown in parentheses are beginning definitions of the properties of those values. Rokeach did a series of very important studies in which he demonstrated that people's attitudes toward political ideas, race relations, and many other critical issues are related to how they prioritize these values.

Rokeach's work demonstrated the importance of priorities in the valuing process, and the importance of personal choice. Along with Maslow, he showed that we also need a named, objective set of values.

Another essential contribution of the work of Maslow and Rokeach is that they are not only suggesting that these values are expressed in human behavior, but that they are also universal in nature. They are value priorities that we all relate to and have, even though we only have time in our lives for a few at a time.

Although what we now call human values have been developed out of what was historically called virtues, values are distinct from virtues. Many people still quite naturally confuse the qualities we are calling values with the traditional idea of virtues as a narrow set of moral norms. When I work with a business organization and I say that I am going to help them assess and measure their values, the client is often offended, thinking that I am planning to do a moral evaluation of the company.

FIGURE 2-1. Rokeach's Value Lists

Terminal Values	Instrumental Values
A comfortable life (a prosperous life)	Ambitious (hard-working, aspiring)
An exciting life (a stimulating, active life)	Broadminded (open-minded)
A sense of accomplishment (lasting contribution)	Capable (competent, effective)
A world at peace (free of war and conflict)	Cheerful (lighthearted, joyful)
A world of beauty (beauty of nature and the arts)	Clean (neat, tidy)
Equality (brotherhood, equal opportunity for all)	Courageous (standing up for your beliefs)
Family security (taking care of loved ones)	Forgiving (willing to pardon others)
Freedom (independence, free choice)	Helpful (working for the welfare of others)
Happiness (contentedness)	Honest (sincere, truthful)
Inner harmony (freedom from inner conflict)	Imaginative (daring, creative)
Mature love (sexual and spiritual intimacy)	Independent (self-reliant, self-sufficient)
National security (protection from attack)	Intellectual (intelligent, reflective)
Pleasure (an enjoyable, leisurely life)	Logical (consistent, rational)
Salvation (saved, eternal life)	Loving (affectionate, tender)
Self-respect (self-esteem)	Obedient (dutiful, respectful)
Social recognition (respect, admiration)	Polite (courteous, well-mannered)
True friendship (close companionship)	Responsible (dependable, reliable)
Wisdom (a mature understanding of life)	Self-controlled (restrained, self-disciplined)

Source: Rokeach, 1973, page 197

What I am actually proposing to do is to evaluate the company's ideals as expressed through their priorities—those values the company holds as important enough to act on and set policy by.

Both Rokeach and Maslow opened the door to a new understanding of values as qualities that are very basic to the understanding of human behavior and that can be defined, standardized, and even measured. For both authors, values have both a subjective and an objective dimension. They recognize that human beings choose their lives, but at the same time each person needs to be exposed to a larger list of possibilities in order to grow as an individual.

Making Sense Out of It All

The work we have just summarized, all quite recent, addresses the issue of human excellence and human potential. Although these researchers' work is contemporary, they all share with Aristotle and Socrates a concern for what it means to be a virtuous person.

We could say that the classical works on virtues up until the nineteenth century are the trunk of a tree. On the left of the tree grow branches that represent recent development in values clarification (Raths, Harmin, and Simon) and the emphasis on values as subjective and personally chosen priorities in our lives. The branches on the right side represent modern concepts of moral development (Kohlberg), which stress values as developed virtues named moral values, and have traditional objective standards.

The work of Maslow and Rokeach grows out of both sides of the tree, because they recognize that values have both a subjective and an objective dimension. In addition, Maslow formed his values into a hierarchy of needs, suggesting that some of the values develop prior to others. Rokeach demonstrated that people's attitudes, even their political ideologies and views about race, are determined by their value priorities. (We will develop this idea further in Chapters 3 and 4.)

The truth is that all of these points of view form a coherent and consistent theory of values, and that traditional virtues are really what Rokeach called a system of values. That is, each of the traditional virtues is underpinned by a specific cluster of values. Kohlberg's stages of moral development can also be seen as underpinned by specific clusters of values. This book is designed to provide an approach to values that incorporates and builds on the work of these earlier researchers. The work described in this book is based on a comprehensive list of 125 standardized values that have been defined in our research.

The Development of the Hall-Tonna Inventory

Starting in the early 1970s, Benjamin Tonna and the author began to collaborate on the development of a comprehensive approach to the assessment, identification, and measurement of values.

Tonna was a sociologist working in Italy and the founder and director of SEDOS, an international documentation center. In his work he collected information from media sources for international service organizations that planned to initiate projects in countries that were new to them. The author's work was also international, with a background in psychoanalysis, religion, and the sciences.

We studied, developed, and tested various lists of values over a period of ten years, collaborating with a group of associates from universities in Europe and the United States. Building on the original concept from Aristotle, we discovered that values are ideals reflected by human behavior that is often habitual, and that it requires skill for human beings to develop them. It also became clear that we were looking for a universal and standardized set of values, values that could be identified through code words in the language.

Over a ten-year period we worked with a number of associates, looking for common words in European languages that were basic motivators in human behavior. We reviewed philosophical, educational, and psychological literature, and finally concluded with an initial list of 100 values in 1976. A team of 15 researchers used this as a test model. We came together in 1979 in Montreal, where we designed the final list of 125 values (Figure 2-2). The concept was that this list of 125 values would represent *a universal list of values common throughout all languages and races.*

From 1980–82 at Santa Clara University, the author and his associates developed instrumentation for measuring these 125 values. The first instrument, the Hall-Tonna Inventory, measured the values of individuals. Standardization and validation of the test began in 1983 under the direction of Dr. Oren Harari from the McClaren School of Business at the University of San Francisco. Multilingual, cross-disciplinary teams of 15 researchers met two days a week over a three-month period to standardize the list of 125 values as well as definitions of the values. These definitions are listed in Appendix A.

Values as Priorities. These 125 values became a rich source of information about the nature of human beings and the institutions they create. Our first discovery was that *these values exist as ideals in our lives, as priorities that reflect our behavior.* Not only this, but they also exist in the institutions within which we live.

FIGURE 2-2.   125 Values Used in the Hall-Tonna Inventory

1. Accountability/Ethics
2. Achievement/Success
3. Adaptability/Flexibility
4. Administration/Control
5. Affection/Physical
6. Art/Beauty
7. Authority/Honesty
8. Being Liked
9. Being Self
10. Belief/Philosophy
11. Care/Nurture
12. Collaboration
13. Communication/Information
14. Community/Personalist
15. Community/Supportive
16. Competence/Confidence
17. Competition
18. Complementarity
19. Congruence
20. Construction/New Order
21. Contemplation
22. Control/Order/Discipline
23. Convivial Technology
24. Corporation/New Order
25. Courtesy/Hospitality
26. Creativity
27. Decision/Initiation
28. Design/Pattern/Order
29. Detachment/Solitude
30. Dexterity/Coordination
31. Discernment
32. Duty/Obligation
33. Economics/Profit
34. Economics/Success
35. Ecority
36. Education/Certification
37. Education/Knowledge
38. Efficiency/Planning
39. Empathy
40. Endurance/Patience
41. Equality/Liberation
42. Equilibrium
43. Equity/Rights
44. Expressiveness/Joy
45. Faith/Risk/Vision
46. Family/Belonging
47. Fantasy/Play
48. Food/Warmth/Shelter
49. Friendship/Belonging
50. Function/Physical
51. Generosity/Compassion
52. Global Harmony
53. Global Justice
54. Growth/Expansion
55. Health/Healing
56. Hierarchy/Order
57. Honor
58. Human Dignity
59. Human Rights
60. Independence
61. Integration/Wholeness
62. Interdependence
63. Intimacy
64. Intimacy/Solitude
65. Justice/Social Order
66. Knowledge/Insight
67. Law/Guide
68. Law/Rule
69. Leisure
70. Limitation/Acceptance
71. Limitation/Celebration
72. Loyalty/Fidelity
73. Macroeconomics
74. Management
75. Membership/Institution
76. Minessence
77. Mission/Objectives
78. Mutual Accountability
79. Mutual Obedience
80. Obedience/Duty
81. Ownership
82. Patriotism/Esteem
83. Physical Delight
84. Pioneerism/Innovation
85. Play/Recreation
86. Presence
87. Prestige/Image
88. Productivity
89. Property/Control
90. Prophet/Vision
91. Quality/Evaluation
92. Reason
93. Relaxation
94. Research
95. Responsibility
96. Rights/Respect
97. Ritual/Communication
98. Rule/Accountability
99. Safety/Survival
100. Search for Meaning/Hope
101. Security
102. Self-Actualization
103. Self-Assertion
104. Self-Interest/Control
105. Self-Preservation
106. Self-Worth
107. Sensory Pleasure
108. Service/Vocation
109. Sharing/Listening/Trust
110. Simplicity/Play
111. Social Affirmation
112. Support/Peer
113. Synergy
114. Technology/Science
115. Territory/Security
116. Tradition
117. Transcendence/Solitude
118. Truth/Wisdom
119. Unity/Diversity
120. Unity/Uniformity
121. Wonder/Awe/Fate
122. Wonder/Curiosity
123. Word
124. Work/Labor
125. Workmanship/Art/Craft

The Barrio Cuba project anticipated all our later research. Reflecting on those events, I realize that my experience was a little different from that of most of the others in the barrio group. I felt affirmed because the time and energy I had put into the experience resulted in success rather than failure. The man and woman who stood up and spoke were affirmed through the discovery that what they said was a common experience for everyone else. They experienced affirmation through solidarity and an increased sense of belonging. Over a period of time, they became aware that they were worth something as human beings.

I was initially worried that I was not going to be successful in what I was doing. All of us experience this at one time or another. I was also afraid that my boss would feel I was wasting my time going to all those meetings that were leading nowhere. I had three value priorities from our list (Figure 2-2):

1. Achievement/Success
2. Self-Worth
3. Security

I experienced achievement and the success of the venture, which made me feel worthwhile, and I found security in my job. As a consequence I changed and became more confident in how I felt about my capacity to work with people.

The people in the group, on the other hand, were dealing with a much more critical and complex set of values. In addition to the discovery of self-worth, which was not originally even in their consciousness, they were coping with the survival of their families in the barrio. Their values, in reference to the 125-value list, were minimally: Family/Belonging, Self-Preservation, Safety/Survival, Community/Supportive, and Self-Worth. Before and after the experience we might imagine they were prioritized as follows:

Before the Experience	After the Experience
1. Self-Preservation	1. Self-Worth
2. Safety/Survival	2. Community/Supportive
3. Family/Belonging	3. Family/Belonging
4. Community/Supportive	4. Self-Preservation
5. Self-Worth	5. Safety/Survival

In my early experience of the people in the barrio, self-preservation and safety/survival absorbed all the energy of most of the families. This was so extreme that the function of the family was to provide what was necessary for survival, even if it meant, in extreme cases, prostituting the children. The values of community support and self-worth were virtually nonexistent. The world was a very alien and hostile place.

In the second experience we see a major shift in the value priorities. A sense of the value of self is evident and is supported by the nurturing community. This in turn leads to a different idea of what a family is. Self-preservation and safety/survival are now prioritized after family/belonging, This led the group to initiate, in the months to come, a family orientation clinic that provided family planning information, child development education, and day-care opportunities for families of mothers who wanted to work.

What happened that caused so much creative energy in this group? We can list the following:

1. Two new values emerged and were recognized: Self-Worth and Community/Supportive.

2. The people's value priorities changed.

3. The change in value priorities altered their perception of what was understood by *family*. Their definition of the value of family changed from something necessary for survival to something that nurtures and loves children and provides a sense of belonging and comfort for its members.

In other words, when the priorities changed, the quality of all their values changed. Putting it another way: their consciousness of themselves and the people around them changed. This in turn radically changed their behavior on a day-to-day basis, and they started using their time and energy in a different way.

Values and Groups. There is also an important group dimension to this experience. Originally, the people in the barrio were a group of separate individuals, all trying to survive independently. Later it became a nurturing community of listeners with common concerns. In fact it can be argued that it was this communal bonding, achieved through the recognition of values, that permitted the group to transcend itself and grow productively. The values in the barrio project came from both the individual's experience and the group's experience, each influencing the other.

In the beginning of the project, this institutional dimension was present in the barrio, reinforcing the value of Self-Preservation. In the second or later experience it was also present, but in a different way. Community interaction was an important ingredient in the process of becoming conscious. Living in today's world means that we must learn to live and work in small groups and institutions. The quality of these institutions radically affects the quality of our lives, just as it did for the people in the barrio.

We were in the process of discovering that values assessment is a way of retrieving information about the human condition. On the one hand, the values point to a deeper internal reality of the individual and can give us information about personal and spiritual growth. The values define the way each of us perceives the world. On the other hand, values underlie the way each of us behaves in the external world. *Values mediate a human being's inner and outer worlds, and enable us to express our inner selves outwardly in our daily activities.*

The Basis for Reality

Without exception, all value theorists agree that any treatment of human values will lead us to this question: What is it we understand by the nature of reality? What we value and give priority to in our life is conditioned by what we think life is about, by what is real for us. We cannot solve the age-old problem of what reality is, but we can address this question: What is the minimal understanding of reality needed to define what we understand by human values? The subjective and objective nature of values suggests that reality is minimally both these things, and that values appear to bridge the gap.

Values then, are the mediators between our inner world—our hopes, ideals, dreams, and images—and the external and observable world of everyday life and human behavior. Our values stand between the two worlds, and are a way of understanding both our inner life and our external behavior.

In *Memories, Dreams, Reflections,* Jung (1963, p. 3) wrote: "My life is a story of the self-realization of the unconscious. Everything in the unconscious seeks outward manifestation, and the personality too desires to evolve out of its unconscious condition and to experience itself as a whole."

In other words, much of the world we human beings have created—civilization itself, in all its forms, from cars to interior design and the very structures of society—is a manifestation of our ideals, our inner dreams and images. Life is not a series of related parts, but an intricately interdependent whole. The inner world of images and dreams is related to the outer world of people, lovers, ships, and cars. This connectedness and its creative consequence has been borne out in working with individuals and institutions to help them assess their values. We call this experience of reality the Genesis Effect.

The Genesis Effect

In 1979 an international organization in Rome asked our research team to develop a method for scanning documents in order to measure the values in their management documents. These documents included vision statements and criteria for executive selection, leadership development, and marketing. The analysis revealed what the top-priority values of the organization were. During the same period, more than 500 executive management personnel were given the Hall-Tonna Inventory, the values questionnaire that provides a computer-generated profile of each individual's values. Both processes were conducted in several different languages.

Much to our surprise, the high-priority values of the majority of executives reflected the priority values of their organization's management documents. The implications were shocking. This meant that the values that describe or underpin an organization's management system, the way it conducts its day-to-day business, actually become internalized in the personal values systems of the people who work in that organization. This is the phenomenon we came to call the Genesis Effect.

The Genesis Effect is the way human beings recreate the world they live in through their values. Each person lives with their feet in two universes at the same time: the external world of societies, institutions, family, and friends, and the internal world of fantasy, images, and the unconscious. This duality has been described in religious literature for centuries. We took our title from the first book of the Bible.

Genesis, which means "beginning," is the first book of the Jewish, Muslim, and Christian sacred literature. Although it was probably not written down until the sixth century B.C., it is perhaps at least 3500 years old in origin. The author of Genesis writes that a personal consciousness, God, acted upon a formless void and brought order out of chaos. The chapter continues with a series of sentences about the creation process, beginning with the phrase "God said":

> God said, "Let there be light," and there was light. (vs. 3)
>
> God said, "Let the waters under heaven come together into a single mass, and let dry land appear." (vs. 9)
>
> God said, "Let the earth produce every kind of living creature: cattle, reptiles, and every kind of wild beast." And so it was. (vs. 24)

The author of these passages has in mind the notion that it is God's spoken word that is the instrument of the creation. When God spoke and named an entity, such as light or cattle or reptiles, then light, cattle, and reptiles became a living reality. For the writer of Genesis, God's word, or language, is the power that causes the world to be created. The author continues:

> God said, "Let us make man in our own image, in the likeness of ourselves, and let them be masters of the fish of the sea, the birds of heaven, the cattle, all the wild beasts and all the reptiles that crawl upon the earth." (vs. 26)
>
> God created man in the image of himself, in the image of God he created him, male and female he created them. (vs. 27)

The heart of the Genesis Effect is the way in which the values mediate the internal and external realities through the medium of language. The book of Genesis explains exactly what this phenomenon means. In the Genesis story, God's image of creation precedes the spoken word that causes the creation to occur. We now know from brain psychology that the same phenomena occurs each day of our lives—that what we speak and say is preceded by our internal images of what we want to communicate.

Not only this, but what we communicate through the language of written words, such as personal letters, newspapers, is the ongoingness of our creating of the created order. It is language—the naming of things—that gives our inner vision outer life in the form of art, music, poetry, and sculpture; or in the form of technology, the marvels of the world of architecture, biological breakthroughs, and electronics.

The Genesis Effect assumes an inner and outer reality for each human being. The internal reality contains our unconscious inner world, and those elements of the unconscious that we become aware of through our dreams and intuition. It is the world of internal images and hidden psychic forces. On the other hand we have our external world, an

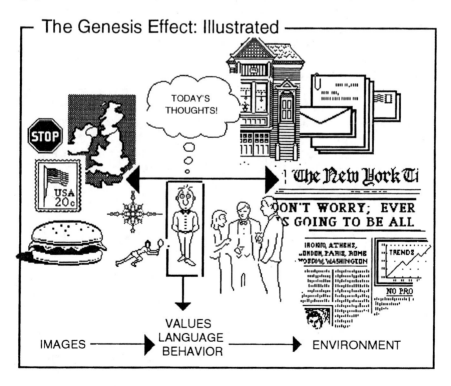

The Genesis Effect: Illustrated

TODAY'S THOUGHTS!

The New York Ti

ON'T WORRY; EVER S GOING TO BE ALL

IRONTO, ATHENS, LONDON, PARIS, ROME MOSCOW, WASHINGTON

TRENDS

NO PRO

IMAGES

VALUES LANGUAGE BEHAVIOR

ENVIRONMENT

individual's external behavior, family and friends, car, the company he or she works with, and everything that is observed and recorded by a person's senses. The inner and outer realities are related through the conscious mind in a circular fashion.

Let me give you an example. One of my students, a 34-year-old woman, was graduating from a master's degree program and beginning a new job. It was Sunday and she was to begin the job on Monday morning at 9:00 o'clock. She quite naturally had some fear and anxiety about the new job. We know that all feelings are accompanied by internal images, although they may remain unconscious. Earlier that day she was asked by some friends why she was so irritable and not talking very much. That night she had the same feelings, accompanied by a dream of being chased by a group of men in business suits. We talked about these experiences, and then she reported to me that she realized that the internal images of fear expressed in her dream were reflected in her external and observable behavior as irritability.

We can also say that the original fear was initiated in the external world by the job that she had interviewed for and accepted. However, this is further complicated by the fact that her anxiety may also be due to her own expectations and internally generated fears, which may have had little to do with the external reality.

What comes first then, the chicken or the egg? Does the external world become internalized as images in the unconscious, or do the images shape our behavior and the interpersonal world we live in? The answer is both; one reinforces the other. Values become the central criteria by which we can assess whether or not our images and external reality are leading to a destructive outcome or to a creative, life-enhancing end.

These conclusions—that language and consciousness are connected, and that language mediates the internal images into an external and recognizable form—are striking. In Genesis, God's image of creation and humanity is mediated through God's spoken word to become the created order. This reality, described centuries ago, is a reality that is given to each of us.

In their book *The Structure of Magic: A Book About Language and Therapy,* Richard Bandler and John Grinder (1975) note that each of us has an inner representational system, an image of what the world is really all about, and that has been logically assembled by the mind as it tries to make sense out of all the data it receives through the five senses.

> A number of people in the history of civilization have made this point— that there is an irreducible difference between the world and our experience of it. We as human beings do not operate directly on the world. Each of us creates a representational world in which we live—that is, we create a map or model which we use to generate our behavior. Our representation

of the world determines to a large degree what our experience of the world will be, how we will perceive the world, what choices we will see available to us as we live in the world. (p. 7)

In other words, each of us creates a practical map of the world based on our experience. Each person's map will be a little different, based on maturity and experience. Later they go on to say:

All the accomplishments of the human race, both positive and negative, have involved the use of language. We as human beings use our language in two ways. We use it first of all to represent our experience—we call this activity reasoning, thinking, fantasying, rehearsing. When we are using language as a representational system, we are creating a model of our experience. This model of the world we create by our representational use of language is based upon our perceptions of the world. Our perceptions are also determined by our model or representation. (pp. 21–22)

They are confirming that there is a relationship between our inner world of images and representations, the so-called external reality, and the spoken language. This again implies that language and consciousness are connected. The concept that internal images prefigure all of our external actions and reality is a little more challenging. Freire (1978) puts it this way, referring particularly to the economically oppressed:

The oppressed, having internalized the image of the oppressor and adopted his guidelines, are fearful of freedom. Freedom would require them to reject this image and replace it with autonomy and responsibility. Freedom is acquired by conquest, not by gift. Freedom is not an ideal located outside of man; nor is it an idea which becomes myth. It is rather the indispensable condition for the quest for human completion.

Freire had discovered that language, particularly when it included literacy in the form of reading and writing, enabled people to image the world differently. Language is the bridge between inner images and the external world. But more than this, when people are able to put their thoughts and ideas onto paper, they see their reality differently. In Freire's words, they become conscientized, or more self-aware of their total reality. This implies that *there is something inherent within written and spoken languages that can alter a person's consciousness. This something is values.*

Values As Mediating Energy

Values are the ideals that give significance to our lives, that are reflected through the priorities that we choose, and that we act on consistently and repeatedly. They are designated by special code words in the spoken and written language, and experienced through our feelings and imagination, and they are experienced in individuals, institutions, and in the products of human effort such as works of art.

Values are units of information that mediate our inner reality into full expression in our everyday lives. Values can be specifically identified in language and in people's behavior. When you know what the values are in a given situation, you have access to a lot of hidden information. This information comes from two sources, an inner world of racial memories and mythical insights, and an outer world of sensory perception.

Reality encompasses both an inner and an outer reality; it is not one or the other. Both realities must be seen as a balanced whole that must be in harmony. Something has to mediate the two realities, and that something is called values. It is the values that we have that carry the life-giving energy of the inner world into the external world of family and society. Each human being is continually experiencing data from two sources simultaneously: from the psyche and from the external world of sensory perception. Values stand between as a brokerage unit that assesses information and enables the brain to synthesize it into everyday decision-making.

Our research has identified a set of 125 values held by human beings, and, more importantly, enabled us to understand what they mean when we are confronted with them. It turns out that there are a limited number of significant values that affect our lives on a day-to-day basis, and that they fall into predictable and readable patterns. In the next chapter we will look at how to read the patterns that occur in value data.

3

World Views and Consciousness Shifts

All communities in all places at all times manifest their own view of reality in what they do. The entire culture reflects the contemporary model of reality. We are what we know. And when the body of knowledge changes so do we.

James Burke, *The Day the Universe Changed*

Several years ago I was working with the president of a small start-up advertising business, who had a particular point of view about his organization that was not at all shared by his partner. The more they talked, the less they understood one another. The president said to me one day, "I guess I'm the optimist, always seeing the bright side, and Jim is always dwelling on the potential downside of things. You know, I just can't understand why he doesn't see my point of view!" That night I had a dream that I later shared with both of them.

In the dream I had invited a group of friends to go sailing. The sailboat was tied up at the end of the pier. I was standing facing out toward the water. It was sunny and I was enthusiastic about having everyone get on the boat. The rest of the group, three people, had their backs to me and were looking the other way. What they saw was dark clouds and a storm coming in. They were afraid and wanted to go home! In the dream, neither I nor the others turned around, so none of us understood what the others saw, felt, or were saying.

When I reported the dream to the clients, they both understood what I meant. I was able to explain that the two sets of people in the dream had different world views. The world of my three guests was an alien world full of danger and foreboding, telling them what to decide about sailing: don't go—it's dangerous! My world view was full of optimism and play and was telling me not to have a care in the world. The gap between the two world views made communication impossible. This dream became a wonderful metaphor that allowed me to explain to the president and his partner that when people's world views differ, so do their values. It's the value differences that explain the communication gap.

Values are the key to understanding the human experience. In the last chapter we saw that values are universal to all human beings; they are what we hold in common. This chapter will show that these values form clusters that shape our world views.

We have found that the 125 values defined in our research fall into four different patterns at different stages of our lives. We call these patterns the Four Phases of Consciousness, and each a different world view. We will look at these four distinct world views, each demanding a different level of awareness or consciousness from the individual as he or she faces the world.

The Four Phases of Consciousness and their world views help us understand human differences, human growth and development, and the development of our institutions.

World Views and Consciousness

It is in the nature of human beings to attempt to make sense out of what we see, hear, and feel in the world around us. What we believe to be the reality of the world around us, however, is in fact an interpretation of what we see. A large grassy plain with a river running through it might be seen by one person as a great place for a vacation, a perfect spot for camping, fishing, and some much-needed solitude. To another person who has never been camping or fishing, it may look like a place where dangerous animals and snakes live, a place to avoid. The way we see and interpret the outer world of nature, things, and people is termed our *world view*.

James Burke (1985, p. 11) speaks about our world views as the way we see the universe: "We abhor complexity, and seek to simplify things whenever we can by whatever means we have at hand. We need to have an overall explanation of what the universe is and how it functions." That is to say, a person's world view is also a description of their awareness or consciousness of the world around them. In fact, each person's world view is based on his or her level of consciousness.[1]

Robert Ornstein (1989, p. 73) says about this consciousness we have of the world about us: "It is easy for us to ignore how limited our view of the world is. After all, our eyes reveal a brilliant, colorful world; our ears help us appreciate the complexity of Mozart. . . . In spite of its seeming limitlessness, the world of human experience and the world of any animal's experience is in truth lilliputian. Modern analysis of the nervous system and the mind yields a surprising conclusion: instead of experiencing the world as it is, people experience only about one trillionth of outside events: a small world indeed!"

Some people are more conscious than others, and we think of them as perhaps having a better handle on reality. Martin Luther King was more conscious of the oppression of black Americans than most, and so he was able to change that reality. Einstein was more conscious of how the world works mathematically and changed modern physics. When our human consciousness expands, our world view changes.

In referring to the way human personality develops, we're going to be using two technical terms from the world of psychology: ego and the self. *Ego* is the "I" we mean when we refer to ourselves—it's the sense of ourselves that develops as we mature through Phases I and II. The *self* is that part of ourselves that, beginning in Phase III, looks for a larger meaning for life; the self operates from a sense of inner authority. It is the self that leads us into a world view that encompasses global concerns.

Figure 3-1 on the next page illustrates the idea that there are four phases of consciousness, each with its own distinct world view. Each phase covers a larger space than the last one, because our awareness of the world around us expands as we become more conscious. With each phase of consciousness, there is a distinct world view.

World Views and Cultural Values

The phrase *world view* is another way of saying "the way we see the world through our values." Each person's world view is associated with a specific set of values, and this set of values is not just self-selected but arrived at through our individual experiences and even through the era in which we live. For example, if you could be transported back in time to medieval Europe, you would find that the dominant world view at

FIGURE 3-1. The Four Phases of Consciousness

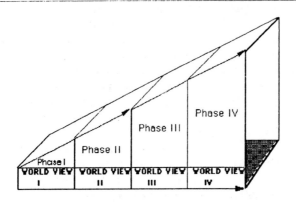

that time was that all of life is a hierarchy flowing from God to His bishops, then the king and queen, then their lords, and finally to the vassals in each kingdom. The values that would have been seen as virtues in that period were such things as Hierarchy/Order, Unity/Uniformity, Membership/Institution (as in the church), Duty/Obligation, Loyalty/Fidelity, and Patriotism/Esteem.

So powerful was this hierarchical world view that when Galileo presented scientific evidence to his superiors that the sun does not circle around the earth but that in fact the earth circles the sun, he was directed to deny his claims. Since he would not, he was put under house arrest for his entire life! Because of the values of hierarchy, the church felt that only its bishops had the right to interpret new information. Galileo's findings were not substantiated biblically, so he was censored.

If you now time-traveled to the mid-1800s in America, which was in the throes of the industrial revolution and the development of a new nation, values such as Independence, Work/Labor, Economics/Success, Technology/Science, Knowledge/Insight, and Achievement/Success would be emerging. This environment gave birth to hundreds of inventors and explorers of ideas—people like Thomas Edison, who invented electricity, and Charles Darwin, who gave us a new understanding of botany and zoology. Unlike Galileo, they were not arrested for their ideas, but their ideas were certainly challenged and debated, and they were finally hailed as heroes in the new industrial society.

Why was their experience different? Because the world view of the society was based on a different set of values such as the pursuit of knowledge and the search for success. In this setting, new ideas were welcomed.

Our experience of the world, the society we live in, and the opportunities we have to dream and grow affect our systems of values and the way we view the world. Derald and David Sue (1990, p. 137), authorities on cross-cultural counseling, summarize how powerful our world views are in everyday activity this way: "World views are not only composed of our attitudes, values, opinions, and concepts, but also they affect how we think, make decisions, behave, and define events."

The Four Phases of Consciousness

The Genesis Effect (see Chapter 2) describes values as the mediators between the inner world of images, an individual's world view, and the external and observable world of everyday life. Our values stand between these two worlds, and are a way of understanding both our inner lives and our external behavior. You might say that values are the most important source of information about our lives and how we view the world. Figure 3-2 illustrates how these elements come together.

The Four Phases of Consciousness form the backbone of our theory and our understanding of the emergence of human and spiritual consciousness. Each of the four phases has its own distinct world view, and each world view has three parts: how the world is perceived by the individual, how the individual sees him- or herself as a consequence, and what needs the individual has to satisfy because of this world view.

At the bottom of Figure 3-2 we see that each phase is associated with its own unique values. These are typical examples from the list of 125 values. Notice that there are goal values and means values. Goal values develop at specific points in our lives, and continue from that point on. Means values are skills-related—values that help us achieve our goal values. As we grow and change and develop new skills, our goal values change in complexity and quality. We adopt new goals that are richer versions of the old values. We will explore this aspect of development in more detail in Chapter 6.

In Figure 3-2 each of the phases is pictured as an ellipse that is circling around. When we are in this world view, we continually try to integrate that phase's values.

Values and the Four Phases

We are now going to examine each of the four phases in detail. You will see that *each phase has a distinct world view that is associated with a specific cluster of values.* It is important to have a common understanding of the meaning of each value, so each of the 125 values was carefully defined using standardized validation procedures (see Appendix B). Each

FIGURE 3-2. Elements of the Four Phases of Consciousness

Elements of World View	PHASE I	PHASE II	PHASE III	PHASE IV
How the world is perceived by the individual	A mystery over which I have no control	A problem with which I must cope	A project in which I must participate	A mystery for which we must care
How the individual functions in the world	Ego is the center of an alien and oppressive environment	Ego seeks to belong by approval of significant others and by succeeding	Self acts and initiates creatively, independently with conscience	Self acts as "we" with others to enhance quality of life globally
Human needs the person seeks to satisfy	Physical needs: food, warmth, shelter	Social needs: acceptance, approval, achievement	Personal fulfillment: meaning, creativity, insight	World community: harmony, by communal action
Types of Values	**PHASE I**	**PHASE II**	**PHASE III**	**PHASE IV**
Goal Values	Self-Preservation	Self-Worth	Self-Actualization	Truth/Wisdom Ecority
Means Values	Safety	Education	Independence	Convivial Technology

definition is unique and reflects the particular phase and world view where it is found.

In the discussion of each phase we will list all the goal values and a selection of the means values for that phase, and whether these goals and means values are Stage A or Stage B values. Stage A values are values that we live by in our personal lives; they are key to our psychological and spiritual growth. Stage B values are also personal, but they are experienced in institutional settings such as work, school, or government.

We will describe each phase's world view and its various dimensions. Since men and women have measurable differences in their values development, we will include a section on how male and female values tend to differ.

Phase I Consciousness: Survival and Growth

Phase I consciousness is the first stage of human development. It is the child's world—but many adults exist in Phase I consciousness, usually

FIGURE 3-3. Phase I Values

A GOALS	B GOALS
Self-Interest/Control	Physical Delight
Self-Preservation	Security
Wonder/Awe/Fate	
A MEANS	**B MEANS**
Food/Warmth/Shelter	Affection/Physical
Function/Physical	Economics/Profit
Safety/Survival	Property/Control
	Sensory Pleasure
	Wonder/Curiosity

because they have grown up in an oppressive environment and been unable to move on, or because they have been thrown back into a world of survival by their circumstances.

How the World Is Perceived by the Individual. In Phase I, the world is *a mystery over which I have no control*. It is an alien and difficult place in which to live, and people have few or no skills with which to cope. The main orientation of a Phase I adult is to "look after number one" first and last (Figure 3-3). The emotional life has little or no priority in Phase I; decisions are made on the basis of physical safety and satisfaction only.

Each phase—even the primitive Phase I—has its positive dimension. Phase I is the world of survival, but it also the world of the growing, naive child whose landscape is uncontrolled fantasy and delight. This world view is illustrated by the popular children's book series by A. A. Milne. In *The House at Pooh Corner* (1928), Milne wrote from the psychological perspective of the small child. In the story "Tiggers Don't Climb Trees," Roo, a kangaroo, is talking to Tigger, a tiger:

> And as they went, Tigger told Roo (who wanted to know) all about the things that Tiggers do.
> "Can they fly?" asked Roo.
> "Yes," said Tigger, "they're very good flyers, Tiggers are. Stormy good flyers."
> "Ooo!" said Roo. "Can they fly as well as Owl?"
> "Yes," said Tigger. "Only they don't want to."
> "Why don't they want to?"
> "Well, they just don't like it, somehow. . . . Tiggers can do anything."
> (pp. 62–63)

In the story, poor Tigger climbs up a tree, but finds that not only can he not fly, he can't even get down from the tree and has to be rescued by his friends. The small child, like Tigger, literally knows no boundaries, because imagination, fantasy, and external reality are still undifferentiated. Tigger felt that what he imagined was the same as what was true! This is the process of growing up from childlike narcissism with the values of Self-Interest/Control in Stage A of Figure 3-3. We all begin life like the small child believing that the whole world is really there for us. When we want food or feel uncomfortable we cry until we get our own way.

Life then literally begins in Phase I and consists of finding out how we must adapt to survive, then to live, and finally to create a better world for others. This innate curiosity is the seed of creativity and remains with us all our lives and is indicated by the values of Wonder/Awe/Fate and Wonder/Curiosity.

On the other hand, Phase I is also the cruel world of survival where millions still go to bed hungry every night—children and adults. Since the dawn of civilization the majority of human beings have lived most of their lives in this phase. In fact we might surmise that before the 1800s most of the human race never left Phase I.

How the Individual Functions in the World.   The ego finds itself at the center of an alien and oppressive environment. Many great works of literature have themes and images from this phase. The ancient Greek dramatists, for example, had no answer to the reality of pain and suffering that afflicted most people. Their tragedies addressed this mystery through plays in which the players and the audience became one in the pain and dilemmas of daily life. These ancient players invented the *deus ex machina*, or god machine. When a play was near its end and there was no resolution to a tragic circumstance, a machine representing a god or a god's messenger would appear upon the stage with an actor inside, who declared that the tragedy was a mystery understood only by divine powers. Characters in this circumstance, a King Oedipus or Electra, were expected to compliantly accept their fate, which was in the hands of the gods.

The work of Sue and Sue, referred to earlier, sheds some light on this experience of helplessness in Phase I. They link the individual's world view and self-concept, both based on where the individual places control and responsibility, or in academic language, the locus of control and responsibility.[2]

They suggest that everyone has the possibility of an internal or external view of responsibility, and an internal or external view of their control over life. This model fits well with the Four Phases of Consciousness, and we will refer to it as we go along. In Phase I we feel that control over our lives is from the outside. As in the "god machine," the cause of our problems is external. Responsibility for problems, especially as viewed by children, is also external.

Consider another great tragedy, William Shakespeare's *Macbeth*. It is a study in Phase I values. Macbeth, obsessed with power, plots with his wife to murder the king while he is a guest at their castle. The story continues with a web of guilt and mistrust as Macbeth is forced to preserve himself—Self-Preservation—by killing anyone who he feels he cannot trust. At the end of the play, opposing forces loyal to the murdered king approach the castle. He hears a scream and learns that his wife, the queen, is dead. He says:

> She should have died hereafter;
> There would have been a time for such a word.
> Tomorrow, and tomorrow, and tomorrow
> Creeps in this petty pace from day to day,
> To the last syllable of recorded time,
> And all our yesterdays have lighted fools
> The way to dusty death. Out, out brief candle!
> Life's but a walking shadow, a poor player
> That struts and frets his hour upon the stage
> And then is heard no more. It is a tale
> Told by an idiot, full of sound and fury,
> Signifying nothing. (act 5, scene 5)

Macbeth is faced with the death of his wife as an omen of what is forecast for him. He experiences life as but a brief moment upon a stage, with little or no significance, and over which the player has no control or responsibility, since the script was written by someone else. Consider some of the related values and their definitions:

Self-Interest/Control. Restraining one's feelings and controlling one's personal interests in order to survive physically in the world.

Self-Preservation. Doing what is necessary to protect oneself from physical harm or destruction in an alien world.

Wonder/Awe/Fate. The ability to be filled with marvel, amazement, and fear when faced with the overwhelming grandeur and power of one's physical environment.

How we function in this world depends on how we perceive the world. Adults in this phase have a world view represented by an absence of control and responsibility. They feel they have no control over their own lives and that responsibility for their actions is due to external circumstances. They struggle to survive in this alien environment. For the child who is protected by a safe home environment, it is different—it is a new world, a mystery to which the ego responds with wonder and awe, but still without control.

Differences Between Men and Women in Phase I

In this phase, a woman's perception of the world develops differently from that of a man. In a survey of 905 men and women, we found that women emphasized Wonder/Awe/Fate as their first value. This value is associated with inward reflection and vulnerability; it leads in later phases to values such as Intimacy and Contemplation. Their second value was Security, which is defined as finding a safe place or relationship where one is free from cares and anxieties and feels protected. Men, interestingly enough, had the same first two values, but the order was reversed, an indication that an outward orientation to the world is typically male.

Human Needs the Person Seeks to Satisfy. When we are in Phase I, we seek to satisfy physical human needs—for food, for warmth, for shelter, and for sexual pleasure. Self-preservation and security motivate us to acquire the skills that will guarantee safety and ensure survival. Notice that in Figure 3-3 a goal value such as Self-Preservation has under it the value of Food/Warmth/Shelter as a means to that end. For many who are disabled by disease or aging, Function/Physical will be a critical means value at Phase I.

Phase I behavior is not limited to adults confined to oppressive environments. Much western advertising is directed to adults who buy products based on sexual images, without reference to more sophisticated qualities. This is reflected in the value of Sensory Pleasure. Consider the appeal used in most ads for cigarettes, liquor, and automobiles. Spy movies and TV detective stories capitalize on Phase I attitudes toward life—personal physical satisfaction and safety.

In Phase I, the ego emerges as a creative entity striving to be itself on the one hand, while striving to preserve itself on the other hand. If self-preservation takes the upper hand, then a state of mistrust is developed, destroying a person's sense of well-being. Erikson calls the first stage of human development the stage of basic trust versus mistrust. In order for us to grow and develop into healthy people, our early experiences must be of security and love.

Phase II Consciousness: Belonging

In Phase II we move from the child's self-interest into a world of other people. We begin to perceive the need to belong to groups, and to develop the skills we need to succeed with other people. We begin to have control over our world through belonging to our families and other important groups.

FIGURE 3-4. Phase II Values

A GOALS	B GOALS
Family/Belonging	Belief/Philosophy
Fantasy/Play	Competence/Confidence
Self-Worth	Play/Recreation
	Work/Labor

A MEANS	B MEANS
Being Liked	Achievement/Success
Care/Nurture	Administration/Control
Control/Order/Discipline	Economics/Success
Courtesy/Hospitality	Education/Certification
Endurance/Patience	Hierarchy/Order
Friendship/Belonging	Law/Rule
Obedience/Duty	Productivity
Prestige/Image	

How the World Is Perceived by the Individual. In Phase II, the world is *a problem with which I must cope.* In this world view, the individual survives and succeeds by belonging, conforming, and adapting to the norms of the dominant society or group, beginning with family. The values listed in Figure 3-4 reveal a peopled world to which one must belong to succeed. Rather than a hostile, alien world over which the ego has no control, it is a social world that has problems with which the individual can cope. This world is ordered, political, and social.

The Stage A* values for Phase II indicate a world in which values related to belonging and pleasing others are given a high priority. The goal values are:

Family/Belonging. The people to whom one feels primary bonds of relationship and acceptance; attachment to the place where one's parents live.

Fantasy/Play. The experience of personal worth through unrestrained imagination and personal amusement.

The most important goal value for our growth at this phase and for the rest of our lives is Self-Worth: The knowledge that when the people that we respect and esteem really know us, they will affirm that we are worthy of respect. The means values expand these dimensions with values such as Being Liked, Friendship/Belonging, Courtesy/Hospitality, and Care/Nurture.

---

* In some versions of the Hall-Tonna Values Management Inventory, the stages are designated by the numbers 1 through 8. Here Stage IA corresponds to Stage 1, Stage IIA to 3, Stage IIB to 4, and so on.

The Stage B values extend these personal social needs with confidence into the wider world of work, play, and religion:

Competence/Confidence.   Realistic and objective confidence that one has the skill to achieve in the world of work and to feel that those skills are a positive contribution.

Play/Recreation.   A pastime or diversion from the anxiety of day-to-day living for the purpose of undirected, spontaneous refreshment that can result in heightened awareness of oneself as separate from daily pressures.

Work/Labor.   The ability to have skills and rights that allow one to produce a minimal living for oneself and one's family.

Belief/Philosophy.   Adherence to a belief system, set of principles, or established philosophy that is based on universally accepted authoritative documents such as the Bible, Koran, or Upanishads, which espouse the concept of reverence for the universal order.

The world in Phase II is ordered like a clock, hierarchically driven, and run by rules of society and the universe. Until recently, the world of science accepted the laws of physical motion proposed by Newton in the seventeenth century. For Newton and generations of later scientists, the universe was like a gigantic clock waiting for us to discover the laws and rules (Law/Rule) that govern it. In this world view, an established order exists in the universe that is governed by recognizable laws (Hierarchy/Order).

When applied, these laws produce predictable results. When laws are respected and used, life is stable and secure in the physical world, and by extension, in the social world as well. Most traditional corporate management structures have Phase II means values such as Administration/Control, Achievement/Success, Productivity, and Economics/Success. Another Phase II means value, Education/Certification, is a very necessary and basic requirement for a stable and productive society.

How the Individual Functions in the World.   The ego seeks to survive by gaining the approval of significant others in order to succeed. At Phase II, we are attracted to people who are important to us because they guarantee acceptance into the group and enhance our sense of competence and confidence. Phase II people function ideally with a lot of internal responsibility, but still feel that their lives are controlled from the outside by people in authority. They are most likely to accept the dominant culture's rules and concept of responsibility.[3]

When we are in Phase II, we are dominated by others' expectations, and there is little distinction between rules and ethics. Personal identity comes from finding our place in the world of work, and in social and religious institutions. This is the phase at which dominant stereotypes of the differences between men and women prevail.

> ## Differences Between Men and Women in Phase II
>
> *At Phase II, the differences between men and women are stereotypical of the values by which men and woman in western middle-class society are supposed to live. Women emphasize values like Endurance/Patience, Care/ Nurture, and Family/Belonging, while men have values such as Competence/Confidence, Economics/Success, Achievement/Success, and Competition. With a world view that reinforces the rules of the status quo, stereotypes between men and women become a rigid pattern that is difficult to change. When this occurs, human growth is stunted, because both men and women need to integrate all the Phase II A and the B values into their lives, rather than excluding some and emphasizing others.*

In Phase II, the function of the ego is to learn how to belong in order to survive and succeed. At Phase II, survival means the ability to cope in society by having sufficient social and job-related skills (Work/Labor). Infants join the social world by winning the approval of their parents. Small children begin to venture out of "our home" onto "our block" into "our neighborhood," and finally into school (Education/Certification), where they learn to read, write, and do arithmetic—the basic skills (Competence/Confidence) on which personal competence and success will be built in "our society."

Associated with school life are a variety of extracurricular group activities—most typically, organized sports. These organized activities share two characteristics in common: (1) to belong, the youngster must live or play by the rules, and (2) to succeed, the youngster must demonstrate personal achievement. Belonging and success are celebrated in initiation rites and secular and sacred rites of passage—induction ceremonies, graduations, bar mitzvah rites.

Human Needs the Person Seeks to Satisfy. At Phase II, our needs or tasks are acceptance, approval, and achievement. We need to conform to the norms of significant people and groups and to become useful and productive. By doing this, we satisfy our social need for acceptance, affirmation, approval, and achievement. As we experience belonging and success, we begin to realize a sense of self-worth. In other words, self-worth is a social phenomenon in a world established by others into which we must fit if we are to experience a sense of personal worth.

When we perceive the world as established and run by others, we must adapt and play by the accepted rules. To become a useful participant in this world, we must contribute in a productive way to society's well-being. We find personal meaning less through the satisfaction of the senses and more through the experience of cooperating in a worthwhile enterprise.

At Phase II, we value work as productive labor because it provides us with the conviction that we are useful and have earned the right to belong. If we overemphasize success, we see competence in work as the only way to achieve a sense of belonging.

At this phase, our primary concerns have moved beyond individual survival to a social perspective. We begin to seriously consider the other person's point of view. Tradition is an essential part of the social aspect of the ego. As we move into the world of work where we provide for our own families, we see social prestige as the beginning of success and affirmation beyond our families.

Phase III Consciousness: Self-Initiating

When we move on to Phase III, we begin to develop an independent sense of ourselves as separate and distinct from our family and other important groups. We begin to honor our own judgment rather than trusting the correctness of the rules and regulations that occur in our environment. This is the phase at which we begin to be self-initiating.

How the World Is Perceived by the Individual.   In Phase III, the world is *a creative project in which I want to participate, to which I have something unique and different to offer.* Stage A is marked initially by a strong sense of independence with a need for equality and liberation (see Figure 3-5). In this phase, authority is viewed as coming from within ourselves; this is unlike the previous two phases, where authority is external, seen as rules and regulations to which everyone must conform. The Phase III person is self-initiating and assertive about his or her creative role in the world.

Stage A values share a strong emphasis on personal expressiveness and development:

> *Equality/Liberation.*   Experiencing oneself as having the same value and rights as all other human beings in such a way that one is set free to be that self and to free others to be themselves. This is the critical consciousness of the value of being human.
>
> *Integration/Wholeness.*   The inner capacity to organize the personality (mind and body) into a coordinated, harmonious totality.
>
> *Self-Actualization.*   The inner drive toward experiencing and expressing the totality of one's being through spiritual, psychological, physical, and mental exercises that enhance the development of one's maximum potential.
>
> *Service/Vocation.*   The ability to be motivated to use personally unique gifts and skills to contribute to society through one's occupation, business, profession, or calling.

FIGURE 3-5. Phase III Values

A GOALS	B GOALS
Equality/Liberation	Art/Beauty
Integration/Wholeness	Being Self
Self-Actualization	Construction/New Order
Service/Vocation	Contemplation
	Faith/Risk/Vision
	Human Dignity
	Justice/Social Order
	Knowledge/Insight
	Presence
	Ritual/Communication

A MEANS	B MEANS
Authority/Honesty	Accountability/Ethics
Empathy	Community/Supportive
Equity/Rights	Creativity
Health/Healing	Detachment/Solitude
Independence	Growth/Expansion
Law/Guide	Intimacy
Search for Meaning/Hope	Leisure
Self-Assertion	Pioneerism/Innovation
Sharing/Listening/Trust	Research

The Phase III means values stress assertion, independence, and law as a guide rather than the Phase II value of law as rule. There is an emphasis on personal growth in values such as Search for Meaning/Hope and Health/Healing. These values give us a whole new sense of ourselves, with a world view that is more self-directed and less ego-centered.

Stage B goal values expand our sense of ourselves and access to power with values that reflect a more institutional and societal level of functioning and concern. For example:

Being Self. The capacity to own one's truth about oneself and the world with objective awareness of personal strengths and limitations plus the ability to act both independently and cooperatively when appropriate.

Construction/New Order. The ability to develop and initiate a new institution for the purpose of creatively enhancing society. This assumes technological, interpersonal, and management skills.

Human Dignity. Consciousness of the basic right of all human beings to have respect and to have their basic needs met so that each person has the opportunity to develop to full potential.

Knowledge/Insight. The pursuit of truth through patterned investigation, motivated by increased intuition and unconsciously gained understanding of the wholeness of reality.

Stage B values are often an upgraded or more sophisticated version of Stage A values. For example, Self-Actualization in Stage A is the self-initiating experience of fulfilling one's own potential, while Being Self in Stage B is an extension of this value because it adds the objective awareness of one's strengths and limitations, transcending the ego in order to act both independently and cooperatively within institutional settings.

Although the values at each phase are separate and distinct, they are also all interrelated. For example, Stage A means values relate to those of Stage B, but they also give clarity to the goal values in each stage. For example, Empathy, a Stage A means value, and Being Self, a Stage B goal value, find depth in the value of Intimacy, a Stage B means value. The definition of Intimacy makes this clear: "Regularly and fully sharing one's thoughts, feelings, fantasies, and realities, mutually and freely, with another person."

How the Individual Functions in the World. Because of the maturity we have achieved in Phase III, we no longer need the affirmation of others to realize our self-worth, and we no longer find meaning in merely living up to the expectations of others. This transition does not usually occur before early adulthood. We have a personal sense of power and authority that replaces institutional control of behavior. We prize creativity and imagination, and we have a newfound sense of honesty that makes conformity hypocritical.

We also begin to respect the authority of our own inner voices—that voice that urges us to be true to ourselves rather than be guided by external society or by the majority opinion. Ira Progoff (1963) illustrates this from Socrates' defense of himself before the Athenian court just prior to his final condemnation and death:

> Socrates there described his intimate feeling of why it was important for him to live his life as he had been living it. It was not a question of intellectual philosophy, but of a calling that came to him from two sources, an outward source and an inward source, which Socrates understood as ultimately not separate at all from one another. The outward source of his calling was the gods of the Greek Pantheon; and to this the Oracle at Delphi testified. The inward source of his calling was the oracle within himself. He described this as the "divine faculty of which the internal oracle is the source." To Socrates the inward and the outward were two aspects of a single principle. It was in the light of this unity that he could state his belief "that there were gods in a sense higher than any of my accusers' belief in them." (pp. 71–72)

Because the locus of control has shifted, we now experience both control and responsibility as internal. We no longer blame problems on externals such as the boss or economic conditions. People with this world view feel that they need to be totally in control of their own choices and that they are responsible for the outcome. They stress independence in thought and action.

At Stage B of Phase III we find meaning in and accept responsibility for revitalizing, even reshaping, the environments in which we live. In our concern for the quality of life and its renewal, we may focus our activity on ensuring human rights and justice in the social order, or on improving the conditions for personal growth within our families or corporations.

We begin to transcend our own limited worlds and become sensitive to the rights of others. The fact that we have equity and rights for ourselves implies that we need to fight for others' rights to protect and enhance our own freedom. People's social concerns—for example, to protect the rights of minorities or to eliminate the causes of poverty, chemical addiction, and institutional injustice—all grow out of a Phase III consciousness.

Human Needs the Person Seeks to Satisfy. At Phase III we need to be ourselves, to seek meaning, and be free to be creative. Self-expression, self-direction, and personal ownership of our ideas and creative enterprises are essential. The two words that best express this are *independence* and *integration*. Independence is a very positive component of any experience of emancipation, either at the personal or societal level. The

---

Differences Between Men and Women in Phase III

Our values surveys revealed that gender differences at Phase III are not in their goal values but in their means values. Both groups have Productivity, a Phase IIB value, and Sharing/Listening/Trust as their highest priorities. The difference is that Sharing/Listening/Trust is the first priority for women but the second for men—more evidence of the emphasis that women put on relationships. The third value for women is Limitation/ Celebration, which expresses a deep inner knowledge of self as a starting point in relationships and work. The third value for men is Adaptability/ Flexibility, indicating a creative response to the demands of the external world. Value differences are less pronounced at this phase, but men and women function somewhat differently, and this is reflected in their means values priorities.

American Declaration of Independence is a strong positive example. It begins:

> When in the course of human events, it becomes necessary for one people to dissolve the political bands which have connected them with another, and to assume among the powers of the earth the separate and equal station to which the laws of nature and of nature's God entitle them, a decent respect to the opinions of mankind requires that they should declare the causes which impel them to the separation.

Phase III is characterized by the formation of conscience. This is the first time a maturing person has had the consciousness and skills to make self-initiating decisions about what he or she thinks is right or wrong, without undue reliance on outside authority. For the first time, the individual recognizes that there are different points of view on significant issues, and begins to move toward a rational, objective view of truth and justice that transcends the individual.

Phase IV Consciousness: Interdependent

Phase IV people have a global context in which they work to enliven and nurture individuals and communities. The interdependent "we" responds to the common call to work for global harmony, to build and renew the face of the earth.

How the World Is Perceived by the Individual.   In Phase IV, the world is *a mystery for which we care on a global scale.* Global consciousness is seen as a series of tasks to be undertaken with other like-minded men and women. The key factor for the self in this phase is a balance of intimacy and solitude, and harmony in the total created order. In Phase IV the world is perceived as a mystery-to-be-cared-for.

Phase IV values (Figure 3-6) are based on a world view that is concerned with universal and global issues. Stage A goal values are:

> *Intimacy/Solitude.*   The experience of personal harmony that results from a combination of meditative practice and mutual openness and total acceptance of another person, which leads to new levels of meaning and awareness of truth in unity with the universal order.

> *Truth/Wisdom.*   Intense pursuit and discovery of ultimate truth above all other activities. This results in intimate knowledge of objective and subjective realities, which converges into the capacity to clearly comprehend people and systems and their interrelationship.

The Phase IV means values include Community/Personalist (a community that maximizes creativity and investigation of the truth), Detachment/Solitude, Interdependence, Prophet/Vision, and Synergy.

FIGURE 3-6. Phase IV Values

A GOALS	B GOALS
Intimacy/Solitude	Ecority
Truth/Wisdom	Global Harmony
	Word

A MEANS	B MEANS
Community/Personalist	Convivial Technology
Detachment/Solitude	Human Rights
Interdependence	Justice/Social Order
Prophet/Vision	Macroeconomics
Synergy	Minessence

Stage B goal values extend these pursuits into practice at a global level. Truth and transcendence become expressed as using technology to allow the earth to become what it was intended to be naturally. Religious concerns become concerns for a just world for all people. For example:

> *Ecority.* The capacity, skills, and personal, organizational, or conceptual influence to enable persons to take authority for the created order of the world and to enhance its beauty and balance through creative technology in ways that have worldwide influence.
>
> *Global Harmony.* Knowing the practical relationship between human oppression, freedom, and creative ecological balance so that one can influence changes that promote greater human equality.
>
> *Word.* The ability to use the power of language to heal and transform the values and world views of the hearers. To communicate universal truths so effectively that hearers become conscious of their limitations, so that life and hope are renewed and the hearers recognize their place in the larger, universal order.

These values are extended into the practical realm internationally with means values such as Convivial Technology (technology that works for world harmony and order, rather than against it), Human Rights, Macroeconomics, and Minessence.

In Phase IV, we see ourselves as being in contact with the creative life forces that make ecological balance on the planet possible from a scientific point of view. This requires the additional consciousness of how global ecological systems interact and work. The phrase *ecological balance* refers here not just to the natural world, but also to the optimal state of harmony for human beings, and is represented by values such as Human Rights and Justice/Social Order. This level of development requires that choices always come from a "we" perspective. From a spiritual viewpoint, "we" includes an experience of divine energy from within, just as Socrates noted in his eloquent defense.

How the Individual Functions in the World.   The individual self acts as "we" with others to enhance the quality of life globally. In Phase IV we see the world as a mystery, but one for which we must take authority by choosing to create and enhance the environment. We view the world as an unfinished work, an incomplete opus. Its present condition is not nearly so important as its future potential.

Phase IV people believe that the individual has internal control and external responsibility for the world at large. This group not only aspires to control their own lives, but will also cooperate with others to change societal and institutional norms. They are often associated with change agents in society.[4]

The self is transcended in Phase IV; not only does the individual "I" become a community "we," but there is a communal call to mankind to renew the face of the earth. In the common interdependent action among men and women and with nature itself, a unity begins to emerge between humanity and humanities-developed technology.

Human Needs the Person Seeks to Satisfy.   Phase IV people have a need to enhance global harmony through communal action and collaboration. People who achieve a harmonious balance at Phase IV seek to see things in their wholeness and to understand the interrelatedness of parts—frequently opposing parts—to each other and to the whole. This is in line with contemporary developments in physics, which now sees harmony as movement and tension in the reconciliation of opposites. Congruence, or the suitable relatedness of things to one another and of parts to the whole, is essential to a Phase IV understanding of harmony.

Differences Between Men and Women in Phase IV

In our survey of men and women business executives, Phase IV men had Truth/Wisdom as their first priority, while Phase IV women gave priority to Interdependence. Even at this high level of development, gender differences remain: men are concerned about the truth as an external investigated phenomena, while women have the relational dimension as their first priority. The value of Justice/Social Order was held by both men and women; it is simply that the first and second priorities were different. Phase IV men prefer to enter into justice issues through reasoned investigation, while women approach the same issues through caring acts followed by reasoned investigation.

The concept of harmony applies to the inner life of the individual as well as to the external world. Insights from psychology and eastern religions have raised in the western mind a new awareness of the potential for personal harmony. At Phase IV, intimacy and solitude become enlightenment. However, the Phase IV person realizes that this harmony must be extended to technology and society at large—the global community.

Inner harmony must be integrated with social harmony through an appropriate technology. Two books that illustrate the Phase IV approach to technology are Ivan Illich's *Tools for Conviviality* (1973), which suggests that man must be in control of his tools, of his technology, rather than a victim of them; and Schumacher's *Small Is Beautiful* (1973), which suggests that we need to develop an intermediate technology that suits the growth needs of the people who use it.

Exploring World Views and Consciousness

In this chapter we have seen that values give meaning to our lives and shape our view of the world as we develop. Not only is our view of the world shaped by our values, but the world we live in shapes our values and world view. As we begin to understand the development of world views and consciousness, many important and interesting questions arise. Here are some of the questions we will explore:

- Is it only our world view that shapes our values, or do other factors such gender, profession, education—even the culture we live in—contribute to our value priorities? This reality of human differences will be the subject of Chapter 4.

- How does consciousness develop? Is there a relationship between the four phases and consciousness development? We have found that consciousness is altered by a pull from future values. This will be the subject of Chapter 5.

- What is the relationship between skills and values? This is the topic for Chapter 6.

- What comes first—the values or the world view? How do we grow to higher levels of values development and consciousness? We will deal with these questions as we look at the seven cycles of human development in Chapters 7 and 8.

- Is there a relationship between values development, world view, and organizational development? This question will be addressed in the last four chapters of the book.

4

Why People's Values Differ

Five assumptions about the nature of human values:

1. The total number of values that a person possesses is relatively small.

2. All men and women everywhere possess the same values to different degrees.

3. Values are organized into value systems.

4. The antecedents of human values can be traced to culture, society and its institutions, and personality.

5. The consequence of human values will be manifested in virtually all phenomena that social scientists might consider worth investigating and understanding.

Milton Rokeach, *The Nature of Human Values*

We all recognize that human beings are different from one another—not only physically but emotionally, psychologically, and spiritually. In the last chapter we saw that our values are a sort of filter through which we view the world as we pass through four identifiable phases of

63

consciousness. In this chapter we will explore the way in which the institutions and cultures within which we live affect our values.

We human beings are driven to create order in the way we understand the world; we want the world to make sense. We are also curious by nature. Everything we have learned in our research indicates that human beings naturally pursue purposeful information retrieval. We seem to want to recreate ourselves and the world in a life-giving way. At the same time, it is evident that our freedom and our values are affected and limited by our environments: our institutions, our cultures, and our personal and shared histories.

To see how our profession, gender, and culture affect our value priorities, we will look at research about human differences—research that was conducted on a range of populations during the last ten years.

Norm Studies of Group Values

In our research we administered the Hall-Tonna Inventory of Values to people in many different groups. This survey consists of a series of forced choices that are analyzed by a computer software program; the result is a printout that identifies a person's values from the list of 125 values (Appendix A), and the priority order of those values. We also developed a method of creating group profiles through a composite of individual scores, and we used this to measure the value priorities of different groups. Studies of this sort that are designed to describe groups are called norm studies.

We carried out norm studies on more that 40 different groups. In this chapter we will look at three different types of groups to see how external influences affect our behavior and our personal values. First we will look at the value priorities of professional groups. For example, can you generalize about the values held by engineers? And are these values different from those held by attorneys? Next we will look at whether the values of men differ from those of women. Is it possible that men and women make assumptions about one another that are actually untrue—that are based on a misunderstanding of the differences between the sexes? The third kind of group that we will look at is that of cultural groups. We will compare the values of several cultures to see whether being from a different culture implies having some value differences.

Remember that norm studies do not predict the exact profiles of individuals. Individuals within a given group differ in the degree to which they hold a dominant value, and some individuals may not hold that value at all. For example, in our cross-cultural studies we found that Americans as a group put a high value on Sharing/Listening/Trust. However, it would be fairly easy to find individual Americans who are

FIGURE 4-1.   Primary Values of Four Professional Groups

Military Recruiters	Engineers
Productivity	Productivity
Rights/Respect	Sharing/Listening/Trust
Responsibility	Competence/Confidence
Competence/Confidence	Responsibility
Work/Labor	Decision/Initiation

Church Leaders	Attorneys
Sharing/Listening/Trust	Competence/Confidence
Belief/Philosophy	Productivity
Loyalty/Fidelity	Sharing/Listening/Trust
Productivity	Work/Labor
Self-Actualization	Rights/Respect

deeply distrustful and unwilling to share. Most other Americans are likely to find those people's distrust very odd, however, because as a culture Americans hold this value as important.

Differences Between Professional Groups

Our norm studies show that with this instrumentation we can measure differences in values priorities between one group and another. For example, Figure 4-1 lists the highest five value priorities for four professional groups.

First let's look at the military recruiters. The Inventory of Values was given to 34 full-time recruiters. Figure 4-1 compares them with 35 full-time engineers, of whom six were women. The first priority of both groups is Productivity, which is defined as:

> *Productivity.* The energy that results from generating and completing tasks and activities and achieving externally established goals and expectations.

Both groups see getting the job done as their primary task. Both groups also share the values of Responsibility and Competence/Confidence:

> *Responsibility.* The ability to be personally accountable for and in charge of a specific area or course of action in an organization or group.
>
> *Competence/Confidence.* Realistic and objective confidence that one has the skill to achieve in the world of work and to feel that those skills are a positive contribution.

Although they share these three values in common, the two groups view the world quite differently because they prioritize the values differently.

The military recruiters place Rights/Respect as their second priority. Rights/Respect is an appropriate priority for someone who has a military career:

> *Rights/Respect.* The moral principle of respecting the worth and property of another as I expect others to respect me and my property.

Engineers, on the other hand, must cooperate to get a job done, and they place Sharing/Listening/Trust as their second priority:

> *Sharing/Listening/Trust.* The capacity to hear another's thoughts and feelings actively and accurately and to express personal thoughts and feelings in a climate of mutual confidence in one another's integrity.

Each group is in a profession that has an overall value orientation that influences its members. In other words, your psychological and spiritual values are in part conditioned by your profession, and the profession you choose influences your value system.

As we might expect, the value priorities of church leaders and attorneys are quite different from those of military recruiters and engineers. They both have Productivity as a value, but it is not their number-one priority. It is in second place for the attorneys, but is much lower for the church leaders. Sharing/Listening/Trust is also shared in common by these two groups, which is understandable since they both work in close cooperation with other people. But here the similarity ends.

The church leaders have Sharing/Listening/Trust as their highest priority, followed by Belief/Philosophy and Loyalty/Fidelity:

> *Belief/Philosophy.* Adherence to a belief system, set of principles, or established philosophy that is based on universally accepted authoritative documents such as the Bible, Koran, or Upanishads, which espouse the concept of reverence for the universal order.

> *Loyalty/Fidelity.* Strict observance of promises and duties to those in authority and to those in close personal relationships.

This makes a lot of sense, since church leaders are those who conduct worship services, marry couples, and call people to be loyal to their faith. Their last value, Self-Actualization, is also related to faith; it emphasizes human and spiritual growth:

> *Self-Actualization:* The inner drive toward experiencing and expressing the totality of one's being through spiritual, psychological, physical, and mental exercises that enhance the development of one's maximum potential.

When we compare the values of church leaders to those of attorneys, we see priorities that lead to a different behavior. Competence/Confidence and Productivity are the first priorities of the attorneys. Their last two priorities are Work/Labor, or being paid for their services, and Rights/Respect.

FIGURE 4-2. **Phases and Stages of Values for Military Recruiters and Church Leaders**

Military Recruiters	Church Leaders
Productivity IIB	Sharing/Listening/Trust IIIA
Rights/Respect IIA	Belief/Philosophy IIB
Responsibility IIA	Loyalty/Fidelity IIB
Competence/Confidence IIB	Productivity IIB
Work/Labor IIB	Self-Actualization IIIA

Differences in Phases of Development. Taking the analysis to another level, if we compare the military recruiters with the church leaders, and look at their overall phase of development, we see another level of difference. Figure 4-2 adds the phase and stage for each value for two of the professional groups.

Generally speaking, the phase and stage of the value given first priority determines the world view of an individual or group. In Figure 4-2 we see that the recruiters have a Phase II world view, which implies that the person sees the world as dominated by those in authority and very rule determined. We verified this in our interviews with the recruiters, who are, after all, following the rules of the military. Notice also that all five values held by the recruiters are from Phase II. The church leaders, on the other hand, reflect a Phase IIIA world view, which is more self-initiating, independent, and self-directed. The church leaders we interviewed were in fact independent operators who led their own congregations with a minimal of external control by their denominational heads.

Our research led us to conclude that the external reinforcement of our work and profession does create differences in values and world views. Values are not developed simply by an individual's choice, but are also affected by corporate reinforcement.

The values that we found were held in common by professional groups do not manifest themselves only in the professional lives of the individuals. Values are internalized, so they will be carried over into every dimension of daily life. Another way of saying this is that the primary institutions in our lives will affect our personal values, so that our behavior and world view is affected not only at work, but at home and in all other dimensions of our lives.

Differences Between Men and Women

In the comparison in Figure 4-1, each of the groups is a mixture of men and women, although men represented the larger percentage of people

FIGURE 4-3. Values of Women and Men in Leadership Professions

Women's Values	Men's Values
1. Sharing /Listening/Trust	1. Productivity
2. Productivity	2. Competence/Confidence
3. Competence/Confidence	3. Sharing/Listening/Trust
4. Rights/Respect	4. Responsibility
5. Adaptability/Flexibility	5. Work/Labor
6. Self-Actualization	6. Adaptability/Flexibility
7. Efficiency/Planning	7. Self-Actualization
8. Family/Belonging	8. Efficiency/Planning
9. Knowledge/Insight	9. Family/Belonging
10. Care/Nurture	10. Decision/Initiation

in each group. Are the values of women different than those of men? Are there differences even in men's and women's world views? Or are the values that are reinforced by the external environment—such as our profession—so overwhelming that there are really no important differences between men and women?

Figure 4-3 compares the values of 355 women with an average age of 39 with a group of 215 men whose average age is 36. All of the men and women were in administrative or leadership positions. In order to get a better picture of the differences between men's and women's values, we have expanded the list to show the top ten values.

Since these are all working men and women in administrative or leadership positions, we can assume that their values are in part related to their professional lives. The two groups have many values in common. For example, Productivity and Competence/Confidence may well be values that are related to their work. However, the priorities are different.

Remember that the first priority that we choose defines the quality of what comes second and third and suggests an individual's or group's world view. For the women the first priority is Sharing/Listening/Trust, which is relational in emphasis. This in turn defines the following values of Productivity and Competence/Confidence, which are now within that relational framework. The male values, on the other hand, begin with the emphasis on Productivity, where behavior is externally oriented. Our work, as well as that of other researchers, indicates that this is an important difference between men's and women's values and world views. Carol Gilligan (1982), for example, found that women see the world in a relational context, while men approach the world from the context of competition and separateness.[1]

FIGURE 4-4. Women's and Men's Values in Retail Sales Professions

Women's Values	Men's Values
1. Sharing /Listening/Trust	1. Productivity
2. Rights/Respect	2. Responsibility
3. Efficiency/Planning	3. Competence/Confidence
4. Competence/Confidence	4. Self-Actualization
5. Productivity	5. Work/Labor
6. Limitation/Celebration	6. Rights/Respect
7. Adaptability/Flexibility	7. Adaptability/Flexibility
8. Work/Labor	8. Achievement/Success
9. Self-Actualization	9. Loyalty/Fidelity
10. Responsibility	10. Competition

FIGURE 4-5. Unique Women's and Men's Values, Combined Groups

Women's Values	Men's Values
1. Sharing/Listening/Trust IIIA	1. Responsibility IIB
2. Care/Nurture IIA	2. Achievement/Success IIB
3. Limitation/Celebration IIIB	3. Loyalty/Fidelity IIB
4. Knowledge/Insight IIIB	4. Competition IIB
	5. Decision/Initiation IIIA

Now notice the differences in phases between the two groups. The female leaders are operating at Phase III, whereas the males are at Phase II. Some might conclude that the women are superior. That might even be the case, but in all likelihood the men are internalizing the values and world view of institutions, which are more rule-oriented and controlled. The women appear to be leaders who are more self-initiating and independent, in that their leadership is primarily relational in character and less oriented toward productivity as a first goal.

Figure 4-4 is a similar comparison, this time between men and women whose profession is retail sales. These groups were smaller, 25 women and 51 men. Again there are several values held in common. Again the feminine values are relational as indicated by the fact that the first value is Sharing/Listening/Trust. As before, the masculine value system begins with the external attention to Productivity, although this time Responsibility has moved up in priority.

Figure 4-5 lists the values that were unique to men and women in the two groups represented in Figures 4-3 and 4-4. In this comparison, the value differences between men and women are very clear. It is easy to see that the four uniquely feminine values have a relational or internal context:

> *Sharing/Listening/Trust.* The capacity to hear another's thoughts and feelings actively and accurately and to express personal thoughts and feelings in a climate of mutual confidence in one another's integrity.
>
> *Care/Nurture.* To be physically and emotionally supported by family and friends throughout one's life from childhood through aging, and to value doing the same for others.
>
> *Limitation/Celebration.* The recognition that personal limits are the framework for exercising one's talents. The ability to laugh at one's own imperfections.
>
> *Knowledge/Insight.* The pursuit of truth through patterned investigation, motivated by increased intuition and unconsciously gained understanding of the wholeness of reality.

The five uniquely masculine values have quite a different tone:

> *Responsibility.* The ability to be personally accountable for and in charge of a specific area or course of action in an organization or group.
>
> *Achievement/Success.* Accomplishing something noteworthy and admirable in the world of work or education.
>
> *Loyalty/Fidelity.* Strict observance of promises and duties to those in authority and to those in close personal relationships.
>
> *Competition.* The ability to be energized by a sense of rivalry, to be first or most respected in a given arena such as sports, education, or work.
>
> *Decision/Initiation.* The ability to feel that it is one's responsibility to begin a creative course of action, or to act on one's conscience without external prompting.

The female values are relational and internal in their perspective. Care and sharing are relational, while insight and celebration of one's limitations are inner qualities. The masculine values are radically different. They emphasize external responsibility to achieve in the world through competition, loyalty, and decision making.

Another clear difference is that the women are functioning at a Phase III level, whereas the men are at Phase II. Minimally, this says something about how men and women are socialized. It also has important implications for the workplace now and in the future, with the increasing number of women in positions of leadership.

These differences in value priorities illustrate that *men and women perceive the world differently and this affects what they choose to prioritize in their day-to-day behavior.* Later in the book we will explore the ramifications of these differences for organizational planning and leadership development.

Differences Between Cultures

We now have evidence that our gender and profession affect our value systems. Does the wider experience of the culture we grow up in also

FIGURE 4-6. Cultural Differences in Educational Administrators

Group 1: U.S.A.	Group 2: Spain
1. Productivity	1. Sharing/Listening/Trust
2. Decision/Initiation	2. Being Self
3. Growth/Expansion	3. Community/Personalist
4. Creativity	4. Authority/Honesty
5. Community/Personalist	5. Education/Knowledge

reinforce certain value sets? Nelson and Jurmain (1987, p. 3) define culture as: "The set of rules, standards, and norms shared by members of a society, transmitted by learning, and responsible for the behavior of those members." These anthropologists believe that culture includes the totality of the behavior of a society—its physical and social behavior, its norms, and its value systems.

Figure 4-6 compares two groups of educational administrators in higher education: Group 1 is comprised of 16 people from a private midwestern university in the U.S.A. and Group 2 consists of 20 people from a similar university in Spain.

The differences between the American and Spanish educators are pronounced. Group 1 places its highest priorities on decision making and organizational growth based on Productivity, a Phase II world view. You may be surprised to see that for the U.S. group education as a value does not appear in the first five priorities. The American administrators themselves felt that the reason for this is that they have to put their energy into enrolling new students to ensure that their schools will be financially viable.

Group 2 places the highest priority on Sharing/Listening/Trust while valuing the communal aspect of the group and Authority/Honesty. By contrast with Group 1, they put a high emphasis on education, priority five. The university in Spain is private, but it is supported by government funds, so they do not have to concern themselves as much with money considerations. Their highest priority indicates that they function in Phase III, making them more independent and self-initiating in their orientation.

Clearly the values are different. Group 2 has a different attitude toward social interaction that is Spanish in character, with less of a separation between education and administration. This study suggests that these value differences might in part be culturally derived.

Figure 4-7 compares Roman Catholic sisters, all in the same international order, all professional educators, all women of course, and all in the same average age range. The four countries they represent are

FIGURE 4-7. Cultural Differences in Catholic Sisters

United States	Italy
1. Sharing/Listening/Trust	1. Generosity/Compassion
2. Rights/Respect	2. Limitation/Celebration
3. Limitation/Acceptance	3. Courtesy/Hospitality
4. Service/Vocation	4. Service/Vocation
5. Integration/Wholeness	5. Sharing/Listening/Trust

Austria	Germany
1. Duty/Obligation	1. Sharing/Listening/Trust
2. Belief/Philosophy	2. Service/Vocation
3. Service/Vocation	3. Duty/Obligation
4. Wonder/Curiosity	4. Loyalty/Fidelity
5. Sharing/Listening/Trust	5. Limitation/Acceptance

Austria, Germany, Italy, and the United States. Each group was approximately 30 in size.

This was obviously not a detailed cross-cultural study. However, since the sisters share the same gender, profession, and religious order, we can conclude that any differences we find transcend profession and gender, and that they are probably related in part to culture.

When this data was collected, the sisters were also individually interviewed about their values orientation. The American group was distinct in its attitude about women's rights and their own personal authority. This feminist orientation is also a Phase III orientation and world view, and is represented through their first three priorities:

Sharing/Listening/Trust. The capacity to hear another's thoughts and feelings actively and accurately and to express personal thoughts and feelings in a climate of mutual confidence in one another's integrity.

Rights/Respect. The moral principle of respecting the worth and property of another as I expect others to respect me and my property.

Limitation/Acceptance. Giving positive mental assent to the reality that one has boundaries and inabilities, based on objective self-awareness of personal strengths and potential as well as weakness and inability. The capacity for self-criticism.

By contrast, the Italian group, although also at Phase III, did not want to do anything until after they had entertained and celebrated with the interviewers. This orientation is very much a part of a culture where eating and drinking is an ongoing celebration that is important to every

Italian family. This spirit of generosity and service is vividly illustrated in their first three priorities:

Generosity/Compassion. The ability to share one's unique gifts and skills with others as a way of serving humanity without expecting reciprocation.

Limitation/Celebration. The recognition that personal limits are the framework for exercising one's talents. The ability to laugh at one's own imperfections.

Courtesy/Hospitality. Offering polite and respectful treatment to others as well as treating guests and strangers in a friendly and generous manner, and to value receiving the same treatment from others.

The German and Austrian cultures are traditionally regarded as more serious, and their values in this study emphasize duty and service. Characteristically, these cultures are less interpersonal and more reserved in their relationships with others. The Austrian group comes from the phase of rules, Phase II. Worship in this case is a part of their work dimension, since these sisters pray daily as a group.

Duty/Obligation. Closely following established customs and regulations out of dedication to one's peers and a sense of responsibility to institutional codes.

Belief/Philosophy. Adherence to a belief system, set of principles, or established philosophy that is based on universally accepted authoritative documents such as the Bible, Koran, or Upanishads, which espouse the concept of reverence for the universal order.

Service/Vocation. The ability to be motivated to use personally unique gifts and skills to contribute to society through one's occupation, business, profession, or calling.

The German group has a Phase III consciousness in the interpersonal dimension, much like the Americans; both groups place the value of Sharing/Listening/Trust first. However, this was followed by the same emphasis on Service/Vocation and Duty/Obligation as in the Austrian group. They also added the value of Loyalty/Fidelity as a fourth priority.

Do I Have a Choice in My Values?

Differences in value priorities underlie the essential human differences that characterize each of us. It makes a difference whether you are a man or a woman. Women in positions of leadership are going to lead and manage differently because their value priorities are generally different than those of men.

The profession you belong to and the culture that you come from will affect your value priorities for the rest of your life. A person from any norm group will have value priorities unique to that group—whether the group is Russians, lesbians, the disabled, or any other group. These values will affect each of us in all sectors of our lives.

What choices do we have about the value priorities we live by? Are our values merely rigid cultural and gender determinants that are programmed into our personalities because of who we are, where we grew up, and the careers we happened to choose?

We believe that these group values do not tell the whole story. They are simply an emphasis, a bias, within each individual's value system. It is important to remember that there are 125 values, and at any given time in our lives we probably do not have room for more than about ten priorities. Even if you and another person had the same top ten values, your behavior will be radically different depending on how you prioritize those ten values. The possibilities for value profiles are almost infinite. Your world view, the culture you were born into, your work, your social environment, and your gender do indeed influence your values, but these factors do not determine exactly what your values and value priorities will be. They are really boundaries and limitations to your freedom.

We do know, however, that these boundaries and your limitations can be expanded almost limitlessly. This is not a contradiction in terms: the key is consciousness. It is important to know what your values are, and what values you have as a man or a woman. It is important to know how your job, your religion, and your culture place certain value expectations on you. If you do not do this, then you may well become what others want you to become rather than choosing life for yourself. To choose life, we need to do two things:

1. Become conscious of the values influences in our lives.
2. Ask: What does it mean to be an excellent human being? What values do I need to be the best person I can possibly be in spite of all the influences in my life?

These first three chapters have laid the foundation for an understanding of values. You should be able to see by now that an understanding of values will provide you with a rich new tool for transforming yourself and the groups you belong to.

If you can now see this possibility, you have probably begun to ask critical questions: What do I need to do to develop the values I want to have? How can I grow through the phases of development? How do I develop values and consciousness? What is the relationship between skills and my growth and development? In Chapter 5 we will look at values as the foundation for personal transformation.

5

How Your Consciousness Develops from the Future

After passing through all the phases of world-experience and self-experience, the individual reaches consciousness of his true meaning. He knows himself the beginning, middle, and end of self-development of the psyche, which manifests itself first as the ego and is then expressed by this ego as the self.
Erich Neumann, *The Origins and History of Consciousness*

In the first four chapters of this book we have looked at what values are and how they affect our behavior and way of looking at the world. Now we are going to see how we can use our knowledge of values to affect personal transformation. That is, we are going to see what values have to do with human growth and maturity.

FIGURE 5-1. Self-Development Track

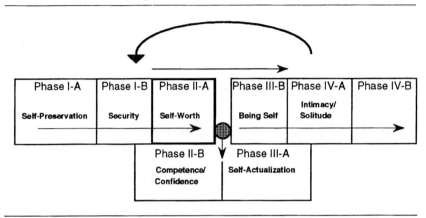

In this chapter we are going to look at what it takes to progress through the Four Phases of Consciousness. First we are going to look at the common tracks that certain values follow through the four developmental phases of consciousness. Then we will demonstrate that it is actually our future values—those that we still have not grown into—that drive us in our choices and actions. We will also explore the effect that memory has on our choices and actions.

An underlying assumption of values development is that values develop in tracks through the four phases. That is, the values and needs we develop early in our life are the foundation for the more complex values at the later phase.

Values Tracking: The Self-Development Track

We have found that values are connected to one another. They develop in somewhat predictable tracks as we progress through the Four Phases of Consciousness. The 125 values that we all have the potential of holding tend to occur at different stages and phases of our development. The values that appear in the later stages are more complex, and are built upon our earlier experience of other values.

The clearest demonstration of this is to see how the goal values naturally track from Self-Preservation to Being Self. It is how the self develops in each of us. Figure 5-1 illustrates how this works.

We begin in Phase I with Self-Preservation. This is the experience of being safe and protected in the world. Ideally, this begins at birth in one's family of origin. Slowly as you adjust you feel less anxious and more comfortable with the world, and the value of Security becomes internalized.

In Phase II the world is completely different and social in its orientation. The key value is Self-Worth. This is a social value, meaning that you need to be valued by others to grow up with trust in other people. Self-Worth in Phase II-A precedes the value of Competence/Confidence in II-B. Why? Because you have to feel worthwhile and good about yourself before you can learn to feel and be competent.

In Figure 5-1 Self-Worth has heavier borders, indicating that it is the most important value in human development. Without self-worth, we do not trust others, which seriously impairs our ability to learn, work, and relate to others.

The bridge to Phase III is Phase II-B's Competence/Confidence, becoming Self-Actualization in III-A. Competence is learning from others what one needs to function in the world of work, but Self-Actualization is learning that takes on a more internal dimension. It includes a wholistic view of one's personal development. It is the development of the self at an intellectual, spiritual, emotional, and physical level—and an integration of all these elements. Their fullest expression is in Being Self, defined as the capacity to own one's truth about oneself and the world with objective awareness of personal strengths and limitations plus the ability to act both independently and cooperatively when appropriate. This is the high point of self-development. Values like Intimacy in Phase III-B and Intimacy/Solitude in Phase IV-A are extensions of this value, where the ego moves beyond itself to a "we" orientation to reality.

There are many natural variations on this basic self-development track. Figure 5-2 illustrates these variations. Each of the goal values in any stage is expanded and particularized in its meaning by any of the

FIGURE 5-2. Variations of the Self-Development Track

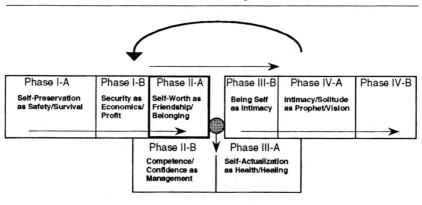

means values in that same stage. This gives rise to an infinite number of tracks that will be unique to each person. For example, in Figure 5-2, Self-Preservation could be expressed as the value of Safety/Survival. An expression of Security by a given individual could be Economics/Profit. In fact, many people are driven by what appears to be greed, when in fact the underlying reality is the need to satisfy Security.

Another example is that Self-Worth can be expressed as Friendship/ Belonging—the place where your self is most valued. It could equally be expressed as Support/Peer, Tradition, or Control/Order/Discipline as activities where you get the self-worth and esteem you need.

Moving on to Phase II, Competence/Confidence could be through Management or any of the Phase II-B means values such as Efficiency/ Planning, Administration/Control, or Technology/Science. Self-Actualization in Phase III-A can be through Health/Healing or any other means values such as Search for Meaning/Hope. Finally, in Phase III-B, Being Self could be expressed as Intimacy or values such as Pioneerism/ Innovation. Phase IV invites the person beyond the self toward enlightenment and global transcendence. We have looked at some basic ways in which values tracks relate to the development of the self. But what about values tracking and the other dimensions of our lives such as our work, our spirituality, and global issues such as the environment?

Three Important Value Tracks

There are three common tracks that our research shows are basic to the way many of the values are interconnected. Interestingly enough, these three tracks are also three common models used in modern psychology, religion, and the social sciences to explain human development and what motivates us to grow. Unlike the self-development track, the high point is not Being Self in Phase III, but the values in Phase IV.

As we discuss these tracks, remember that they are presented in a simplified form. In fact, as we saw above, there are other values within each stage that could substitute for a given value. The means values connect in each track, creating a rich and complex description of human development. Figure 5-3 illustrates these three common tracks.

Track One: Vision

Track One deals with the need of the human being to survive, get along in the world, and finally cooperate with the environment in order to build a better world. This struggle to survive and then see a vision for a better existence for ourselves is the innate experience of hope. It is the need for each of us to have goals and to envision a future.

FIGURE 5-3. Three Common Value Tracks

Phase I	Phase II	Phase III	Phase IV
Track One M Self-Preservation	Vision Work/Labor	Service/Vocation Construction/ New Order	Ecority Human Rights
F Wonder/Awe/Fate	Family/Belonging	Justice/Social Order	Justice/Social Order
Track Two Security	Courage Self-Worth	Search for Meaning/Hope Faith/Risk/Vision	Truth/Wisdom
Track Three Self-Interest/ Control	Compassion Loyalty/Fidelity Family/Belonging	Empathy Intimacy Human Dignity	Intimacy/Solitude

Our earliest self-awareness is of the body with its predominantly masculine or feminine characteristics. According to Gilligan (1982), feminine and masculine perceptions of the world seem to develop differently. Girls perceive survival in terms of the preservation of relationships, and communication arises as the means to get along in the world. Boys, on the other hand, see survival in terms of rules and rights, and competition arises as the means to get along in the world. Feminine ego development, then, is influenced by a psychology of interconnectedness, and masculine ego development by a psychology of separateness during Phases I and II. However, it is the task of both genders to integrate aspects of the other to grow beyond Phase II.

One view of human beings is that, like most animals, we are primarily motivated by the need to survive and preserve ourselves. This initiating reality for men most often shows up as the value of Self-Preservation, an external reactive orientation to the world. The equivalent for the majority of women is a more internal and introspective way of dealing with reality, the beginning value being Wonder/Awe/Fate. It is fascinating to see what happens when these values develop through the Four Phases of Consciousness.

Stereotypically, for men the value of Self-Preservation in Phase I becomes Work/Labor in Phase II as an extension of survival. Other Phase II values such as Achievement/Success, Management, and Productivity are extensions of this. When Work/Labor in Phase II is experienced at Phase III, it becomes a chosen vocation, a self-initiating personal choice.

A man is not simply surviving; his value has become Service/Vocation—
or even Construction/New Order, where he creates his own organization
and contributes to society as a whole by who he is and what he does.

At Phase IV, preserving oneself and surviving become Ecority, or taking care of and preserving the planet itself. In other words, the beginning
value of Self-Preservation has graduated into Ecority as preserving all
things and not only oneself.

The stereotype for women follows a parallel track, with a process that
is similar but different. Self-Preservation is often present at the beginning
as a more inward reaction that implies vulnerability: Wonder/Awe/Fate.
This then manifests itself as Family/Belonging in Phase II-A, the biological extension of Safety/Survival in Phase I. In today's world women
have the value of Work/Labor, but it originates in Wonder/Awe/Fate,
and it is often experienced more relationally and introspectively in leadership. In Phase III, Service/Vocation is common to men and women.
Construction/New Order often emerges with women as a concern for
the Justice dimension of a new institution or society. In Phase IV, Ecority
is there as Human Rights and Justice/Social Order at an international
level—the relational dimension of Ecority.

It is important to understand that values do cross over between the
sexes. Many women feel that Work/Labor is as important as Family/
Belonging, or that ecology (Ecority) is an essential dimension of our future.
These tracks are there for all human beings regardless of gender, but differences between men and women can help build more collaborative futures.

Another important assumption is that all women and men have both
feminine and masculine sides. These value tracks recognize that as human beings develop they become more successful at integrating and balancing their masculine and feminine values.

Ecority as the development and survival of all humanity is an expansion
of Self-Preservation, which is survival of oneself. Work/Labor, Service/
Vocation, and Justice/Social Order are extensions of (Self) Preservation on
the one hand and dimensions of the vision of Ecority and Justice/Social
Order on the other hand. *What is most significant is that the values in Phases I to
III are partial dimensions of the more complex values in Phase IV; therefore it is our
Phase IV values that shape and motivate each of us in our development.* It is not
Self-Preservation and Wonder/Awe/Fate that push us; it is the need to
express our creativity and freedom through Service/Vocation, Justice/Social
Order, and Ecority that pulls us into the future.

Track Two: Courage

The second track is courage (Figure 5-4). This is the ability to live as if the
vision you have for your life is true now. People on the second track

FIGURE 5-4. Track Two: Courage

Security	Self-Worth	Search for Meaning/Hope Faith/Risk/Vision	Truth/Wisdom

move from Security to Truth/Wisdom. A central theme of this track is faith—a powerful value that is by no means held only in a religious context. Faith implies personal courage and independence.

A person with faith or courage is willing to behave now as if what he or she envisions for the future were true. For example, entrepreneurs are business people who are willing to act out of faith in their vision of a technological breakthrough, risking their financial and professional security to bring their dreams to reality. When Martin Luther King, Jr. said "I have a dream," he was living out that dream by risking his life, by living as if the dream were already a reality. His vision was driving his behavior in the present.

The initial value on Track Two is Security. At its extreme, Security emphasizes control, comfort, and maintaining the status quo in a stratified society. In Phase II, the personal comfort of Security gives way to the need to find real security and comfort in the support and affirmation of others in Self-Worth. Values like Friendship/Belonging, Support/Peer, and Care/Nurture are all extensions of Self-Worth.

In Phase III, Self-Worth becomes the ability to give worth to others through Search for Meaning/Hope, and having faith (Faith/Risk/Vision) in others. The ultimate opposite of Security is the exploration of Truth/Wisdom. The pursuit of truth is a motivator that transcends the need for security. Great leaders of history have died for their need to express and pursue the truth as they saw it—Socrates and Gandhi are both examples of people who pursued truth at a level of integrity that made them willing to die rather than compromise their beliefs.

At Phase IV, other values work together with the pursuit of truth. For Gandhi, for example, the pursuit of truth was striving for justice—Justice/Social Order and Human Rights. The values in the early phases are partial fulfillments of their Phase IV manifestations. *The future pulls us from an internal vision we have of wholeness as expressed by the values in Phase IV, which are a fuller and more wholistic expression of Phase I–III values.* Security as personal comfort becomes Truth/Wisdom, which, combined with Justice/Social Order and Ecority, becomes an investigation of how Security can be accomplished globally.

FIGURE 5-5. Track Three: Compassion

Self-Interest/ Control	Loyalty/Fidelity Family/Belonging	Empathy Intimacy Human Dignity	Intimacy/Solitude

Track Three: Compassion

The third common track is that of compassion or love (Figure 5-5). This track is the means to make a vision happen through courage. It is really what courage is about: building a safe, new world that has compassion for its inhabitants regardless of gender, race, or ethnic origin. In other words, Track Three is the glue that makes the other two work.

Track Three goes from Self-Interest/Control, which is narcissism or self-love, to Intimacy/Solitude, which is the ability to love oneself, transcend that love, and love others without limitations. When we are born, we are very narcissistic; we believe the world is there for *us*. More basically, we actually believe that we are of infinite worth. Track Three moves from this basic experience to the realization that all human beings are also infinitely valuable.

This journey begins at birth. We feel that the universe is there for us, and then we encounter the family, with its components of loyalty and fidelity, and we find that others also have to be taken seriously. When these values evolve to Phase III, they become Empathy, or the ability to see the world through the eyes of others and to appreciate their points of view and perspectives. The individual experiences this as Human Dignity, and finally as Intimacy and its counterpart, Intimacy/Solitude, which is the transcendent experience of feeling that love extends to all human beings and beyond to the source of life itself. The most wholistic perspective is in Phase IV, which is drawing us forward into continuing growth. The other side of this picture is that values at the lower end of the continuum can exert a resistant force that moves us away from growth toward our dark side.

The Dark Side

The values of Self-Preservation, the implicit fears of Wonder/Awe/Fate and Security, the need to avoid pain, and Self-Interest/Control as a tendency to be self-centered and mistrustful are with us all the time. Whenever business is bad, we have a crisis at home, or even when we have to take an examination, these values raise their heads and draw us back. In the extreme these earlier values provide motivation, in a sense dominating our personal vision. These foundation values can become future values, and we cease to grow.

When Self-Preservation dominates our lives, we become tyrannical and insensitive to externals and can even allow desecration of the environment. This was the case, for example, in the Gulf War of 1991, when Saddam Hussein ordered troops to set oil wells on fire and to release oil into the Persian Gulf. An overdose of Security prevents risk taking and the ability to see the truth of anything outside of our own opinions. Finally, Self-Interest as narcissism means creating a world, a family, or an administration where only you know what decisions can be made. In the extreme it becomes a total denial of the worth of anyone's opinion about any decision of consequence that you do not guide and control yourself.

There is a natural tendency for these values to combine coercively and draw us away from development. Historically, the world has been in a Phase I world of survival, where the orientation of a person in power has been to have total disregard for the environment and human life. Napoleon and Hitler represent the extreme of this; for them, the idea was to make the world look like them and become their vision for how things ought to be.

Living into the Future

There is a remarkable richness in the possibilities of these tracks. The patterns of human development they represent are the basis for both human survival in society and the preservation and development of global society. When we put them in relationship to the negative pull of the dark side, we perceive very quickly that life is basically a struggle—not to survive, but to develop the innate potential within each of us.

Remember that we have shown only the dominant values in each track in order to illustrate the concept of value tracking. An individual holds as many as ten dominant values at any one time, and all of these values are related. Each person's means values are linked to his or her goal values. Each of us is drawn mysteriously forward by future phases and stages, and we grow and develop in complexity as we evolve. The question we now want to address is: How do we move forward and prevent ourselves from being drawn back into the despair of Phase I?

Foundation, Focus, and Future Values

Over the last five years more than 10,000 people have taken the Hall-Tonna Survey. The survey is designed to identify each person's top 15 to 20 values, and to sort them out into the Four Phases of Consciousness. The scores are analyzed by a computer, which prints out individual profiles.

FIGURE 5-6. Example of Focus Values for a Phase II-B and III-A Person

═══FOUNDATION═══		═══FOCUS AREA═══		═══FUTURE VALUES═══			
Phase I		**Phase II**		**Phase III**		**Phase IV**	
Stage A	Stage B	Stage A	Stage B	Stage A	Stage B	Stage A	Stage B

When we analyzed all these profiles, we found that the majority of a person's values always fall within two adjacent stages in the Four Phases: a Stage A and the following Stage B, or a Stage B and the following Stage A. We call this the *focus values area*, because this is where a person's first priorities lie. Figure 5-6 is an example of how this is organized for a person whose focus area is Phase II-B and III-A. The focus area can be any two adjacent stages—stages II-A and II-B, I-B and II-A, or any other adjacent combination.

Everyone we tested had values in all four stages of development, but the computer analysis identified the two stages on which each person was currently focused. The *focus area* is identified in Figure 5-6 by the two stages that are gray. The values that fall into the stages preceding the focus values we call *foundation values*, and the values that fall beyond the focus values we call *future values*, as the diagram illustrates. All three categories are important and essential to our development, and they are closely related:

1. *Focus values* are those value priorities in our day-to-day lives that describe our present world view, our criteria for decision making, our attitude toward relationships, and the focus of most of our energy.

2. *Foundation values* represent our basic needs and are the foundation for being able to act on and live out our focus values. Foundation values dominate during times of crisis or stress. People who are habitually very stressed can live out their whole lives in this arena.

3. *Future* or *vision values* represent the motivational force in our lives. They are our future because they are not yet fully developed, although they are present, motivating us to move forward. They form the vision that pulls us into the future every moment of our lives.

All three value areas are essential if you are to grow and develop in a healthy way. Your foundation values are not values that you discard as you evolve to a higher stage of consciousness and develop more complex values. They are an essential part of your life no matter where you are in your development—they are just not what you are concentrating on right now. If something goes wrong in the area of your foundation values, your focus values will become weak and you will be unable to act forcefully on your current priorities. If your current focus then becomes weak, your vision for the future will be ignored, and your life may seem meaningless and confused.

Your future values act powerfully on your current focus values as well. They give meaning to what you are doing right now. A mother with a newborn child is an example of this powerful effect. Her current focus is on caretaking and nurturing, but it is her vision of the man or woman the baby will grow into that motivates her to learn everything she can about good child care and to train the baby to be healthy and happy. Feeding the baby in the middle of the night and handling piles of dirty diapers are not her idea of meaningful work, but given her vision of the well-adjusted human being she is nurturing, she does these tasks willingly and without punishing the baby for creating more work for her. Her future vision gives meaning to her current priorities and shapes how she relates to the baby.

Consciousness-Shift

Each of us has the possibility of actualizing any of the 125 values, but we only have room in our lives for about ten priorities. Very few of us are aware of what our value priorities are, or how they sort themselves out into future, focus, and foundation values. When you become aware of what your values are, it is as if you have been given a clear map into your future. In our work we have found that when people are clear about their future or vision values, meditate on their meaning, and make an effort to take care of their foundation values, a shift occurs in their conscious behavior.

Example: Margerie. Margerie was a second-year university student who wanted to see if her values profile would shed some light on some of her present confusion and sadness. She told us that she was confused and unclear about where she was going in life. She filled out the Hall-Tonna Survey. Figure 5-7 on the next page shows where her initial focus values are in the phases of development, and her foundation, focus, and future values. In the second part of the diagram we have blown up the picture to see her focus more clearly and what her specific values were. Notice that some of the columns have two groups of values; the top group is the goals values, while the bottom group is the means values.

The figure illustrates that the focus area is where our present energy is. At the same time the focus values are really transitional, in that they are between the foundation and future, where most of the dynamic action is. It is the future that motivates us to grow, but we are successful

FIGURE 5-7. Margerie's Values Profile

═══FOUNDATION═══		═══FOCUS AREA═══		═══FUTURE VALUES═══			
Phase I		**Phase II**		**Phase III**		**Phase IV**	
Stage A	Stage B	Stage A	Stage B	Stage A	Stage B	Stage A	Stage B

FOUNDATION ────────▶ **FUTURE OR VISION**

Phase I-A	Phase I-B	Phase II-A	Phase III-B	Phase IV-A	Phase IV-B
	Security	Self-Worth	Knowledge/ Insight	Truth/Wisdom	Ecority
		Care/Nurture	Intimacy		

FOCUS

Phase II-B	Phase III-A
Competence/Confidence Work/Labor	Service/Vocation
	Independence
Achievement/Success Education/Certification	Search for Meaning/Hope
	Equity/Rights

only to the extent that the foundation is in place. When this happens, the focus becomes very active because it provides the necessary bridge values to make forward movement possible.

1. *Margerie's Foundation Values.* I asked Margerie to look at the definitions of her foundation values of Self-Worth, Security, and Care/Nurture. She talked about how the values spoke to her. She came from a very caring family where she was very secure. Everything was provided for. Now she was living at the university, on her own for the first time. She had to manage her own budget, which was very limited. She had few friends and had to get to know new people. She had to meet the expectations of her professors with her work and grades. She was afraid, lonely, and unsure of what others thought of her. The values described her reality, and she began to understand her feelings of insecurity.

2. *Margerie's Future or Vision Values.* The combination of Knowledge/Insight, Truth/Wisdom, and Ecority confirmed for Margerie that her values were pulling her toward a career in the natural sciences, doing education or research. Knowledge/Insight and Truth/Wisdom confirmed her interest in education and possibly in teaching as a career. Ecority confirmed that she wanted a career that dealt with global environmental issues, particularly in the field of biology, which was her major.

3. *Margerie's Focus Values.* Margerie told me that school was hard work and that learning new things made her doubt her competence. We noticed that the more lonely she felt, the less confident she was. In other words, when her foundation values of Self-Worth and Care/Nurture were not taken care of, it affected how she felt in her focus area of Competence/Confidence, a goal value. Achieving and succeeding at school were important to her because they were the means for achieving her goals of confidence and employment.

We talked about the Phase III-A values in her focus area. Her values of Service/Vocation showed that she wanted to do something significant with her life when she graduated. But she said that she wasn't sure what she wanted to be. Search for Meaning/Hope expressed this exactly for her. I asked her what Independence and Equity/Rights meant, and she said, "Are you kidding? I'm a woman, and I want my own career; I don't want to be dependent on a man for the rest of my life! I want independence through my own career!" She was adamant that she wanted to be independent, but she was frustrated that she had no clear sense of what she should do. I suggested that the future values area might point in the right direction.

The value of Intimacy in her future area—a means value—reminded her of her foundation need for Care/Nurture. She said, "I want to be independent, but I would also like to be close to someone who cares enough about me to support my career; someone I can care about."

The experience of confronting and understanding her values caused Margerie to have a consciousness shift. When she recognized that her foundation values of Care/Nurture and Self-Worth were connected to her future value of Intimacy through the focus value of Equity/Rights, she had an entirely new perspective on her personal needs.

She stated her needs this way: "I would really like to date, but I'm a little afraid of men." Margerie's father died when she was twelve years old, and she was naturally anxious about relating to men because she had so little experience with them. After a couple of weeks and several discussions, she decided to go out with someone who had been asking her out for three months. She started dating, and soon found a relationship that was supportive and meaningful to her. At this point her foundation values of Self-Worth and Care/Nurture were being taken care of, and her life began to change.

When her foundation values fell into place, the future suddenly became clear. She was able to see that, for her, truth and knowledge was related to the value of Ecority, and that she wanted to follow a career that would allow her to use her knowledge to improve the global environment. She had a consciousness-shift that eventually enabled her to pursue a career in politics and the environment. Marjorie grew in the consciousness of her own future, and she was able to do this by acting on her focus values when she had taken care of her foundation values. But she had to overcome anxiety about her foundation area before this could happen. What was the source of this anxiety?

Existential Choosing and Acting

The existential perspective proposes that we are born into the world as finite human beings with natural limitations, as diagramed in Figure 5-8.

The first and most basic limitation is that we have physical bodies that will eventually stop functioning. This limitation is called "Contingency." It means that life is full of contingencies and risks. We may become ill at

---

A Theoretical Diversion

The way we understand anxiety as well as other emotional symptoms comes largely from our perspective on human development. We might consider these different views of how a person grows as different ways of getting quality information about the person.

One way of looking at human growth is to see it as a developmental process—another way of saying that we go through stages of development on our life's journey. This view is held by psychologists such as Piaget, Erikson, and Kohlberg; it assumes that life is hierarchical and that we have specific tasks to accomplish at each stage.[1] In this framework, the four phases or eight stages would be seen as a journey for which Phase IV-B values are the ultimate goal. This perspective is a valid way to gain information about a person. We will visit this perspective in more depth in Chapters 6 and 7.

The existential perspective is equally valid but different, in that it gives us different quality information. Important existential thinkers include the philosophers Soren Kierkegaard, Jean-Paul Sartre, and more recently philosopher-psychologists like Thomas Oden, Peter Koestenbaum, and Irvin Yalom. The existential perspective sees values wholistically and relationally. This book assumes both these perspectives.

FIGURE 5-8. Existential Limits

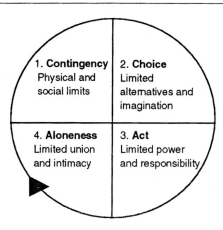

some point and die, or we can be killed by some natural disaster. We may even be born into this world with physical or mental limitations such as Down's syndrome. We are also born with social limitations: you can be born into a rich or a poor, educated or uneducated family.

Everything else flows from this reality, since the only way you can change or improve your reality is by facing the choices that you have. "Choice" here does not mean *acting* on the choices, but rather seeing the alternatives available to you within your limited circumstances. The ability to see your choices is connected to imagination—the innate ability to imagine alternatives.

In order to grow and survive you must "Act" on those choices in order to achieve your goals. To act means to act on or take responsibility for your choices. Positive outcomes from acting on our choices empower us. But in everything we undertake, we may succeed or we may fail. *This uncertainty about the outcome of our choices is the natural cause of our anxiety.* Life is a struggle to survive in which we learn to choose and act wisely.[2]

Finally, there is the condition of "Aloneness," or the reality that you are separate from others and ultimately responsible for everything that you do. In the existential perspective, intimacy is essential to growth and to coping with this reality. Loneliness and responsibility, then, are the source of a lot of our anxiety.

Anxiety is a natural part of living and expressing ourselves in the world. We experience anxiety as we develop physically and emotionally and discover ourselves to be separate people from our families; we experience loneliness as Margerie did. As we develop, we must make choices and act on them. When we make choices with courage and have

---

Insights

The existential way of looking at life and the growth process gives us many insights about our basic needs. For example, Aloneness and Contingency are linked, because the more we feel at risk in our lives, the more we feel the need to connect with others and be comforted. We must all deal with Contingency, because we are at risk all the time. We have to be careful what we eat, when we cross the road. We worry about getting old, flying in airplanes. The basic antidotes are to make wise choices and to take responsibility for the choices and for intimacy and caring from others. Another important insight is that meaning in our lives requires us to experience intimacy and to develop the ability to make choices in our lives. Without these two abilities, we experience despair.

---

faith in ourselves and others, we experience hope and overcome our feelings of aloneness, isolation, and separateness. We see our actions as having meaning, and we experience intimacy and union with others.

This is what happened to Margerie. Her ability to trust in a new relationship shifted her whole view of the world from a Phase II perspective that was dominated by loneliness and a need for belonging to a Phase III and IV perspective, in which she was free to become concerned about global environmental issues.

The Positive Effect of Memory on the Future

Our foundation values are also more a part of the past than other values that we have, because they emerge from our family of origin—particularly values related to care and belonging. One way we experience the past is as memory. A good memory from the past gives you positive images of the future. The future is then often experienced as imagination. Figure 5-9 illustrates these possibilities.

When we can remember successful action in the past, we have confidence, and we can imagine creative alternatives for the future; this in turn generates possible new choices. For example, if you have had several very positive job interviews in which you got personal affirmation for your experience and marketability, the anticipation of a new interview will not intimidate you and may even be something you look forward to. Successful experiences in the past enable us to recognize that we have values, skills, and abilities; this feeds our positive imagination, allowing us to fantasize about possible futures.

This process is related directly to the power of our future values to motivate us to grow and change. A mind- or consciousness-shift depends

FIGURE 5-9. How Positive Memories Affect Us

PAST	PRESENT	FUTURE
Memory	**Choice and Act**	**Imagination**
Success experienced as reconciliation and affirmation	Success experienced as powerfulness and confidence	Sucess experienced as hope and vision

Positive thoughts, images, and fantasies

Possible Positives
1. Relaxation
2. Celebration
3. Creativity
4. Collaboration
5. Harmony

very much on whether we have cataloged positive rather than negative experiences. Figure 5-9 illustrates how this works in our memory.

A positive experience, perhaps of a holiday you took with close friends, automatically triggers images and generates thoughts of new possibilities for the future, such as another holiday next year. Now when you remember, you have a memory of that event, and your imagination is positively stimulated about future events. The past memory was positive; you felt affirmed. If, when there had been arguments or disagreements, you and your friends talked it out and came to reconciliation, the memory elicits a future anticipation of hope. When this happens many, many times you become a person who can imagine the future, set goals for yourself, and have a strategic plan or vision for your life. When this happens, a mind-shift occurs and your future values begin to be actualized, as in the case of Margerie.

As Figure 5-9 illustrates, these good experiences of the past and positive hopes for the future feed into the present, and over the long haul they affect your day-to-day decision making. You become more relaxed, you celebrate rather than deny your limitations, you even become more creative and collaborative. At a spiritual level, the final outcome is inner harmony and peace.

Connecting the Values: An Experience of Success. When my daughter Christie was six years old, she was having a particularly difficult time with her friends. Her schoolwork suffered, and she was spending more time at home alone, which was not at all her usual style. She had been given a bicycle for her birthday two weeks earlier, but she still hadn't taken it out of the house.

Finally I asked her if anything was bothering her. She said, "Nothing is the matter, but none of my friends like me!"

"Why do you think that?" I asked.

"Well, they all have bicycles and go everywhere on them, and I can't go with them."

I reminded her that I had volunteered to teach her to ride, but that she had said that she wanted to wait for a week or so. Finally she admitted that she was afraid to try to ride, because she might not be able to learn how, and then her friends would think she was stupid.

The next day was a Sunday. Very early in the morning when no one was around, we went over to her school playground for a training session. She pedaled and I ran beside her with my hand on the seat so that the bicycle would not tip. She kept saying that she would never be able to do it on her own, and that she was not going to try because she would fail. But I kept insisting that she get back on the bicycle.

Finally, I told her that we were going to cycle down the playground and then turn and come back without stopping. "Only this time," I said, "I am going to hold you up from behind the bicycle where you can't see me."

"You make sure that you hold on," she said.

Off we went. I ran along beside her as before, talking all the time, but halfway down the playground, holding my breath, I let go, but kept running and talking to her.

"When do you want me to turn?" she said.

"Whenever you want to," I said. "You make the decision; after all you have been cycling without me for half of the playground!" And I ran past her. Her smile is something I will always remember. Her confidence grew so much that both her schoolwork and her popularity with her friends improved overnight.

Christie's foundation values (Figure 5-10) were Self-Worth and Friendship/Belonging. Because she couldn't ride her bicycle, she thought that her friends wouldn't value her, and she couldn't do things with them.

Before she learned to ride, I noticed that her self-confidence was eroding more each day. This is represented by the value of Competence/Confidence in her focus area. The confidence she gained affected her schoolwork enormously. As she grew up, learning (Knowledge/Insight) became her future value and she choose a vocation as a mathematician.

FIGURE 5-10. Christie Learns to Ride Her Bike

PAST	PRESENT	FUTURE
Memory	Choice, Action	Imagination
Foundation Values	**Focus Values**	**Future Values**
Self-Worth Friendship/Belonging	Competence/Confidence	Knowledge/Insight

The power to act and create one's own life is critical to what reality is all about. When you act on a choice that is successful, you are empowered to be confident not only in your future choices but in your interpersonal interactions, as my daughter was.

We all have some level of anxiety about making the right choices in our lives and creating something for ourselves in the world. Since life is full of unexpected contingencies and we can never make perfect choices, some failure is inevitable, and so is its natural consequence, guilt. These negative feelings have a positive side: they motivate us to change. My daughter felt guilty and anxious about rejection by her friends before she learned to ride her bicycle. In fact, however, she had not been rejected by them, but in her perception, she had failed by not learning to ride her bicycle. These are all natural feelings and a part of what motivates us to be responsible, to risk, and to live.

That Dark Side Again

On the other hand, when a person has had negative experiences in the past, the imagination catalogs foundation value experiences and draws us back to a Phase I view of the world. In the extreme, a person's internal images may become limited to negative outcomes, damaging his or her ability to generate positive dreams for the future. Figure 5-11 on the next page describes the relationship of memory and imagination to the past and the future when the experiences are negative.

The memory of failure causes guilt that is experienced as anxiety. I remember talking to a student who did not show up for her final comprehensive examination for a master's degree. Joan claimed she was ill, so a new time was set up for her. She did not appear a second time.

When I talked to her about the problem, she reported that when she was a young girl first going to school, her father beat her when she got poor grades. It stopped when Joan was ten years of age—when her mother divorced her father and he went away. This negative memory

FIGURE 5-11. How Negative Experiences Affect Us

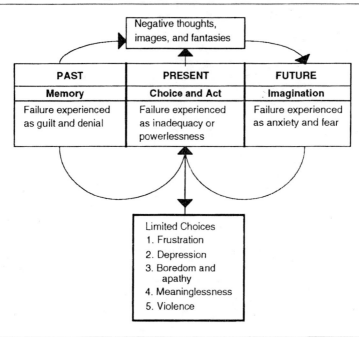

recurred when she took exams as an adult, and the negative images immediately became the experience of anxiety and fear.

Past experiences of failure are always experienced as guilt. This is transferred into the future as the experience of fear and anxiety. But what is even more dramatic is that both these elements get transferred into the present as the experience of frustration and an increased inability to act. Joan was totally unable to act and simply did not show up for the exam.

When the past experience is traumatic and experienced long-term, as in the case of severe grief, the symptoms can be anger turned into depression, boredom, and apathy. Finally, a person can feel that life is meaningless and enter into despair. In the extreme, the final end of this despair can be chemical dependency, physical abuse of others, or even suicide.

For some people it is anxiety-producing just to think about alternatives. For others, choosing is a simple matter, but they get anxious when it is time to act on their choice. Anxiety is particularly likely to show up if a person's past experience with making choices and acting on them has been very negative. For example, I have counseled many students who failed an examination and were so anxious that when they took it for a second time, they were unable to remember anything—they were unable to act. This is the dark side, where not only are our values negated, but our foundation becomes our future. On the other hand, when people

FIGURE 5-12. Relationship Between Negative Choices and Values

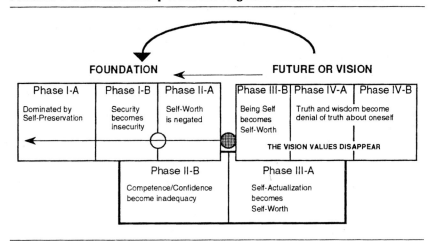

overcome this anxiety and act successfully, they experience a new sense of themselves.

Earlier we looked at different values tracks. We saw that a central values track is related to the development of the self: Self-Preservation (I-A), Security (I-B), Self-Worth (II-A), Competence/Confidence (II-B), Self-Actualization (III-A), and Being Self (III-B). When an individual becomes overwhelmed with negative images, the value of Self-Worth in Phase II-A becomes diminished. When this is a severe problem, it affects the totality of one's future. Figure 5-12 illustrates the relationship between negative choices and values in the extreme scenario.

In the movie *Ironweed*, Jack Nicholson plays Francis—"a worthless bum," a homeless alcoholic during the depression years before World War II. The story contains several flashbacks portraying Francis in a childhood surrounded by unemployment in his family. This leads to continual guilt for past violence culminating in the death of his son, who he drops and kills after drinking several bottles of beer. The story indicates that he never recovers from the guilt. He enters into a life of deprivation that can best be described as hell. In the story he is scrounging for the next dollar each day, and looking for food and somewhere to sleep each night. Hell is where his foundation literally becomes his future.

What occurs is the negation of Self-Worth through the death of his child; this in turn subverts Competence/Confidence into a feeling of inadequacy. Then Self-Actualization and Being Self deteriorate into the struggle to regain self-worth, and Truth/Wisdom simply flips and becomes a denial of everything he has done. His life slides back into Phase I and is dominated by anxiety (the reverse of Security) and Self-Preservation. At another level, we see him overwhelmed by depression and meaninglessness.

Choices become meaningful to us as we learn that they enhance cooperation rather than alienation from other people. This is the source of creativity and intimacy in our lives. We create only by having the freedom to choose, and we gain perspective on reality only as we can relate to others with care and intimacy. Very often, as in the case of Margerie, this means confronting the anxiety we have about our foundation needs, rather than denying it as Francis did in *Ironweed*. This occurs because our personal foundation values lie behind our experiences of failure and success. These foundation values automatically move to the future as either hope or despair. Hope is the activation of our future values; despair is their negation.

A Case: Values, Idolatory, and Ethics

John was 30 years old and had been married to Diane for seven years. They were good friends with another couple of about the same age. Every Sunday they all went to a local church and had lunch together afterward. John was attracted to the other man's wife, Joyce, but never mentioned it; he felt that the attraction was natural. One day Joyce's husband George was killed in a car accident in a city three hundred miles away.

John agreed to take Joyce to the mortuary and to help with the funeral arrangements. They would be gone for three days over a weekend. Diane stayed at home and looked after both sets of children while they were gone.

After the funeral John and Joyce stayed overnight in a local hotel. In their mutual grief they had a few too many drinks, and ended up sleeping together and comforting one another physically. John came to see me a week later in a deep depression about what he had done. He had told his wife and she was making life miserable for him. His wife blamed him and felt that he had taken advantage of a friend at a time of tragic loss. John's depression was increasing and he had missed several days of work. He was beginning to become dysfunctional, sitting in a chair at home for long periods of time without moving.

After several weeks of counseling it became clear that John believed very much in marriage and loved his wife Diane. He felt that Intimacy and Loyalty/Fidelity were the two values that were most important to him. Diane agreed. He agreed with Diane that they had taken life vows together in church for better or for worse, and that divorce was out of the question. But in fact John had broken the vows. They seemed to be deadlocked and trapped in each other's anger.

All she would say to John for the first two sessions was, "I can't believe you could do this to me. Maybe it's my turn now." This would end in a shouting match and more depression on John's part. There was no movement until one day I suggested that the real problem was not adultery on John's part but idolatry on both their parts.

Idolatry could be said to be a narrow set of values or an object—a car or a job—that is given ultimate significance; the values or object become like a god. When your central value system—those values that contain the total source of your life's meaning—is given a godlike significance, it will always eventually fail because it can only cope with the narrowest of situations. If, like John, you make a choice that leads to circumstances that threaten your central value system, then the value of Self-Worth becomes negated or at least severely damaged, the future becomes threatened, and security and survival dominate. Exaggerated anxiety and guilt over perceived failure are the result. The initial failure, in this case John's physical experience with Joyce after the funeral, challenged John's and Diane's joint central value system.

In reality, each of us needs values that can cope with any situation that may arise. John's and Diane's values were their faith in each other based on the values of Family/Belonging, Intimacy, and Loyalty/Fidelity. Why was this not adequate in their case? The critical missing value was Limitation/Celebration, or the ability to realize that they were not perfect. Limitation/Celebration implies that we can keep learning from our mistakes no matter how bad they are.

John recognized that he had broken the rules, contravening his own ultimate values, so guilt followed, plus the anxiety of what the consequences might be. He could no longer imagine anything good happening to him. Another example of the catastrophic results of the failure of a central value system is what happens to some people who suffer an economic disaster and suddenly find themselves in poverty. Self-blame, paranoia, and even violence may follow. These feelings may result from an inadequate central value system whose values cannot transcend the failure, making forgiveness and alleviation of the guilt and anxiety impossible. This is the condition of idolatry, of giving exaggerated importance to a set of finite values.

Once Diane and John had revisited their values and filled the hole in the breach, their foundation took on new depth and meaning. A consciousness-shift occurred that allowed them to live their marriage with a renewed vision.

Values and Ethics

Values are priorities that are given to each of us; all 125 values are potentially present in each of us. Ethics is that discipline that points out that it is necessary for everyone to know the minimal values priorities they must hold to lead a creative rather than a destructive life for themselves and for those they influence.

If you are to develop and grow, you must choose certain value priorities at given points in your life. It is essential for you to choose and internalize the values of Security and Self-Worth at an appropriate stage of your life. To be an integrated person, you must consult your conscience and intelligence to decide what values you are going to live by, and what priority order you will give them. For example, what are the essential values needed to maintain a faithful marriage? What are the essential values needed by counselors to carry out their task under any contingencies? What are the bottom-line values for an executive, a surgeon, or an attorney?

Ethics is not a subjective discipline. Every society and each profession has its own ethical guidelines that represent the minimum values that everyone must agree to. The United Nations Charter tells us that a bottom-line value for international human rights is a priority on Human Dignity. The marriage vows used in most cultures represent the minimal values necessary for a couple to hold if they are going to have a faithful and productive marriage. These include Loyalty/Fidelity, Intimacy, Care/Nurture, Self-Worth, Family/Belonging, and Limitation/Acceptance and Limitation/Celebration. Education in any culture must have as its goals the minimal values of Self-Worth, Education/Certification, Knowledge/Insight, and Truth/Wisdom.

The healthy development of consciousness depends on our finding balance and a harmony of values in our lives. You will find that, like Margerie, you are helped to grow to a healthy maturity when you balance your foundation and future needs as they are reflected through your values. Consider the following questions about your values:

1. What values and priorities do you need to live your life by, alone or with another person, to ensure a meaningful and productive existence for yourself (and for a partner if you have or want one), no matter what contingencies you encounter?

2. What values do you need to act on to ensure that you can fulfill your maximum potential as a gifted person as you grow and mature through the different stages of your life?

3. How can you discover how your gifts, potential, and inherent values fit into your overall life strategy and that of those you live with? What is your moral and ethical obligation as a human being? Do you have the right values or all the values that you need to operate ethically within your chosen vocation or profession?

We know that we have the potential of holding any of 125 values, and that we need to choose our priorities if we are to live to our maximum potential. But once you know what values you need, how do you develop them? The initial answer is that values are also inventories of skills, and that your values can be realized only if they are translated into sets of skills. In the next chapter we will explore values and skills.

6

How You Develop Values: The Skills Connection

Personal mastery is the discipline of continually clarifying and deepening our personal vision, of focusing our energies, of developing patience, and of seeing reality objectively.

Peter M. Senge, *The Fifth Discipline*

Your future values, your hopes, and your imagination contribute to your maturity and fulfillment of personal potential. But what does it take to move through the phases of development? Once you identify your future values, you still have to acquire the skills to apply them.

For example, when Christie learned to ride her bicycle, she regained her confidence, thus meeting her foundation need to belong with her peers. As she continued to develop other skills, she gradually moved toward her vision of becoming an educator. However, first she had to learn to ride the bicycle! She learned new skills that made the connection between her foundation, focus, and future values real for her in that moment, and she became a lifelong learner of new skills.

FIGURE 6-1. Skill Development and the Four Phases of Consciousness

Phase I		Phase II		Phase III		Phase IV	
Stage I-A	Stage I-B	Stage II-A	Stage II-B	Stage III-A	Stage III-B	Stage IV-A	Stage IV-B
Instrumental Skills →				Imaginal Skills			
		Interpersonal Skills →				System Skills →	

In this chapter we are going to describe the relationship between skills and values. We have found that important life skills fall into four categories related to our abilities to do things, to relate to other people, to use our imagination, and to master systems. When we look at these four kinds of skills, we can make a useful connection between these four categories, the values, the Four Phases of Consciousness, and the other developmental factors that can cause a shift in personal consciousness. We will also take a look at what you need to know and what support systems you need in your journey through the phases and stages of personal development.

Skill Development and the Four Phases of Consciousness

There are direct connections among the phases of development, values, and skills. We found that values can be seen as inventories of skills, and that there are basically four types of skills:

- Instrumental skills
- Interpersonal skills
- Imaginal skills
- System skills

Each of these skill types are related to specific values that develop in relationship to the Four Phases of Consciousness. Figure 6-1 shows the relationship of the development of these four skill types to the Four Phases of Consciousness.

Instrumental skills develop early in life, since they are related to basic survival. Development of instrumental skills usually ends at Phase II-B, which emphasizes education and training for the workplace. Interpersonal skills start developing in the family at Phase II-A and reach their high point in Phase III-A with the ability to empathize with others. Imaginal skills are at their peak in Phase III-A. System skills do not begin to develop until later in life, at Phases III-A to IV-A.

Since human development is related to the development of the imagination, the emergence of imaginal skills at Phase III-A is critical to personal growth. We know that memory is stored in images, and that images prefigure language and therefore rational thinking and discourse. Many great thinkers like Einstein have said that they thought primarily in images first, and in logic and language second.[1]

We're now going to examine these four skill types in more detail. We will begin each skill section with its definition and a sample list of skills.

Instrumental Skills

Instrumental skills have that peculiar blend of intelligence and manual dexterity that enables one to be professional and competent. They include the ability to manipulate ideas and the immediate external environment, the skill of handicrafts, physical dexterity, and academic or cognitive accomplishments.

A sample inventory of instrumental skills includes the ability to:

- Read, write, and count.
- Speak clearly and correctly.
- Think logically.
- Coordinate your physical self (for example, drive a car).
- Master new skills in your profession (for example, bookkeeping).
- Retain primary information processes.
- Be competent in your work.
- Logically integrate and process new technical data.
- Manage a given amount of money per year.
- Diet, exercise, and keep physically fit.

After birth, an infant receives sensory data from the environment and acquires basic instrumental skills, such as learning to suck its mother's breast for food. This acquisition of sensory data, combined with the conscious and unconscious activity of the psyche, enables the child to learn and grow. Once language develops, this process is accelerated, because the child can now transfer inner images into the external world in precise ways, and can begin to experience the inner world of others through imitation and then later through conversation.

Instrumental skills are related to the body and tools. Indigenous peoples have used tools as extensions of the body—the flint rock swung by the arm as a hammer, or down across an animal skin as a cutting implement—for millenia. For indigenous peoples as well as for us, our physical condition and dexterity are forms of tools, since the body itself is an instrument that acts on an external environment.

Slowly through history tools became separate from the body and had the ability to extend the power of the body. For example, spears and boomerangs extended the power of the aborigines to touch and slay animals at great distances. Like these, all tools are some form of extension of the body. For example, television is in fact an extension of someone's inner fantasies as we watch a comedy or a drama. Light bulbs when turned on extend our optical system.

Tools, through time, have become very complex. The body's ability to adapt to temperature change was extended by animal furs, and eventually evolved into modern clothing. A more complex adaptation is the development of primitive shelters as a kind of group clothing; these shelters eventually became houses, buildings designed for specialized functions, and cities.[2] The modern hospital is an example of the combination of hundreds of tools that are extensions of the body's ability to heal itself.

Instrumental skills combine tools and the intellect—a combination required in any profession. For example, a craftsperson such as a weaver must have a basic knowledge of the materials he or she is working with as well as physical dexterity to create patterns and to weave them into a completed design.

The Skills–Values Connection.   We have noted that each of the four skills occurs within certain phases of values development. Instrumental skills tend to dominate the values in the first two phases, because they are basic skills for physical and social survival. *We have discovered that skills are related to value clusters, not individual values. We have found values always occur in binary combinations of a goal value with a means value, so that the skill is related to the means value within the confines or boundaries of the goal value with which it is associated.*

We have further found that the means value is normally within one stage of the goal value—that is, at the same stage as the goal value, or one stage before or after. For example, here are two Phase II-B means values that require instrumental skills to be activated: Administration/Control and Economics/Success. Both these examples are in relationship to the goal value of Competence/Confidence, also a Phase II-B value.

Example 1: Administration/Control.   *Skills:* Learning skills in administration such as bookkeeping and time management to improve efficiency and productivity in your work. You must be able to:

- Clarify responsibilities and assignments.
- Draw up an organization chart with roles and responsibilities and consider alternative approaches to organizing for maximum efficiency.

- Maintain standards and procedures; organize files so that items can be readily located.
- Select personnel; develop selection criteria and interview questions for new hires, and check references.
- Identify key positions and desirable potential candidates to fill these jobs in the future.
- Develop job descriptions for each position.
- Maintain sound financial controls. See *Economics/Success,* below.
- Become computer literate with the ability to use a wide range of business technologies.

Example 2: Economics/Success. *Skills:* Planning and understanding how to use financial resources to accomplish your goals. You must be able to:

- Establish sound financial controls.
    * Learn to read annual quarterly financial reports.
    * Become involved in the budgeting process.
    * Learn your organization's system of financial reporting.
- Develop your analytical skills.
    * If you have difficulty with math skills or math anxiety, take a course at a local community college or university.
    * Learn how to use personal computers and spreadsheet programs.
- Learn to incorporate financial and quantitative data into your decision making. Determine the kind of quantitative data that would be useful and create a plan to obtain this information.
- Improve the quality of financial data submitted by your work group.
    * To improve the financial data submitted by your subordinates, meet with them and review key items with them.

As we have seen, imagination plays a key role in the integration of instrumental skills. The role of imagination becomes even more evident when we look at interpersonal skills.

Interpersonal Skills

Interpersonal skills are related to the ability to act with generosity and understanding toward others, an ability that comes from having self-knowledge. These skills involve the ability to objectify personal feelings so that you are able to cooperate rather than remain isolated.

A sample inventory of interpersonal skills includes the ability to:

- Show and share emotions appropriately.

- Identify feelings accurately.
- Identify another person's feelings accurately.
- State anger objectively.
- Objectify your own and others' feelings and hold others accountable.
- Articulate personal goals.
- Remain calm in times of stress and anxiety.
- Affirm the worth of others.
- Project your imagination into another's world.
- Be present with someone who is dying and reflect their feelings in a way that increases their comfort level.
- Be creatively assertive.
- Cope with conflict.

Our interpersonal skill potential grows out of our family relationships and our early social experiences. The family and early social experiences are the condition out of which our interpersonal skill potential grows.

Interpersonal skills begin to develop at Phase II-A, but become an important factor in Phases II-B and III-A. In the second phase, language is a central developmental issue. Then, as we move into Phase III, we become skilled in dealing with feelings, and we acquire the ability to mobilize feelings creatively. First we become able to recognize and objectify our own feelings. For example, we master the appropriate expressions of anger: we learn to state our anger to someone else in a controlled manner and within a short time after our anger occurs, and in a way that allows the other person to react by cooperating rather than retreating.

To acquire mature interpersonal skills, you must become self-aware and have a knowledge of your past and present emotional and imaginal life. This awareness and the skills that come with it cannot be learned intuitively; they must be learned formally through education. The values that would motivate you to know yourself in the emotional arena—such as Empathy—do not occur until the third phase. However the means value of Empathy does require prior development in other interpersonal values such as Care/Nurture. Let's look at these two means values as examples.

Example 1: Care/Nurture. *Skills:* Learning how to emotionally and physically care for and look after others so they feel acknowledged and loved. You must be able to:

- Care for and take a personal interest in your friends.
- Take time to know the personal side of others and show a genuine interest in their families, leisure activities, and work lives.
- Consider having social events where you can get to know people personally.

- Do not allow phone calls to interrupt personal discussions.
- Develop listening skills and resist the temptation to problem solve. If you sense that the person needs help with the problem, say so in a kind, supportive way.
- Keep all personal discussions strictly confidential.
- Keep a calendar of birthdays and recognize people on significant dates by sending them cards and notes.

Example 2: Empathy. *Skills:* The ability to see the world through another's eyes, recognizing the differences between the two of you, allowing the other person to reflect more in depth on who they are, and not to feel judged, but accepted by you. This includes being able to objectively identify another person's feelings, including negative feelings, without personalizing the interaction. You must be able to:

- Understand the agendas and perceptions of others.
- Speak to others in a manner that keeps in mind their level of development, their tendencies, their mental makeup, their character, and their capacity to understand a particular question.
- Identify feelings accurately.
- Identify another's feelings accurately.
- State anger objectively.
- Objectify your own and others' feelings and hold others accountable.
- Imagine yourself in situations where you are unfamiliar and the responsibilities or ground rules are unclear. Try to envision how you could respond.
- Encourage bringing conflict out into the open, especially when you are personally involved. Learn to express feelings in a constructive manner.

The art philosopher Susanne Langer (1957) has demonstrated that you cannot have feelings without images. Any internal images that we have through dreams or sudden recall have feelings that go with them. In other words, the feeling is the effect of an internal image on the body. For example, if you are driving to work and you suddenly remember that you left your lunch at home, you experience a feeling of annoyance or disappointment as soon as you have the image of your lunch sitting on the kitchen counter.

The imagination is an integral part of the skill of interpersonal communication. But as we move from Phase II to Phase III, something very critical occurs: the imagination not only begins to integrate our feelings in the formation of social skills, but it begins to integrate our instrumental and interpersonal skills in a way that radically alters our world view. This is the arena of imaginal skills.

Imaginal Skills

Imaginal skills use that peculiar blend of internal fantasy and feeling that enables us to externalize our ideas effectively. Imaginal skills include the ability to see and make sense out of increasing amounts of data. We develop a capacity to learn from direct experience, and to be creative about our choices and how we act on them. Imaginal skills act as a synthesizer that integrates our other skills.

A sample inventory of imaginal skills includes the ability to:

- Make your values conscious.
- Combine and adapt new information.
- Initiate totally new ideas from seemingly unrelated data.
- Perceive hidden meaning in standard data.
- Dream and imagine new futures—that are possible.
- Generate new ideas and images by:
  * brainstorming
  * using "think tank" techniques
- Utilize several modes of communication, such as poetry, music, and dance.

Imaginal skills enable you to make sense out of increasingly complex data and to synthesize it into new patterns. Imaginal skills help you envision new possibilities where none existed before. When combined with instrumental, interpersonal, and systems skills, the results are a highly developed human being who has the capability to generate creative solutions to complex problems and who can work interdependently for the good of society.

Imaginal skills only develop with emotional maturity. The process begins as the imagination and the skills related to its development blend, first with instrumental skills and then with interpersonal skills. Until Phase III-A, imaginal skills are simply a dimension of the development of your instrumental and interpersonal skills.

At Phase III-A, imaginal skills arise as a separate and unique entity. Strange as it may seem, it is as if the psyche, that internal universe, begins to assert itself into the external interpersonal world, and you are motivated to creatively act on, rather than react to, the world. You begin to recognize the independent authoritative value of your own inner uniqueness, capability, and life experience.

The acquisition of imaginal skills is a critical stage in our emotional and spiritual growth. Their major function at this stage in our lives is:

1. To integrate our personalities and to enable us to transcend the preservation and procreation dimensions of the imagination. At any sign of

threat, our instinct for preservation sets off internal images that cause the defensive action of anger—a return to the Phase I value of Self-Preservation. To become mature in both the imaginal and interpersonal arenas, we must develop the skill of expressing emotions creatively, without fear, with productive consequences for all concerned. This is a basic ingredient of Self-Actualization, Equality, Independence, and all the Phase III-A values.

All human beings have a physical, sexual side—the drive for procreation—that is activated by images of sexual fantasy. These are often only felt as one becomes sexually stimulated at the sight of an attractive man or woman. The key imaginal skill is to be unafraid of such feelings, and to be able to discuss them in an adult, responsible manner with any mature person of the opposite sex, without becoming inappropriately physically involved.

The procreation aspect of life is important because it is a powerful source for the realization of our full creative potential. Each of us has both a masculine and feminine side, whether we are male or female. When we creatively manage our images of sexuality, we begin to integrate the masculine and feminine sides of our inner lives, which gives us much richer and more powerful imaginal skills.

2. To enable us to explore our own unique gifts, skills, and potential. This of course includes the recognition that masculine and feminine psychologies are different, and that each makes different demands on the individual.

3. To enable us to look for authority from within, as conscience, rather than from an external source. This is the essential difference between the first and last two phases of development. When we move from Phase II-B to Phase III-A, we experience a consciousness shift, with an emergence of imagination and creativity and the experience of a sudden expansion of consciousness that is unequaled by any other growth movement in our lives. This occurs with integration of our instrumental and interpersonal skills.

One reason for this remarkable growth experience is that the self-image is largely reflected through our confidence in our gifts and skills, and through validation and affirmation from those whom we trust. Once this integration of instrumental and interpersonal skills occurs through the imaginal dimension, we rely less on external validation and more on our own inner authority. We enter the stage Erikson termed *generativity*, and our concerns become focused on service to others.

Imaginal Skills as Integration. Figure 6-2 illustrates how the imaginal skills cause the instrumental and interpersonal skills to form an integrated whole. At the top of the figure we see that instrumental skills develop in

FIGURE 6-2. Imaginal Skills as Integration

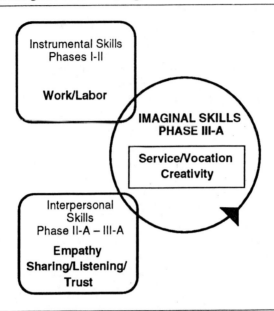

the first two phases. The value that summarizes their purpose is Work/ Labor. This value is a means of survival and is an extension of the skills initiated in Self-Preservation.

Interpersonal skills begin in one's family of origin (Phase II-A), and develop into Empathy and Sharing/Listening/Trust (Phase III-B), with the emergence of the ability to imagine and affirm the feelings of others.

Imaginal skills become engaged at the point when you actively employ imagination in the service of your reason and emotions to envision and act on the world with a new sense of yourself.

The values of Service/Vocation and Creativity summarize this concept of imaginal skills. Creativity is the self-initiating of original ideas and actions. Service/Vocation is the recognition that work is not simply labor for coping with and surviving in society, but an opportunity to make a contribution that arises from personal, unique abilities. Service is the beginning of taking responsibility for the world. Figure 6-2 shows that imaginal skills have the critical integrative function of upgrading interpersonal and instrumental skills so that they take on expanded meaning.

Let's take a look at two examples of means values—Creativity and Limitation/Celebration—that place a priority on imaginal skills.

Example 1: Creativity. *Skills:* The ability to use brainstorming, research techniques, and personal reflection and investigation to bring new ideas and images into a practical and concrete reality. This ability includes the use of new technology such as computer software to enhance this possibility. The purpose is to enhance the goals and mission of an organization or project. You must be able to:

- Make your values conscious.
- Synthesize new facts.
- Initiate totally new ideas from seemingly unrelated data.
- Perceive hidden meaning in standard data.
- Dream and imagine new futures—that are possible.
- Generate new ideas and images by:
  - ∗ brainstorming
  - ∗ using "think tank" techniques
- Utilize several modes of communication, such as poetry, music, and dance.
- Fantasize a different universe with differing universal laws and see what new possibilities exist for solutions.
- Talk about ideas with people from different disciplines or who have different perspectives.

Example 2: Limitation/Celebration. *Skills:* Recognizing that your limitations are the other side of what constitutes human potential for you, and being able to celebrate this and laugh at your mistakes and errors and grow from the experience, and help others to do the same. You must be able to:

- Acknowledge failure and ask, "What have I learned?"
- Seek ways to make a unique contribution and take calculated risks to demonstrate that contribution.
- Confront poor performance in yourself.
- In handling a disagreement with peers, remember that your ideas are valuable and that problems must be addressed if they are going to be resolved.
- Have issues clear so that you can focus on the issue and not on personal skills.
- Frame problems in light of a positive outcome and offer solutions or next steps.
- Trust your intuitive side and make decisions under uncertainty. This can mean putting your reputation on the line.
- Avoid a tendency toward perfectionism and allow others to make mistakes.

As imaginal skills develop, we experience an expanded awareness of how we can function creatively in the world of work and relationships. This expanded self-awareness enables us to see the world wholistically with a systems perspective.

System Skills

System skills are a peculiar blend of imagination, sensitivity, and competence that gives rise to the capacity to see all the parts of a system as they relate to the whole. They include the ability to plan and design change in systems—institutions, societies, and bodies of knowledge—to maximally enhance the growth of the individual parts. System skills require the integration of all the other skills.

A sample inventory of system skills includes the ability to:

- Use money as means.
- Move comfortably with process.
- Differentiate in small group settings between interpersonal and system needs.
- Clarify group complexity.
- Synthesize complex data, statements, and emotional input.
- Set priorities creatively in the face of internal and external pressures.
- Speak with clarity and be understood by people of differing educational levels, cultures, and walks of life.
- Engage in long-term system planning and goal setting.
- Make sense of disparate data and see new possibilities.
- Set limited design criteria.

System skills enable us to see the parts in relation to the whole, to grasp the interrelationships among the parts, to plan interventions to change existing systems, and to design new systems. System skills are the last to be developed because they depend on the development and integration of the other three sets of skills.

The full development of system skills becomes possible only after the system perspective occurs. There are at least three basic kinds of systems with which a person must learn to cope:

- The human body
- The family
- Societal institutions

We naturally begin to understand the body and its functions through instrumental skills early in life. The family as a system is appreciated and primarily accessed through interpersonal skills. But seeing the body as a

FIGURE 6-3. The Systems Perspective

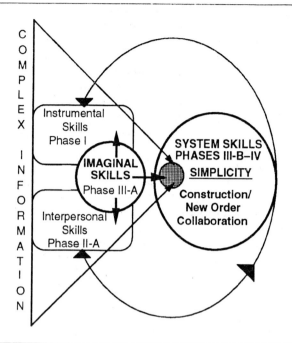

whole or family as a system rather than a series of individual relationships takes a jump in consciousness, and what we are now referring to as a systems perspective.

Figure 6-3, an expansion of Figure 6-2, begins to explain these phenomena. We see that imaginal skills are those that integrate instrumental and interpersonal skills. When you acquire minimal skills in these three areas, a consciousness-shift takes place whereby you suddenly gain a systems perspective. When you have this perspective, you are able to see the whole first and the parts second—the simple unity of it all.

Before this consciousness-shift occurs, life appears to become more and more complex, because all that you learn and know is cumulative. Once a system perspective is gained in Phase III, you experience simplicity, where the whole is evident and all the detail and parts fall into place. System skills require minimal integration of the other three skills. Let's look at an example.

Case Example: Don's Promotion. Don was the chief executive of a chemical manufacturing company. He had been trained as a research chemist. At a time when the market was concerned about the incidence of lead poisoning in children, he invented a new paint that was not lead-based. As a result the company made money and he was promoted from the laboratory to a fairly high management position.

He had excellent instrumental skills as a professional research chemist. These were in his foundation area. He wanted to accept the position and had the vision of one day becoming vice president of the company. As a chemist he had been trained to break things up into their component parts, and then to work with the chemical parts to discover new applications. His imaginal capacity was related more to categorizing and assessing data, not to coming up with new ideas. His whole life had been very rational in its orientation. When he got into management he suddenly found himself in a world of not only technical problems but also complex human problems for which he was not equipped.

His vision and his ability to act effectively were separated by a lack of skills that he suddenly needed but had no training or background for. Since he badly needed interpersonal skills, which take training and time to develop, he was unable to cope with the job and finally had to resign. This story is not untypical.

Don did eventually recover his sense of dignity through counseling and training in stress management and meditation. We eventually introduced him to a series of training seminars in group dynamics, an essential skill area for management personnel. This combination of counseling and group skills shifted his consciousness into a systems perspective.

Interestingly enough, some two years later he did return to a significant leadership position. He told us: "You know, when I was first in management I used to worry about all the guys in the shop, or how my secretary felt today. Everyone's problem was my problem—you know? Then something happened. Like this last week one of the employees that I have known for years came in. I knew he had been drinking on the job. He sat in my office and just gave me hell for about fifteen minutes. I don't even know what he was yelling about.

"A year ago I would have gotten an instant ulcer worrying about him. I was really calm, I mean calm inside. I just said to him, 'You can feed me all the garbage you want, but I really don't have to eat it!' I then asked him what he was going to do about his drinking problem, because it wasn't just a problem for him and me, but for his family and the whole division he was working in. Do you know, I don't know what happened, but he changed after that—he has been reliable ever since."

We discussed this incident at some length, and discovered that Don was able to be clear, supportive, and assertive with his employee because he simply viewed the world more wholistically and simply than he had before. All the management skills and training that he had acquired suddenly took on a new perspective and he was able to use them in a whole new way. He had gained a systems perspective and all the past skills he had were collaborating to give him system skills: the ability to see problems within a greater context. When he conveyed this perspective or vision to his employee, it inspired the man and enabled him to take responsibility for himself in a new way.

The following are examples of system skills related to two means values with different goals that Don felt were important to him: Management and Collaboration.

Example 1: Management. *Skills:* Learning and studying how to improve competence in management skills that can improve efficiency and productivity. You must be able to:

- Make timely and sound decisions.
- Assign responsibility, provide clear direction, and set priorities.
- Build effective teams committed to organizational goals and use the teams to address relevant issues.
- Encourage and motivate others to achieve and set high standards of performance.
- Accurately assess strengths and development needs of employees by providing challenging assignments, managing implementation effectively, and understanding the agenda and perceptions of others.
- Establish liaisons to integrate the work of different activities.
- Ask for input from other similar departments for how to best organize.
- Delegate decisions to the lowest possible level.
- Clarify steps and procedures necessary to accomplish important tasks.
- Conduct an annual performance review with each employee.
- Keep notes on accomplishments and difficulties.
- Review and summarize accomplishments and identify skills that they represent.
- Reflect on limitations and identify one or two areas that would most help the individual improve. Discuss these with employees in a constructive manner.

Example 2: Collaboration. *Skills:* The ability to cooperate interdependently with all levels of management to ensure full and appropriate delegation of responsibility to enhance the forward movement of the organization to fulfill its goals and vision. You must be able to:

- Foster collaboration between team members and other teams and develop give-and-take relationships with others.
- Seek input from other departments on how to best organize to promote cooperation.

- Learn how to develop win-win solutions to problems and formal relationships with other groups and companies.

- Hold others accountable for delegated tasks while giving encouragement and support, but without taking back the responsibility. If you lack confidence in running a team, begin with lesser tasks and build skills gradually.

- Understand the needs and motives of those with whom you work and collaborate.

- Meet informally with team members to discuss the working relationship; ask them for comments on what can be done to improve the working relationship.

- Listen and let them know that you will think about what they have said; you don't have to resolve the issue on the spot.

- Ask others for information as well.

Case Example: Julia and Bryan's Ambitions

Julia and Bryan had been married for one year. Julia was disappointed that they were unable to buy some furniture to replace some of their second-hand tables and chairs. Bryan had aspirations to be in management in the electronics industry, and wanted very much to buy their own house.

He was not earning a high enough salary to accomplish what he wanted, and when they had been married only six months, Julia began complaining and communicating to him that she was sorry they ever got married. They were both disappointed and experiencing insecurity and frustration.

Bryan had started work in a fairly good job, but without actually finishing high school—he had only one class to finish to get his diploma. Julia, on the other hand, had completed two years of college but had given it up to get married, and was frustrated in the job she had as a part-time secretary.

Bryan was told that in order to move into management training in his company, he would need a high school diploma, and that he would need to be enrolled in a university or college in either a science or business degree program. The company was even willing to pay for him to go to college part-time. Bryan was willing to do this, but he was afraid to tell his wife because she had already given up college to marry him. However, Julia was actually angry at him because he was not trying to improve his education. She did not say anything, because she was also angry in her job, where it was difficult to get anywhere as a woman in a man's world, especially without a degree.

Their difficulties were basically all skill related. Many of the values that were inspiring them were really future or vision values. They both wanted to own their own house and new furniture, and to be successful in jobs that interested them. It was a simple matter to identify their skill value combinations as Competence/Confidence—Education/Certification, Family/Belonging—Care/Nurture, and Service/Vocation—Achievement/Success. But it was not until we began to convert these values into skills that we made any practical headway.

When we looked at the skills that they already had, they were impressive. Julia had excellent skills in writing, typing, bookkeeping, and some crafts such as finishing old furniture. Bryan was very good at mathematics and calculus, and at mechanical things around the house. In the foundation area they both had a lot of basic instrumental skills ranging from crafts to educational skills.

The problem areas were in interpersonal and imaginal skills. Historically, Bryan had a problem with completing things. He had a negative imagination that made him afraid that he would fail in anything to do with schoolwork. Julia was very rational and competent but did not share her feelings and concerns about him in a way in which he could hear her without being defensive and angry. Their difficulty lay in the focus area—the one where what we want to do and accomplish (vision) intersects with what we can do well (foundation).

The development of a particular skill often releases many potential skills in a person, or in this case in a couple. What helped them was simple. First they identified through a values survey the means values that were important to both of them. These were as follows:

> **Education/Certification:** *Skills:* Studying and getting the education required to develop the trade or professional skills you need.
>
> **Care/Nurture:** *Skills:* Learning how to emotionally and physically care for and look after others so that they feel acknowledged and loved.
>
> **Achievement/ Success:** *Skills:* Understanding how to be more productive and efficient in order to succeed and accomplish your goals. Envisioning and being clear about your goals.

These skill descriptions were of course only a beginning. We now had a 30-minute training session in brainstorming and planning. We had Julia and Bryan write down on a large sheet of paper what it was they wanted to accomplish. They did this without discussion but with our support. Then we prioritized what was on the paper and looked for the values behind what they had written down. Within an hour, Bryan was able to state that his need for Achievement/Success required some schooling. Julia was able to say that she wanted to finish college but felt that Bryan should finish high school and do a couple of years of college first.

In a second session they brainstormed about what they had to offer each other and what their limitations were, again writing them down on a large sheet of paper with our guidance. The difference this time was that they reported on their experience of each other. Once everything was written down, we looked at the skills that lay behind what they had written down.

Finally, at home, they put these skills together with their goals from the first session and came up with a strategic plan. I saw them only once after that—we ran into each other several months later while shopping. They reported that less than a month after the second session Julia had assisted Bryan with a written English examination to complete work for his high school diploma. He was enrolled in a local junior college with an emphasis in science. Since the classes were paid for by his company, Julia was enrolled in one of the classes with him; this enabled him to be supported while she continued to work on her own education. They were planning to buy an inexpensive fixer-upper house, and to rebuild the inside of it themselves.

What was interesting to me was something Julia said: "You know, we're still using that goal-setting technique we used in the counseling session. It's funny, but when we write things down and look at them, we can laugh at each other more easily. But what is really nice is the way Bryan thinks about himself now."

"What do you mean?" I asked.

"What she means," piped in Bryan, "is that I don't have a crummy attitude toward myself like I did before. You know, I do almost as well in math as she does, and I'm getting better at it. We also talk more now—well, not more exactly, but more caring and deeper maybe."

This is an example of how skills are important to growth. Naturally, not all counseling and guidance sessions turn out this way. But it does illustrate that often what is often felt and seen as a problem is actually a lack of skills. Both Julia and Bryan had strong instrumental skills in the foundation areas. They had internalized values and skills related to crafts, education, and success in the past. They had a great deal already in place that they brought to the relationship—values and skills in their foundation areas. The counseling revealed that their hopes and future vision were being frustrated.

Foundation and future values and skills intersect at the middle ground of the focus area—those values and skills we need to concentrate on in the present. To move forward from past to future, you must build on your present gifts, or foundation skills, by choosing to learn the skills that will produce your vision for the future.

How to Support Personal Growth

You can create the conditions that are necessary for journeying successfully through the phases and stages of personal development. We have identified two kinds of knowledge and support systems that you need.

Take Care of Your Foundation Values. To move beyond Phase I and Phase II development, you need at least the basic skills for actualizing your values in the foundation and focus areas. You must have integrated your Phase I goal values into your life, typically values such as Self-Preservation, Security, Family/Belonging, Self-Worth, Work/Labor, and Competence/Confidence.

In working with more than a thousand individual profiles, we found that when foundation values are not being taken care of, people tend to act out their worst selves. In our last example, Bryan discovered that an important value for him was Care/Nurture, which he was not getting from his wife when they first came to see me. Because Care/Nurture was a foundation value that wasn't being taken care of, his already difficult behavior became worse.

Develop Skills in All Four Skills Areas. In order to become an integrated, mature person, you must develop at least minimal skills in all four skills areas, especially in the adult stages of your life. In order to develop your instrumental, interpersonal, and system skills, you must have access to your imagination at each cycle.

Skills and values are very interrelated. Your growth may be retarded, not because a lot of skills are absent, but because a particular skill that affects all the others is absent. This was the case in the example of Bryan and Julia as a couple.

When our skill development is not minimally integrated or is incomplete in some central way, we may unconsciously behave in an immoral or destructive way. This happened to Don, the paint company chemist and executive. When he was first in a management position, he made personal decisions about people based only on the technical requirements of the job and was overwhelmed by the interpersonal realities of management. His management style alienated so many people that he finally had to be asked to resign.

When we consult with adults who are not handling their responsibilities well—particularly when they are in executive positions that have considerable pressure—we find that there is a marked deficiency in one of the four skill areas. We are able to monitor this by using surveys that not only tell individuals what their values are, but give them information about the relationship between the skills and the values that they have chosen.

When we work with young people or people at an early stage of development, we usually find that their instrumental skills percentages are high and their system skills low. This is because people normally develop instrumental skills during in their early educational and professional lives. We also find that executives who are over thirty-five years of age normally have low percentages in the instrumental area, since they learned most of those skills earlier in their professional lives. But when there is an imbalance in interpersonal, imaginal, or system skills, serious problems often result.

For example, people who lack imaginal skills are unable to take creative risks, so they continue to manage tasks as they have always been managed. People who lack system skills are particularly at a loss in complex settings; they become increasingly distressed and may burn out or leave. People in management who have insufficient interpersonal skills unconsciously use the system against an individual and cause emotional problems for personnel. Integrated skill development is essential for everyone's personal growth, and it is even more critical for people who are in leadership positions.

Summary

As we develop, moving through the Four Phases of Consciousness, our particular clusters of values lead us to develop essential skills in four areas: instrumental, interpersonal, imaginal, and system skills. We become fully mature when we have a balance among these four skills areas, and when our skills allow us to fully express our personal values.

We know that people can stay at different phases of consciousness and never move. We know that people regress. This is reality. We noted in an earlier chapter that life is a very basic struggle to grow rather than regress into comfort or over control due to worry and anxiety. Basically we know that a shift in consciousness takes a lot of hard work and the right kind of institutional reinforcement to grow. Knowing what our values are, and getting the skills is a good start, but what else is involved? We are going to begin to address this in the next chapter as we examine the cycles of human development.

Part II

Human Transformation: People, Leaders, and Organizations

7

Phases, Stages, and Cycles of Development

Personality can be said to develop according to steps predetermined in the human organism's readiness to be driven toward, to be aware of, and to interact with, a widening social radius, beginning with the dim image of a mother and ending with mankind, or at any rate that segment of mankind which "counts" in the particular individual's life.

Erik H. Erikson, *Identity and the Life Cycle*

"All is change," observed the Greek philosopher Heraclitus over 2500 years ago. In this century, the processes of human change have been studied extensively, and the research has yielded several theories of human development. While the context of the theories may vary, they share an underlying tenet: that the process of human development is predictable.

In Part I of this book we looked at values and the Four Phases of Consciousness. We saw that as each of us grows and develops, our view of the world expands. This expansion of our consciousness affects not only the way we see the world, but also how we react to it.

121

This chapter will provide background on how the four phases break into seven cycles of development, the relationship of the cycles to other theories of development, and what it is that enables a person to grow through the cycles.

Stages and Cycles of Human Development

That human development is predictable was first understood within both eastern and western mystical traditions many centuries ago. Different paths described in the Hindu and Buddhist traditions, as well as those in the Jewish, Christian, and Islamic faiths, are all remarkably similar and show amazing convergence. The stages of mystical development are related to individual experiences of consciousness, and stand outside the aging process. Recent theories about psychological stages of development, unlike those in the mystical traditions, are related to the aging process. For the most part, they are an outgrowth of the early work of Sigmund Freud, which gave rise to the psychoanalytical traditions and the work of Piaget and other structural developmentalists, which in turn gave rise to modern educational psychology.

As we constructed the paradigm of the Four Phases of Consciousness, or values development, we studied more than 40 theories of human development to identify the common themes and underlying values that relate to the various stages that different theorists would propose (Ryckman, 1978). When I began this work, I naturally assumed that all the different theories of development would relate to the four phases, or at least to the eight stages. But when I initially tried to line up different developmental theories involving stages, I was not always able to find any satisfactory correlation with the Four Phases of Consciousness!

There were stages of human development that did not exactly fit into the phases and stages of values development, but that seemed to occur between them. Upon further study we noticed that correlation occurred when we reordered the values stages to include B-A as well as A-B pairings. These additional pairings gave rise to the Seven Cycles of Development.

In Figure 7-1, rows 1–3 summarize the four phases and eight stages of values development. The four pairings that constitute the four phases are: I-A and B, II-A and B, III-A and B, and IV-A and B. These are four distinct cycles of development. However, between each of these four cycles, there are pairings of Stage B of one phase and Stage A of the next phase, creating the following pairings: I-B and II-A, II-B and III-A, and III-B and IV-A. Each of these is a distinct cycle of human development, thus making seven complete cycles. We then found that these Seven Cycles of Development correlate with most of the theories of human development that we examined.

FIGURE 7-1. Seven Cycles of Development

Elements of World View	PHASE I	PHASE II	PHASE III	PHASE IV
1. Individual's Perception of the World	A mystery over which I have no control	A problem with which I must cope	A project in which I must participate	A mystery for which we must care
2. Goal Values / Means Values	Self-Preservation / Safety	Self-Worth / Education	Self-Actualization / Independence	Truth/Wisdom Ecority / Convivial Tools
3. Phases and Stages	IA IB	IIA IIB	IIIA IIIB	IVA IVB
4. Phases and Cycles	IA IB	IIA IIB	IIIA IIIB	IVA IVB
5. The Seven Cycles	1 2	3 4	5 6	7

The Seven Cycles and Human Development Theories

We assumed that all theories of deve'. pment, whether religious or psychological, are a part of a single wholistic process; that each of the theories, with their different stages and formulas for human development, would be comparable; and that you could use values theory to clarify each theory. This is illustrated in Figure 7-2. The first two rows of the figure show the cycles of development and their relationship to the four phases.

Sigmund Freud. Freud, one of the earliest developmentalists, wrote at the turn of the century. He is noted for his discovery of the unconscious processes that are the basis for human growth and suffering. He saw human beings as goal-directed, with each person passing through a hierarchy of developmental stages; each stage requires tasks to be completed and skills to be developed. He also saw that, beginning at birth, psychological and physical development are related.

In Freudian theory, the oral stage marks the beginning of a child's social existence; it compares to Cycle 1 values. The oral stage is tied to

FIGURE 7-2. The Seven Cycles and Human Development Theories

PHASE I-A PHASE I-B	PHASE I-B PHASE II-A	PHASE II-A PHASE II-B	PHASE II-B PHASE III-A	PHASE III-A PHASE III-B	PHASE III-B PHASE IV-A	PHASE IV-A PHASE IV-B
Cycle 1	**Cycle 2**	**Cycle 3**	**Cycle 4**	**Cycle 5**	**Cycle 6**	**Cycle 7**
Freud Oral	Anal | Genital	Latency Adolescence				
Eastern and Western Mysticism	Human and Psychological The Primal Stage of Development		Conversion	Purification	Illumination	Enlightenment
Erickson Trust vs. Mistrust Autonomy vs. Shame & Doubt	Initiative vs. Guilt Industry vs. Inferiority	Identity and Role Confusion	Intimacy vs. Isolation	Generativity Creativity vs. Stagnation	Integrity vs. Despair and Distrust	
Fowler 1. Primal* Intuitive Projective Faith	2. Mythic Literal Faith		3. Synthetic Conventional Faith	4. Individuative Reflective Faith	5. Conjunctive Faith	6. Universalizing Faith
PRE-CONVENTIONAL		**CONVENTIONAL**		**POST-CONVENTIONAL**		
Stage 1 **Kohlberg** Fear	Stage 2 Self-Interest	Stage 3 Conformity		Stage 4 Social Order	Stage 5 Others Rights	Stage 6 Universal Principles
Maslow's Hierarchy of Needs Basic needs: Survival Food/Warmth/Shelter	Achievement Needs: Self-Worth Competence and Success			Self-Actualizing Needs: Self-Actualization, Transcendence, Creativity		

* Fowler actually calls Primal Faith, Stage 0.

the child's experience of eating, and his or her initial experience of the mother as caring and nurturing. The anal stage, initiated in the first year or so, is related to toilet training and the child's capacity to control basic anal muscles. This is emotionally related to discipline, control, and letting go of a part of oneself. The genital stage addresses the sexual part of development between the ages of three and six years, when the child works out bonding and role model adherence with the parents. Latency refers to the period when the child leaves home for the first time and goes to school and begins training to enter the world in a independent way. For Freud, adolescence was the end point, since from his point of view all seminal development takes place in the early years. He believed that disruptive experiences at any of these stages had lifelong consequences for development.

Freud had many disciples who have contributed depth and new insights to his initial work. His followers expanded on his new and very radical ideas about the human condition. Jung studied the inner psychic processes; Adler and Sullivan placed special emphasis on the interpersonal dimension; Erikson put his emphasis on identity and development.

Eastern and Western Mysticism. Historically, mysticism has described five stages of experience. The terminology for the stages varies with the school of thought. Writers like Evelyn Underhill (1955) and Ken Wilber (1983) have demonstrated that a developmental view of the spiritual life has been around since at least 600 B.C. The stages of development represented in western religious experience through writers like Saint Bonaventure and in eastern Hindu and Buddhist literature show remarkable congruence.[1]

The pursuit of truth is expressed in different ways. For Einstein, it would be expressed in mathematical terms; for others like Gandhi, it would be human justice; for Buddha or John of the Cross, it would be enlightenment. Underhill notes that a study of all these exceptional people enables us to look at the high end of human development, and concludes that the journey they describe breaks down into five stages. The first is the primal stage, the stage of initial human and psychological development. It is equivalent to Cycles 1-3. It is the basic requirement of Psychosocial Development as described by Freud, Erickson and Kohlberg. Cycles 1-3 prepare a person to grow through the seven cycles of development. Looking at all theories we are exposed to different dimensions of Human and Spiritual Development.

Conversion, relates to an individual's initial awareness of the transcendent dimension in life. The individual begins to pay attention to life-giving values and to see objectively that they are essential to personal growth, and therefore makes a commitment to these values.

The third stage is purification, initiated by the experience of conversion. The individual chooses a way of life that enables him or her to conform to chosen values through personal discipline. This is precisely what occurs in the development of one's values at Cycle 4.

The stage of illumination relates to the values in Cycle 5. It is the description of a state of internal integration through values like Integration/Wholeness and Being Self.

The fifth and last stage is an experience of enlightenment. Some mystical theorists call this stage the unitive experience, unity consciousness, or ultimate reality. This stage is anticipated by the values in the fourth phase of development—values such as Truth/Wisdom and Intimacy/Solitude.

Erikson and Kohlberg. Figure 7-3 spells out in more detail a comparison of the developmental models of Erikson's and Kohlberg, which were summarized in Figure 7-2.

FIGURE 7-3.   Comparison of Erikson's and Kohlberg's Developmental Models

ERIKSON'S LIFE-CYCLE STAGES	KOHLBERG'S STAGES OF MORAL DEVELOPMENT
1. Trust vs. Mistrust (Age 1–1-1/2 yrs) Initial need for securing care.	**PRE-CONVENTIONAL LEVEL** Moral choices reside in external authority.
2. Autonomy vs. Shame and Doubt (Age 2–6 yrs) Need for parental care and affirmation of will.	**1. Stage of Punishment and Obedience** Doing right to avoid breaking the rules and being punished.
3. Initiative vs. Guilt Need for positive role models who provide creative fantasy.	**2. Stage of Individual Instrumental Purpose and Exchange** Doing right is based on meeting one's own needs and upon fair exchange, while recognizing that others have individual interests that may sometimes conflict with one's own.
4. Industry vs. Inferiority (Age 7–12 yrs) Need to experience success in tasks at school and work.	
	CONVENTIONAL LEVEL Moral choices are based on performing the right role and maintaining the expectations of others.
5. Identity vs. Role Confusion (Age 13–21 yrs) Adolescents need to integrate past tasks in order to direct their own lives.	**3. Stage of Mutual Interpersonal Expectations, Relationships, and Conformity** Right is living up to one's role expectations, having good motives, and showing concern for others in order to have a positive self-image.
6. Intimacy vs. Isolation (Age 21–35 yrs) Capacity to make committed relationships.	**4. Stage of Social System and Conscience Maintenance** Right is fulfilling obligations, upholding the social order, and maintaining the welfare of the group. Law is the final word in social conflicts.

continued

FIGURE 7-3. **Comparison of Erikson's and Kohlberg's Developmental Models (continued)**

ERIKSON'S LIFE-CYCLE STAGES	KOHLBERG'S STAGES OF MORAL DEVELOPMENT
	TRANSITIONAL LEVEL Individual bases choices on emotions and makes decisions without a commitment to society. Picks and chooses obligations and while these may be defined by particular groups, the individual has no principles for the choices.
	POST-CONVENTIONAL LEVEL Morality resides in personal conscience.
7. Generativity vs. Stagnation (Age 35–60 yrs) Extension beyond personal concerns to embrace global concerns and future generations.	**5. Stage of Prior Rights and Social Contract or Utility** Right is upholding basic rights even when these conflict with the law of the group. Concern that laws and duties be based on "greatest good for the greatest number." Some rights, such as life and liberty, must be upheld regardless of majority opinion.
8. Integrity vs. Despair and Disgust (Age 60+) Final stage of meaningful life satisfaction and affirmation of self-transcendence as death approaches.	**6. Stage of Universal Ethical Principles** Right is based on universal principles. When laws violate these principles, the individual acts in accord with universal principles.

Erikson's stages outline emotional development. Based on Freud's original construct that described adolescent development, Erikson's model is expanded to include all of the life cycle from birth to death. There are eight stages. Lawrence Kohlberg based his work on the cognitive developmental scheme of Piaget; he showed that personal decisions about what is right or wrong are also developmental and depend upon the cognitive level of individual development. His model has three levels and six stages and is much like the first three phases of the values model of development. Now it is clear that they do not line up by the numbers, but that they are parallel in levels of value development.

For example, our Cycle 1, which includes Phase I values such as Self-Preservation, Self-Interest/Control, and Security, is parallel to Erikson's first two stages. Basic trust, for example, is the value of Security. On the other side, Kohlberg points out that at the pre-conventional level all decisions are based on what is satisfying to an individual, and on reward and punishment. Egocentricity and self-interest dominate one's moral decisions. This information helps us determine what the values and the world view are at Cycle 1. For example, the criteria for the values in Cycle 1 (Phase 1) are that they are physical in nature, such as Sensory Pleasure/Sexuality, Physical Delight, and Food/Warmth/Shelter.

Erikson's stages 3 and 4, initiative and industry, relate to the child's early experiences in the family and at school that prepare him or her for work. This is parallel to Cycle 2 with its values of Family/Belonging and Self-Worth. Self-Worth is the most important value for giving individuals the encouragement to learn and to relate to others and eventually to form families of their own.

In Kohlberg's conventional level, stages 3 and 4, morality is based on rules and mandates from others. It is the social world of belonging that parallels Phase II, Cycles 2 and 3 of values development. For Erikson, this is first the period of identity and then intimacy (stages 5 and 6). During this time, the adolescent integrates previous tasks in order to develop an identity that will enable him or her to succeed in the world of work, and then go on to establish a lifelong committed relationship with a mate. Values important to development at this time are Being Liked, Family/Belonging, and Competence/Confidence.

Kohlberg's post-conventional level, stages 5 and 6, is a world view that is dominated by self-initiation and social responsibility based on a personal conscience. Erikson's equivalent is the generativity of stage 7 when the individual, having succeeded at work and family life, expands his or her world view to include the global society and future generations. In values development this is Phase III, or Cycles 4, 5, and 6, and includes such values as Service/Vocation, Accountability/Ethics, and Being Self.

Finally Erikson's stage 8, integrity, relates to values development at Cycle 7. The mature individual, who has made a conscious and deliberate life passage, begins to review that life, and develops detachment as preparation for death. The well-integrated person at this stage has developed such values as Detachment/Transcendence, Truth/Wisdom, and Intimacy/Solitude/Enlightenment.

James Fowler.   Fowler (Figure 7-2 on page 124) built his theory of faith development on a model that integrated the work of Kohlberg and Erikson. Fowler describes faith as grounded in the values that empower us. For Fowler, faith "involves people's shaping or testing their lives, defining directions and relationships with others in accordance with co-ordinates of values and power recognized as ultimate" (1981, p. 93). What the individual sees as "relationship" and "ultimate" then changes with each stage of development.

At Fowler's mythic literal stage, our parents are godlike and their values are also ours. At the conventional stage, faith is related more to institutions and what they say is ultimate and valuable. The individuative stage reflects our initial attempt at a personal values orientation, much like the classical idea of conversion. The conjunctive stage is that of personal integration and development that leads finally to the recognition of universal truths and has to do with commitment to a future vision that relates to the greater purpose of what it means to be human. Fowler is unique in that he integrates the developmental theories of Piaget, Erikson, and Kohlberg into his lifescape, and he also recognizes that values are central in human development.

Abraham Maslow. Maslow's hierarchy of needs relates directly to the first three phases of values development through a graduated values hierarchy. His first two stages—basic needs and achievement needs—are what he called "D" or deficiency cognition, because if they are not met, they create a developmental deficiency that makes further growth difficult. These are basically foundation values. His third level, "B" or being cognition, relates to what we call future values, including values such as Creativity and Self-Actualization.

How We Develop and Grow

Comparison of other developmental theories with the phases, stages, and cycles of values development gives us a richer background for understanding the world views and values that stand behind the Seven Cycles of Development. Are all these models really saying the same thing? Are Erikson's stages, for example, simply parallel to the cycles? I believe that Erikson's schema is an important contribution, but that the seven cycles are a unique perspective that is enhanced by the contributions made by other scholars' models of development.

In Chapters 8–10 we are going to see that the cycles of development are not simply descriptions of how we grow psychologically, or even spiritually, but of how we function in relationship to the institutions that influence our lives. Remember that each phase has an A and a B stage. Stage A values are essential to our growth as individuals. Stage B values are also essential, but they are the values that we internalize through the institutions we are part of, such as our families, schools, places of worship, and workplaces.

This idea was anticipated by developmentalists such as Erikson, who emphasized the family and the effect of school on a child's life. But we are saying in addition that institutional experiences affect the way our values develop or fail to develop. In fact, the way we design or manage our families, classrooms, or even corporate offices is going to affect the values and therefore the emotional and spiritual lives of everyone within that setting. We are really addressing a more basic question: What factors enable a person to grow through the Seven Cycles of Development?

Journeying Through the Cycles

In order to develop a meaningful life, one that energizes us and originates in our unique values, it is necessary to pass through the Seven Cycles of Development. This passage introduces us to an intricate network of values patterns that will be examined in the next chapter. In preparation, let's look at the four minimal conditions that are necessary to move through the Seven Cycles of Development and to achieve personal transformation.

1. Each cycle of development presents opportunities to integrate the values of the individual and institutional/relational stages (A and B). Cycle 1 represents the early stages of a person's life, the period during which the values in individual and institutional/relational stages are integrated. An individual who is experiencing I-B values becomes aware of II-A values and begins to grow toward them, initiating the journey through the cycles.

   But it cannot be assumed that once a person has passed through a certain stage of values development he or she will never need to develop new values in that cycle. Since this process is cyclical and not linear, it may be necessary as one matures to revisit an earlier stage in order to integrate certain skills associated with a value.

   For instance, if a person in III-B has been promoted into a position at work that requires skills of collaboration, which is a highly developed interpersonal skill, that person may first need to learn the basics of negotiation, team building, and active listening. This requires the II-B values of Education/Certification and Communication/Information. Figure 7-4 illustrates this process.

2. At each cycle a person must develop minimal essential values in that stage, along with the necessary skills to actualize those values. Some of the more obvious values that must be developed are Self-Preservation in Stage I-A, Security in Stage I-B, and Self-Worth in Stage II-A. We need minimal values and skills from every stage.

FIGURE 7-4. Journeying Through the Seven Cycles of Development

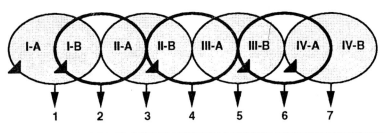

During the later cycles, a balance of the four skill types—instrumental, interpersonal, imaginal, and system—must be developed for healthy and integrated development to occur.

3. At each cycle, we must address our fears or dark side. Each cycle has its own fears. At Cycle 1 it may be insecurity (Security); at Cycle 2 it might be not being validated by others (Self-Worth); or at Cycle 5 it might be fear of intimacy.

4. At each cycle we must experience positive institutional reinforcement for our stage of development and for the next stage ahead of where we are. For example, a child in Cycle 1 who feels insecure and who is held by other children (Security, Stage I-B), but who does not receive reinforcement one stage ahead from caring adults (Family/Belonging, Stage II-A) may not grow. To grow, children need caring and comfort when they are frightened and anxious, but they also need the comfort that comes from the consistent institutionalized reality of the family.

In the next chapter we are going to look at the early cycles of development, Cycles 1–3. In Chapter 9 we will revisit the conditions for development, especially as they relate to leadership and organizational transformation. Then in Chapter 10 we will review the last four cycles of development.

8

The Early Cycles of Development

Cyclical implies going in circles, with the repetition of familiar patterns—night and day, the four seasons, birth and death. From this perspective, the purpose is to master the repetitive patterns in our ever-changing experience. Cyclical thinking looks for human meaning in the ongoing flow of human experience, from world news to family events to personal concerns. It assumes that life can make good sense in good times and bad, in growth and decline, in the beginnings and endings. Cyclical thinking tolerates high levels of ambiguity and finds pathways for living in dark and unseemly places.

Frederic Hudson, *The Adult Years*

In this chapter we are going to explore the first three cycles of development. We will begin by examining the world view and values of the two stages that comprise each cycle. This will be followed by a discussion of the ethical issues and discernment questions raised by the values. Discernment questions are those that, when answered "yes," indicate that the individual is currently living in that cycle's values. This will be followed by a skills section that describes the basic skills/values clusters that an individual must master to move forward.

We will also look at the leadership and institutional styles that emerge at each cycle. Institutions, just like individuals, operate at identifiable stages of development, often influenced by their missions and environment. The question of leadership and management will be addressed in more detail in Chapter 8.

Cycle 1: Safety and Security

The Cycle 1 person views the world as an alien and mysterious place ruled by distant authority. The adult is motivated by the need for security and material ownership, and the struggle for physical survival (Figure 8-1). Ethical choices are based on self-interest, which is viewed as the most practical way to survive. In this cycle, it is important to develop a creative and positive imagination in order to have a healthy movement into future stages.

Ethical Choices. In Cycle 1, choices between what is right and wrong are based on a perspective of self-interest, where our personal physical needs must be taken care of first, whether they be finances, eating and living arrangements, or sexual and physical issues in relationships. In this cycle we begin to build basic trust in life and ourselves. Kohlberg describes this as pre-conventional morality.

FIGURE 8-1. Cycle 1 Values

STAGE I-A	STAGE I-B
Goals Values	**Goals Values**
Self-Interest/Control	Security
Self-Preservation	Physical Delight
Wonder/Awe/Fate	
Means Values	**Means Values**
Food/Warmth/Shelter	Affection/Physical
Function/Physical	Economics/Profit
Safety/Survival	Property/Control
	Sensory Pleasure
	Territory/Security
	Wonder/Curiosity

FIGURE 8-2. Cycle 1 Sample Discernment Questions

Self-Preservation
■ Is life a daily physical struggle for you?

Wonder/Awe/Fate
■ Do you see life as mysterious and awesome much of the time?

Safety/Survival
■ Do you feel that outside forces are threatening your survival?

Security
■ Is comfort and certainty important to you?
■ Does worry or anxiety take a lot of your energy at this time?

Sensory Pleasure
■ Is being touched and held important to you?

Economics/Profit
■ Do you have sufficient skills in money management?
■ Is your financial future a problem at this time?

Discernment Questions. Discernment questions are designed to find out more about a person's values than they themselves are aware of. For example, those who put a lot of emphasis on security in their lives but are not aware of it will exhibit insecurity in their behavior. An example of a related discernment question for Cycle 1 values would be: "Is a minimal amount of certainty and security important to you?" By asking a question rather than giving an answer, the subjects are invited to see themselves at a deeper level.

Discernment is the ancient art of asking sensitive questions in order to enlarge the perspective of the person and enable him or her to see deeper within themselves. Sample discernment questions in this and the following cycle descriptions will appear in figures. Figure 8-2 lists example discernment questions related to the values in Cycle 1.

Cycle 1 Skills. The ability to function at any cycle and to grow toward the next cycle depends on the skills that the individual has or develops for taking responsibility for his or her life. First there are the positive skills. In Cycle 1 basic instrumental skills are necessary in order to feel secure and to survive. Some of these are fundamental skills involved with physical functioning—for example, hand-eye coordination—that are learned in childhood. Others are educational skills such as reading,

FIGURE 8-3. Examples of Cycle 1 Skills/Values Clusters

Economics/Profit

Skills: Practical know-how and skills in accumulating and managing the money you need to survive and support your lifestyle. Bookkeeping skills to control expenditures and to protect yourself from the avarice of others.

Food/Warmth/Shelter

Skills: Obtaining and securing minimal resources to feed, protect, and clothe yourself, and to find an adequate place to live in order to survive. Maintaining healthful and economical eating habits.

Sensory Pleasure

Skills: Appreciating and understanding the fears of another, and imagining how to please another with physical tenderness in order to experience personal gratification without anxiety.

Self-Interest/Control—Property/Control

Skills: Obtaining and maintaining real estate or property to provide for personal physical survival needs and comforts.

Physical Delight—Affection/Physical

Skills: Receptivity to being touched, held, and cared for physically by another and the ability to do the same with those who are close to you.

---

writing, and mathematics, which enable people to survive in their cultures and form basic competencies later in life. Figure 8-3 shows some of the skills that are acquired in Cycle 1.

However, foundational to all skills is the ability to tolerate pain and discomfort in order to delay gratification, to make sense out of pain or discomfort, and to see it as growth-producing. Developed in Cycle 1 and carried throughout a person's life, the ability to cope with physical and then emotional pain enables an individual to endure and finally to transcend discomfort, thus becoming autonomous, the value of Being Self.

The classic example is that of a youngster who is playing a game of catch with her friends. She misses a catch, and the ball crashes through the neighbor's window. Her friends dash for home, and she is left holding the empty mitt as her neighbor glares from behind the broken glass. She could deny doing it—after all she didn't hit the ball; but instead she owns up to the fact that she was at least partially responsible for the broken window. That is a painful moment, but growth occurs because she has been honest about her role in the accident. She feels good about herself. She may even arrange to help pay for the damage by doing yard work. That would mean the further discomfort of knowing her friends were out playing while she worked in the neighbor's yard. The consequences of our actions are not without pain or discomfort. But when we face them and accept responsibility, we mature and grow toward autonomy.

Early in life parents help young children learn about discomfort, pain, and growth. They do this by placing limits on behavior and having clearly defined consequences for misbehavior. The disciplining of a child should never be physically abusive, and should always have a rationale associated with it that the child can understand. Whatever the consequence or punishment, the parent's goal should always be the growth and development of the child toward eventual autonomy.

Negative Skills. It is possible at any cycle to develop skills that avoid and deny inner feelings and images, thus keeping the person from realizing the full potential of life at that cycle of development.

At Cycle 1 these avoidance mechanisms are especially strong, creating resisting forces that may impede a person's progress through the cycles of development. Negative skill formation happens when the individual perceives that survival is at stake when the environment is in fact secure. Negative skill development also involves both conscious and unconscious techniques that delay or impede a person's ability to take responsibility for his or her life. Any of the Phase I means values coupled with Self-Preservation or Self-Interest/Control can result in forms of narcissism and obsessiveness.

In the case of the girl who missed the ball in the game of catch, if Self-Preservation had linked with the value of Safety/Survival, she might have attemped to lie her way out of the situation or blame others and claim total innocence. Such a scenario would not have promoted her growth and development toward autonomy or Being Self.

An adult who lives in Cycle 1 can become obsessive about means values, resulting in an individual who is demagogic and dictatorial. For example, Tom has more than enough money in retirement to meet his basic needs of food and shelter. He lives alone in a two-bedroom condominium that is part of a retirement village that has become a national model. Tom pays cash every two years for a new car. He eats breakfast out each morning by himself.

Recently a group of residents formed to develop a nature trail that would take advantage of the beautiful grounds, which include a woods and a quiet pond inhabitied by wild ducks and geese. They raised the money and drew up the plans themselves. Tom wanted no part of it. From the beginning, he criticized the project, from the materials that were used for the walk itself to the "scrawny flowers" that were eventually planted along the trail. However, he complained most bitterly when the plans placed a bench within 30 feet of his back porch. He felt that his privacy was threatened.

Tom is a person who is unnecessarily concerned with issues of Territory/Security, Property/Control, and Economics/Profit. He has spent most of his life in Phase I. Phase II values such as Belief/Philosophy and Duty/Obligation have provided his motivation—in other words, they are his future values. Throughout his life, Tom has denied his own development for the purpose of perceived threats to his survival, when in fact his environment has always been secure. This is an example of negative skill formation.

Alcohol and drug abuse are extreme means of avoiding growth. In more moderate forms, self-narcotization by means of sex and even too much television has helped people avoid the discomfort of developing their full potential. Even a seemingly benign avoidance technique such as manipulating others to get what we want is a means of not taking responsibility for our own needs. Anything that prevents our taking personal responsibility for our own lives is negative skill development, a barrier to reaching our potential.

Cycle 1 Leadership Style: Dictatorial.   In adults, each cycle of development gives rise to a related style of leadership. Leadership defines the way in which an individual influences others. Because Cycle 1's values are based on survival, the leadership style is going to be autocratic. Cycle 1 people feel that all major decisions have to be made personally by themselves. When a Cycle 1 person is in leadership or management, they will feel that they need to keep tight control over their subordinates.

Survival on a day-to-day basis, control of property, profit margin, and financial flow are of utmost importance. Loyalty to the organization through its leadership is seen as a number-one priority and the overriding criterion for ethical choices. Robert Townsend, speaking tongue-in-cheek and quoted in Hall & Thompson (1980, p. 56), put it this way: "The best two guarantees that the chief executive will work full time are hunger and fear. He has to hunger for the company to succeed; and he has to have so much of his own money and ego tied up in the company that fear of failure is constantly with him."

This level and style of leadership is absolutely essential when the environment is alien. In other words, when the values of Safety/Survival and Self-Preservation are objectively occurring, a dictatorial leadership style is probably the only thing that will work. If you are in charge of a jungle search team in wartime, your leadership style had better be autocratic. If your house is burning and your children are trapped, someone has to be dictatorial to avoid disaster.

Autocratic leadership is hardly ever elected; it is usually appointed out of survival necessity. Churchill was asked to be prime minister at the beginning of World War II, but as soon as the war was over, he was voted out of office. Why? Dictatorial leadership was needed in the war years. Any leadership style has a consequence for those who are working for the designated leader. For the follower of an autocratic leader, the experience is that of oppression. Therefore when the environmental threat is removed, the people if they have a choice will change the leadership—as they did with Churchill.

I remember being on an overseas assignment in Costa Rica for a Canadian company. I was with my wife and a small child. All our baggage had been lost for six weeks, and we had heard nothing from our superiors in Toronto for two months. It was in August and they were on holiday! There were a lot of serious questions from local people in Costa Rica about the work we were doing there. I put my concerns in a letter to my boss, asking for an urgent reply.

A short letter came back three months later that said: "Hall, please remember, we are all members of a soccer team, and you are one of the linebackers. Team members do not ask questions, they wait for orders. Hope all is going well. Yours sincerely . . ." Followership with this style of dictatorial leadership is primarily an experience of distance, with a lack of interpersonal sensitivity.

When leadership operates autocratically in a physically nonthreatening environment, it becomes dictatorial and destructive. Leaders with Phase I values and autocratic leadership styles need to be certain that their circumstances really demand such a style. When this is not the case, the situation is emotionally unhealthy for the followers and the leader.

This style of leader is over-controlling of employees and possibly of family and friends. The leader's primary loyalty is to him- or herself and close confidants. There is also a tendency to place unrealistic expectations on others.

Cycle 1 Institutional Style. Traditional, hierarchical institutions are examples of Cycle 1 institutions. They are very structured, top-down hierarchies, where the leadership's authority goes unquestioned, especially in times of crisis. There are many examples of institutions that need to run autocratically for the protection of the institutional members and their development. An example is the intensive care unit of any hospital.

A family must be run this way for the first year of a child's life; otherwise the child would go hungry and never learn the most basic skills of Cycle 1 existence.

However, it is essential not to set up a Cycle 1 leadership and institutional style when the environment is at a higher level; if a leader adopts autocratic methods when there is no environmental threat, the membership feels oppressed and demeaned.

It is important in all the cycles to assess the values appropriate to the environment and the needs of the people in that situation, then to design the management structure and provide the leadership style that is based on these needs. Generally speaking, the leadership should always be at least one cycle ahead of where the people in the institution are, or where the environment demands they be. In other words, in Cycle 1 environments such as a military operation or firefighters battling a fire, a Cycle 2 leadership style will produce the best results.

Cycle 2: Security and Family

Cycle 2 is between Phases I and II. Figure 8-4 shows the values of this cycle. Cycle 2 people have moved from a physically oriented world to a social orientation, stressing family and belonging. In Cycle 2, the person progresses into wider realms of learning and social encounter.

The central dynamic of this cycle is the awareness that survival in the world must include the valuing of other people, particularly members of your family. The world may appear to be hostile outside the boundaries

FIGURE 8-4. Cycle 2 Goals and Means Values

STAGE I-B	STAGE II-A
Goals Values	**Goals Values**
Security	Family/Belonging
Physical Delight	Fantasy/Play
	Self-Worth
Means Values	**Means Values**
Affection/Physical	Being Liked
Economics/Profit	Care/Nurture
Property/Control	Control/Order/Discipline
Sensory Pleasure	Courtesy/Hospitality
Territory/Security	Dexterity/Coordination
Wonder/Curiosity	Endurance/Patience
	Equilibrium
	Friendship/Belonging
	Obedience/Duty
	Prestige/Image
	Rights/Respect
	Social Affirmation
	Support/Peer
	Tradition

FIGURE 8-5. Cycle 2 Sample Discernment Questions

Family/Belonging
■ Is your family a priority concern for you?

Self-Worth
■ Do you feel sufficiently respected by those who know you?
■ Are there aspects of yourself you cannot share with others?

Being Liked
■ Is being liked by others an important issue for you?

Care/Nurture
■ Do you feel cared for?

Control/Order/Discipline
■ Do you have sufficient skills in orderly discipline in your work, hygiene, and play?

Tradition
■ Are family traditions and annual festivals important to you?
■ Do you enjoy historical reading, drama, and film?

Social Affirmation
■ When you make a decision, do you wonder what others will think?
■ Do you take care to positively affirm those close to you on a regular basis?

of your home, but your family provides the security and belonging essential to your well-being. The world view of this cycle is a blend of Phase I and II, where your living situation, home, and friends shelter you from an unfriendly or uncaring society. The predominant task is to integrate personal security needs with those of family and friends.

Ethical Choices. Ethical choices are based on fairness and mutual respect. We are "good" when we follow the rules that fair authority has laid down. In this cycle, education, the avoidance of perfectionism (over-attention to following the rules), and hospitality are essential for growth. This cycle is moving in the direction of personal and familial integration. What is right is based on personal self-interest, with a minimal recognition that the perspective of others is important.

Discernment Questions. The discernment questions for Phase I-B have already been addressed as a part of Cycle 1. Additional example questions related to values from Phase II-A are listed in Figure 8-5.

FIGURE 8-6. Examples of Cycle 2 Skills/Values Clusters

Tradition

> *Skills:* Promoting family traditions such as major holidays and birthdays to enhance the feeling of worth and pride in our family, religion, and country.

Care/Nurture

> *Skills:* Learning to care for and nuture all the members of one's family, including their emotional as well as physical needs.

Economics/Profit

> *Skills:* Practical know-how and skills in accumulating and managing the financial resources that permit you to gain the respect of those you work with.

Cycle 2 Skills.   The skills at Cycle 2 are a continuation of instrumental skills with an emphasis on the basics of reading, writing, and simple mathematics. In this cycle the beginnings of interpersonal development occur, stressing courtesy and hospitality, caring, nurturing, and being supportive of friendship. Examples of Cycle 2 skills/values clusters are shown in Figure 8-6.

The most basic skill that needs to be nurtured for the future is the skill of rote learning, which combines control and discipline with the interpersonal component of obedience and respect for authority. This skill is always essential, as in the example of needing to learn a foreign language or a computer program.

A positive experience of these values at each cycle helps development occur at the next phase with its expanded world view. Once individuals are able to experience the values, they are often able to convert them into images. This often becomes a description of a personal aspiration of hope for the future. For example, Christine and Joe, a young couple who were in premarital counseling, were able to talk about their dreams, as reflected in their goal values, but they occasionally substituted means values. An example of their goal values is shown in Figure 8-7.

Christine and Joe owned a small fish shop. She spoke from their values when she described their shared vision: "We have both had a difficult upbringing, and have both been divorced before. So we are hoping to buy some property in the country and slowly build our own house by buying more materials each month from the money we make in our business. This captures my hopes for Joe and me. But the more we concentrated on the money [Economics/Profit], the more distant we got from

FIGURE 8-7. Christine's and Joe's Values

Goal Value 1: Security	Goal Value 2: Family/Belonging
Means Values:	Means Values:
Economics/Profit	Sensory Pleasure
Property/Control	Care/Nurture

each other. Now we have balanced our lives with the other values" (Sensory Pleasure and Property/Control).

She continued, "We get a lot of pleasure just being with each other and cuddling up in front of the fire or the television at night. Anyway, we want to have several children and build a family for all of us, so that they can have what we could not have—a place where we belonged and felt secure." Obviously the values were being defined by Christine as she spoke. They reflect the depth of feelings that she had about the internal images she expressed.

This illustrates that a values cluster is a shadow of an internal reality that is, in turn, a plan for future behavior. This attachment to a cluster of values that enpowers a person to grow is what James Fowler calls a Faith Center.

Negative skills at Cycle 2—those skills that reflect the darker side of our nature—involve neurosis, which is developed to defend the self against external threat. They are associated with a mistrustful attitude to the world with an over-attention to perfectionism and a fear of failure. The most direct negative behavior is an overt resistance to change and to learning anything new. A Cycle 2 person in a negative state can be in a state of high anxiety coupled with circular feelings of guilt, anger, and depression. The consequence is to block growth by a tendency to be cliquish and isolated from a wider range of persons. It can also be experienced as arrogance and discrimination against other people. At this cycle it very often takes on the form of sexual and racial discrimination.

Cycle 2 Leadership Style: Benevolent. The Cycle 2 leadership style is one of caring authority, or benevolent paternalism or maternalism. The style is autocratic, as in the first cycle, but with an emphasis on careful listening. The leader is very much aware that he or she is ultimately responsible for decisions. Consequently, loyalty to designated superiors and following the rules they set down is important. Credibility and resistance to change often mark the leader's style. He or she cares about the employee but would never consider what the follower or employee has to say to be of any significance as far as decision making is concerned. •

The subordinate of the benevolent autocrat still feels oppressed, but feels cared for much like a child feels about a parent. This is a common style in administrative settings, and was the normal style of operating for most executives until the late 1960s. This style of leadership is most appropriate in an environment where the founder or executive of the organization is highly skilled and the support people are not. In this setting, the leader very often has to take a parental or teacher role in order for the system to survive. However, this role would be a disaster with competent peers.

The Cycle 2 Institutional Style. The Cycle 2 institutional style, like the leadership style, is that of a benevolent hierarchy that is managed from the top down, and where all the decisions are made by appointed leadership, or by leaders that own or founded the corporation. There is an inherent danger in this style in a tendency to hire friends and family into the business.

The benevolent organization can very often exaggerate the already dominate stereotypes of men and women in society. In systems where the male leader is a father figure as in religion or sometimes medicine, it is very difficult for women to function and break the stereotype. Likewise, in professions where women are parental role figures, as in teaching and nursing, there is a similar danger of exaggerating and falling into stereotyped roles.

Cycle 3: Family and Institutions

The Cycle 3 values and world view are those of Phases II-A and II-B (Figure 8-8). The world is viewed as a problem, but one with which you are able to cope by becoming educated and by making an adequate living. Your chief struggle is to be successful and to please those who control your work future and still be able to take enough time to be with your friends and family. This cycle expands personal awareness of weaknesses and strengths in the world of education and work. As a consequence, interpersonal skills and facility with emotions begin to expand the possibilities for personal growth.

Ethical Choices. Ethical choices in Cycle 3 are are similar to those in Kohlberg's conventional morality. What the individual sees as right is what those in respected authority see is right. Initially this may be attached to certain personalities such as one's parents or boss or a minister. Later in the cycle, morality becomes more sophisticated and choice is related to laws and rules of respected institutions such as government and religious organizations. The important skills acquired in this cycle are interpersonal skills, skills of administrative effectiveness, and the ability to look critically at the values of family and the policies of respected institutions. In this cycle the

FIGURE 8-8. Cycle 3 Goals and Means Values

STAGE II-A	STAGE II-B
Goals Values	**Goals Values**
Family/Belonging	Competence/Confidence
Fantasy/Play	Play/Recreation
Self-Worth	Work/Labor
	Worship/Faith/Creed
Means Values	**Means Values**
Being Liked	Achievement/Success
Care/Nurture	Administration/Control
Control/Order/Discipline	Communication/Information
Courtesy/Hospitality	Competition
Dexterity/Coordination	Design/Pattern/Order
Endurance/Patience	Duty/Obligation
Equilibrium	Economics/Success
Friendship/Belonging	Education/Certification
Obedience/Duty	Efficiency/Planning
Prestige/Image	Hierarchy/Order
Rights/Respect	Honor
Social Affirmation	Law/Rule
Support/Peer	Loyalty/Fidelity
Tradition	Management
	Membership/Institution
	Ownership
	Patriotism/Esteem
	Productivity
	Reason
	Responsibility
	Rule/Accountability
	Technology/Science
	Unity/Uniformity
	Workmanship/Art/Craft

individual moves from a family-based orientation to the larger social context—institutions beyond the family that influence personal choices and make demands on personal time, such as work and church or temple.

Discernment Questions. Figure 8-9 on the next page lists discernment questions related to Stage II-B values. Stage II-A discernment questions were discussed in Cycle 2.

FIGURE 8-9.   Cycle 3 Sample Discernment Questions

Competence/Confidence
■ Do you feel competent in the work you do?

Belief/Philosophy
■ Are your religious beliefs very important to you?

Play/Recreation
■ Do you feel the need for recreation?

Achievement/Success
■ Do enjoy competitive sports? Is winning important to you?
■ How important is success to you?

Loyalty/Fidelity
■ Is loyalty a high priority for you?
■ Is commitment to your partner a significant issue for you?

Education/Certification
■ Is completing your education important to you?

Law/Rule
■ Do you think of yourself as living within the rules?

Cycle 3 Skills.   In Cycle 3 the continuation of instrumental skills dominates as individuals fulfill their places in society by completing their professional and formal education (Figure 8-10). An essential skill at this level of development occurs through a good experience of a rigid institution, where one learns all the basic administrative skills needed today to be competent in all areas of life. Among these are: word processing; using a telephone, fax machine, calculator, and copying machine; placing and filling orders; filing; and managing one's personal life or the life at the entry level of any institution.

To do well in management in this cycle and beyond, one must have Stage II-A skills such as Care/Nurture, which men often have not developed. It is critical for managers or executives to work hard to develop interpersonal skills. Men who lack these rudimentary skills of caring and relating, natural to most women, will alienate the people they work with. These interpersonal skills include the ability to listen well and to clarify communication, and the ability to keep calm during times of conflict. In this cycle, peer support is important, with an emphasis on pleasing others and being friendly and outgoing. The essential interpersonal skills are most often related to Stage II-A means values, as shown in Figure 8-11.

FIGURE 8-10. Examples of Cycle 3 Instrumental Skills

Reason

Skills: Learning how to think, plan, and apply rules of logic to problems in work.

Productivity

Skills: Understanding how to be more productive at work through time management, quality control, and education at work. This involves developing effective plans and reaching goals.

Membership/Institution

Skills: Thinking, planning, and executing procedures to make your place of work successful and productive.

FIGURE 8-11. Examples of Cycle 3 Skills/Values Clusters

Social Affirmation

Skills: Developing personal affirmation and respect for and from the people one respects the most.

Support/Peer

Skills: Feeling the support and being supportive of one's friends and equals at work.

Rights/Respect

Skills: Learning to esteem and receive rights, respect, and honor from those whom one respects and admires.

Courtesy/Hospitality

Skills: Creating ways to be courteous and hospitable to those one works and plays with.

A poor experience of an institution or an excessive dependence on institutional life can lead to minimal skill development. Institutions such as the church, the military, and even the government can totally absorb a person's life. This is very common in some industrial corporations, in which all of an employee's education, medical bills, and life needs—from family security and recreation to death—are taken care of.

Some companies expect the same loyalty from an executive as the military expects from one of its officers. If a person in this situation is not well-developed emotionally, a negative experience of leadership can become life-threatening and damaging to the person's system of meaning. This experience can lead to passive-aggressive behavior that manifests itself negatively in later experiences of leadership by the individual.

A person who is excessively dependent on an institution and who has acquired all of his or her skills from that setting has experienced accomplishment within a limited environment. Such a person may have difficulty envisioning the future in a meaningful way. I have known several people who did well in electronics companies. They were making so much money that they did not finish their education, but the skills they learned were esoteric and specialized, so that when the company collapsed they were unable to get other jobs. They lacked balance among instrumental, interpersonal, imaginal, and system skills. Their success within a limited environment stunted their ability to envision a future outside that environment. This influenced their decisions to forego the education process, later preventing them from employment in other environments after the collapse of the company.

Skills and a Consciousness Shift. There is a dramatic consciousness shift that occurs during Cycle 3. Let's illustrate this by continuing with the example of Christine and Joe, the young couple with the small fish shop. There are many possible combinations that reflect the development across the cycle; some of Christine's and Joe's are shown in Figure 8-12. They had values ranging from Phase I-B all the way to II-B, which is not uncommon as people grow and develop.

Christine and Joe have now been married for two years. Joe is working on the value of Security by doing well in his business (Economics/Profit). He spends a lot of time in the community making himself known (Social Affirmation) and feels esteemed (Self-Worth), and as a consequence he also feels that he is achieving and succeeding through his work.

The result of all of this is that he feels more confident (Competence/Confidence). What was originally an experience of insecurity about his work is becoming an experience of security through the family. This in turn altered his image of himself, and now he has a vision of a possible future.

FIGURE 8-12. Christine's and Joe's Values, Cycle 3

STAGE I-B	STAGE II-A	STAGE II-B
Goal Value 1: Security	**Goal Value 2:** Self-Worth Family/Belonging	**Goal Value 1:** Competence/Confidence Work/Labor
Means Value 1: Economics/Profit	**Means Value 2:** Social Affirmation	**Means Value 1:** Achievement/Success

This brings us to the important consciousness shift that takes place in Cycle 3. The traditional understanding of development assumes that we grow emotionally and physically by completing different tasks at different stages. There is a hierarchy of tasks, and integrated development comes about as these tasks are completed at each stage of maturity. Erikson, Fowler, and other developmentalists refer to a circling back to earlier tasks, but basically this is simply a readdressing of past incompletions.

But there is something more than this. In the first integration of two values across the phases, in Cycle 2, the individual's consciousness is altered and he or she is able to see the future and its possibilities differently. Now, in Cycle 3, Achievement/Success alters the values back in Phase I-B. As Joe began to understand and experience Achievement/Success, his perception of his past and of the values from an earlier stage was altered. He had a new consciousness of all that had been before.

His perception of Security altered and expanded beyond making a profit to include accomplishments in the community. This new internal re-imaging of reality had moved into the future, giving Joe a whole new confidence about his work and himself. In other words, *the value clusters and their skills are not only a bridge to the internal images we have of reality and how we express them behaviorally, but they are also a part of the dynamics of the development of consciousness.* They appear to be an energy form that transcends ordinary growth processes, rewriting our past and our future.

Cycle 3 Leadership Style: Efficient Management. For a person in a leadership position at Cycle 3, the priority is on efficient management. Business is seen as ordered and productive. The institution is ordered in layers, each layer having different functions and levels of power and authority. The system is governed according to the principles of scientific management. Management by objectives would be an appreciated methodology. Respect for superiors and the rules and policies of the organization are viewed as being of paramount importance.

Cycle 3 institutional authority has replaced parental authority. Good experiences of institutional leadership are necessary for a person to develop into the later and more complex leadership styles. This is the last of the autocratic styles, characterized by set hierarchical structures that view the system as being made up of leaders and loyal members.

The rank and file experience leadership as considerably less distant than in Cycles 1 and 2. Cycle 3 leaders, at their best, are sensitive listeners who take everything that followers say into consideration as long as it reflects loyalty to the institution and helps make the system more efficient in accomplishing its given tasks and goals. Just as Cycle 1 was oriented to the Self-Preservation of the individual, so Cycle 3 is oriented to the preservation of the institution.

Cycle 3 Institutional Style.   The Cycle 3 institution is the large, efficient, ordered bureaucracy—an ordered, layered, and hierarchical system. This ordered system has been the backbone for all major institutions—from hospitals to industrial giants—for most of this century. For the most part, leadership in these institutions is elected or chosen through the hierarchy itself. The system consists of the president and his or her board, the vice-presidents of operations, marketing, R&D, and finance, then the general managers, and finally department heads.

The system is political and requires loyalty and obedience if it is to function well. In fact, the higher the level of obedience in the system, the more efficient it is; for example, in the modern Japanese corporation, the values and philosophy of the founder or CEO and president are carried out through every cell of the system, making an single, efficient mind.

A form of institutional narcissism can occur if the system begins to protect itself against any kind of change. In the late 1960s, as opposition to the conflict in Vietnam increased, the reaction of many leaders was to see those who held opposing views as traitors turning their backs on the country. This is the negative aspect of this stage of institutional development.

Summary

In this chapter we have looked at values growth through the first three cycles of development, growth that is basic to early human development. At Cycle 4, enormous shifts in consciousness occur that are reflected also in present shifts in organizational and global consciousness. In the next chapter we will look at the implications of the consciousness shift that occurs in Cycle 4 and continues to Cycle 7. Each of these cycles involves higher levels of integration of the skills, and an increased consciousness of the human, spiritual, and organizational dimensions of day-to-day living.

9

Transforming Consciousness: The Values Gap

To lead change the leader must believe without question that people are the most important asset of an organization.

Charles Joiner

We like to think that each of us possesses freedom individually. We are thus reluctant to give up a part of that freedom in order to create an integrated society. Durkheim offers the opposite view. He argues that freedom is the social creation of the body politic and that each of us draws his or her individual liberty from that social body.

William Ouchi

In the last chapter we described personal development through the first three cycles. In this chapter we will complete the cycles by reviewing what occurs in Cycles 4 through 7.

This is an important time, because at Cycle 4 people experience a dramatic shift in consciousness in the area of the institutions in their lives.

151

Institutions—schools, employing organizations, churches, and so on—have a special role in personal development. In order for us to grow from cycle to cycle, the institutional influences in our lives need to be supportive, and they need to reinforce our values at a level that is a stage ahead of our development, encouraging personal growth.

There are two factors in this shift of consciousness: (1) When a person gets to a Cycle 4 level of development, the critical institutions of influence are likely to be in the workplace. (2) At this stage, people begin to be more direct and self-initiating in exercising leadership.

As people become self-initiating, they begin to alter the institutions that affect their lives—they begin to *create* institutional life rather than simply react to it. Consequently, a major factor in human transformation at Cycle 4 and in the following cycles is leadership and its ability to reshape organizational life.

This chapter will address the "Values Gap," which is the jump from previous cycles of development (Cycles 1–3) and their reactive view of the world, to the new paradigm where the individual creates the world he or she lives in. We will also look at the critical leader/organization connection that reinforces and makes this consciousness-shift possible.

The Last Four Cycles

The Seven Cycles of Development appear at first to be a linear path of human development: in the first three cycles it appears that we simply grow from childhood until we complete our education and enter into the life of family and work. However, each cycle represents a jump in human consciousness that is not so evident in our earlier years as it is when we are more mature. Figure 9-1 represents another look at the seven cycles. Each ellipse represents the field of awareness at that cycle, and this field expands as the individual grows; this is a visual representation of the expanding consciousness that comes with personal growth. The horizontal line through the seven cycles represents the normal psychological view of development, where time is linear. In this view, you can get to Cycle 4 only after having completed the minimum tasks at Cycles 1, 2, and 3.

In the paradigm of the Seven Cycles of Development, the integrated person is conscious of the larger field of awareness, indicated by each cycle's ellipse, which encompasses all the possible value combinations in that cycle of development. If a person in Cycle 3 were fully aware, his or her consciousness would encompass all the possibilities in Cycles 1, 2, and 3. A person who was well integrated at Cycle 6 or 7 would be able to imagine how the person at Cycle 1 or 2 felt in a given situation.

Well-integrated people have fully developed psyches with a personal consciousness of both inner and outer reality. They live by a set of values that result in health and integration, enabling them to fulfill their potential.

FIGURE 9-1.   Expanding Consciousness Through the Cycles

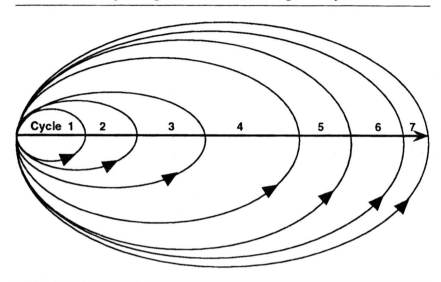

Integration is the ability to see the world more wholistically as one matures, and as a consequence to act in a way that is consistent with that consciousness. In Figure 9-1 the arrows attached to each cycle represent the process whereby the person is constantly integrating the stage A and B values. At each cycle, this circling around encompasses not only the values that come with that cycle, but the values and consciousness that go all the way back to Cycle 1. For example, a person in Cycle 4 who is working on the value of Integration/Wholeness may also be re-addressing the value of Self-Preservation from Cycle 1 in a new way, as he or she decides to take on a new job or pursue a new vocation.

Mind Shift

Each cycle represents an enormous expansion of consciousness. The linear model is based on time that is sequenced as we normally experience it in the everyday world. However, we know that the future pulls us forward to live by our future or vision values; the values in Cycle 7 pull us forward from the cycle where our lives and world views are currently operating.

When we move into Cycle 4, the pull is even stronger, because our world view changes so radically from this point on. There is a paradigm shift that bridges the Values Gap, and the world begins to take on significantly wider dimensions. It is a basic change in world view that alters our behavior in our relationships with others, but more basically in the way we see and relate to institutions.

This alteration in world view contains the following elements:

1. There is an internal shift in our perception of who runs and directs our lives. In the first three cycles our lives appear to be outer-directed by authority, whether it be that of parents, church, rules, or laws. Beginning in Cycle 4, we become inner-directed in all aspects of our lives.

2. We recognize that we have leadership abilities, that we have a unique contribution to make to the world. This is a movement from values emphasizing Independence in Stage III-A to an emphasis on Interdependence in Stage IV-A. Leadership from Cycle 4 on is seen as a cooperative venture rather than as the job of one person.

   We first recognize that we are equal among others (Equality/Liberation) and that we have special gifts and skills that are unique to us (Search for Meaning/Hope and Service/Vocation). This gives way to being happy with one's talents in a cooperative environment (Collaboration and Interdependence).

3. Growth is more than ever dependent upon institutional reinforcement, and there is a growing symbiosis or relationship between leadership and the management design of the institution the leader functions in.

   Leadership is now seen as a group or team reality, rather than an emphasis on one person. In Cycle 4 the leader is an enabler, enabling others to function cooperatively. Later, in Cycle 6, the person is one among a prescribed group of equals with a common interdependent task. The mind shift in values, skills, and world view occurs as the person recognizes that optimum development, especially in the area of leadership, can occur only when there is a concomitant shift in organizational structures.

4. The values shift requires a shift in skills. The shift begins with a higher level of interpersonal functioning demanded by values like Empathy in Cycle 4. This in turn causes a development of imaginal skills such as Expressiveness/Joy and Creativity. Finally, the move toward Interdependence in Cycle 6 causes the development of system awareness and systems skills with values such as Mission/Objectives and Corporation/New Order.

Leadership and Skill Development

Beginning at Cycle 4 the relationship of the individual to institutional reinforcement is critical to the growth process. *The person is not so much an individual relating to other individuals in a totally free environment, as an individual in a system interrelating with other systems or institutions, such as family and work.* An institution, its management style, and its products—whether they are television sets or the services of a day-care center—are some individual's visions and ideas projected onto the world through his or her values. This individual is the founding leader of the organization.

One could have the view that it was the leader's power and administrative ability that resulted in a given organizational form or style. Let's take a look at the relationship between leadership development in large institutions and the development of skills.

Instrumental Skills. Instrumental skills combine intelligence and manual dexterity; they enable one to be professional and competent. They are the skills that stand behind your profession, whether you are a banker, chemist, secretary, or engineer. They are the first set of skills that a leader develops as a part of his or her education. Instrumental skills are developed early on in our lives through formal education in grade school, high school, technical school, and college. It is only recently that instrumental skills directly related to leadership have been taught in schools.

Before the 1850s, leadership in Europe and America was for the most part conferred on men in the aristocracy or the ruling classes. Although there was a merchant class from the beginning of civilization, it started to grow significantly at the end of the Middle Ages with the development of an international banking system. But it was the American and French Revolutions and the English Industrial Revolution that really unleashed the power of the merchant class. Even though these merchants were thriving in the nineteenth century and early in the twentieth century, leadership was viewed as something that was literally bred into someone born into the upper classes or at most that it was God-given; leadership was not thought to be something that could be taught.

The idea that leadership could be learned was a new and novel idea that appeared in the early 1900s when the concept of scientific management was introduced by Frederick Taylor. Taylor suggested that managers need to be scientific in their approach. They must acquire specific technical skills essential to systematically improving production and control. These skills included accounting and standard business procedures. Sales and marketing techniques were acquired by studying the methods of the great entrepreneurs such as John D. Rockefeller, J. P. Morgan, and Thomas Watson, Sr., Peter Drucker (1969, p. 42) notes that: "The inventors of this period had to know how to convert their technical work into economic performance and their invention into a business. It was then that the big businesses of today were founded."

The leader during this period was the man whose technical skills could increase efficiency and productivity; his style was authoritarian;

his organization, hierarchical and bureaucratic. Since the early 1900s, instrumental skills have been an essential part of what leaders need to do the job efficiently. In the earlier part of this century, little or no attention was paid to the needs of employees.

Interpersonal Skills.   Interpersonal skills involve the ability to express and manage emotions so that we elicit cooperation rather than alienation from those we work and relate to. These skills are initiated in Phase II and have their high point in Stage III-A. It is in Cycle 4 that they reach their high point.

The study of sociology and psychology in the first half of this century caused a breakthrough in our understanding of the interrelationship between human emotions, motivation, and mental health. In the same time period the group dynamics movement gave rise to new system theories of family interaction; this opened up organizational studies to the field of human relations training and the introduction and acceptance of the importance of interpersonal skills.

The emphasis on the human side of management was particularly advanced by the group dynamics movement in the 1960s. The study of small group interaction by psychologists and sociologists has been in effect for at least seventy years. It was the pioneering work of the National Training Laboratories and the Center for Group Dynamics Training at the Massachusetts Institute of Technology that did much to advance the acceptance of training in human relations into education and business organizations. Now anyone who wants to be an efficient and productive manager of a bank or an effective member of a high-tech research team must have at least minimal interpersonal skills.

McGregor, in the *The Human Side of Enterprise* (1960), wrote about this shift from one management approach to another; he called the two styles Theory X and Theory Y. Theory X is his name for the conventional concept of management evident in the first half of the twentieth century. This approach assumes that the worker is (1) indolent, (2) dependent, preferring to be led, and lacking in initiative, (3) resistant to and even fearful of change, and (4) less intelligent than the leadership.

Theory Y on the other hand sees management as responsible for organizing the elements of productive enterprise in the interest of economic ends, but adds the following proposition:

> People are not by nature passive or resistant to organizational needs. . . . The motivation, the potential for development, the capacity for assuming responsibility, the readiness to direct behavior toward organizational goals are all present in people. The essential task of management is to arrange organizational conditions and methods of operation so that people can achieve their own goals best by directing their own efforts toward organizational objectives. (Vroom and Deci, 1970, p. 315)

Anyone who wants to develop interpersonal skills must begin by working in a group. The group is a laboratory of interpersonal training, and it is not possible to learn interpersonal skills in solitude, out of a book, or even on a one-to-one basis.

Of course, you cannot develop a person's interpersonal, emotional side without affecting his or her imaginal development. It is the development of the imagination that enables individuals to see a vision of reality that is needed to transform them into effective leaders. As they develop interpersonal skills and can see the world empathetically as others see it, they grow in their ability to engender cooperation, encouraging others to exercise their potential with confidence.

Interpersonal skills nurture the values that cause the significant mind shift from Phase II to Phase III thinking in individuals and leaders at Cycle 4. They are the readiness skills so essential to the development of the imagination of effective leaders.

Imaginal Skills. Imaginal skills are the capacity to learn from direct experience, to choose and to act creatively on complex alternatives, and to see and act on new ideas not previously thought of. They emerge naturally at Cycle 4 when a person has minimal instrumental and interpersonal skills. Interpersonal skills focus on human relations and social or outer harmony. With imaginal skills the focus is on inner harmony.

We know that interpersonal development develops the readiness for imaginal skills. But there is also a consciousness shift to a Phase III world view. Imaginal skills are the ability to manage complex information such as hard data and emotional issues such as conflict. But it is also the ability to transcend the moment and to own and externalize our ideas in an effective and practical manner. Central to this ability is the balance of work and play in our lives, because it is in the play area that the values related to creativity emerge.

In the first three cycles, authority is seen as external to the person. It is with the development of the imaginal skills that the moral side of the leader develops together with a sense of internal authority. James MacGregor Burns (1978) recognized that exceptional leadership has this imaginal ability, and gives us a further clue to what is going on:

> The ultimate test of moral leadership is its capacity to transcend the claims of the multiplicity of everyday wants and needs and expectations, to respond to the higher levels of moral development, and to relate leadership behavior, its roles, choices, style, commitments, to a set of reasoned, relatively explicit, conscious values. (p. 46)

A critical part of imaginal skill development is to become conscious of your values and to choose a set of values that you feel are essential to maximize your personal development. But Burns also points out that the leader *declares* a set of values:

> Given the right conditions of value conflict, leaders hold enhanced influence at higher levels of the need and values hierarchies. They can appeal to the more widely and deeply held values, such as justice, liberty, and brotherhood. They can expose followers to the broader values that contradict narrower ones or inconsistent behavior. Most important, they can gratify lower needs so that higher motivations will arise to elevate the conscience of men and women. (p. 43)

To put it another way, leaders know the connection between values and virtues; they are aware of those universal clusters of values that everyone needs to adhere to in times of conflict. Imaginal skills are related to our imaginations, our system of internal images, our dreams and visions, which are based on our future or vision values. But we also have values that are basic and foundational for us, values from the lower end of the need hierarchy, and Burns is saying that talented leaders provide for their followers' foundational values so that they are free to follow their future values.

In the development of leadership, imaginal skills are bridge skills that make the vision and moral components of leadership possible. But once the mind shift has occurred, the leader needs skills to implement the vision and make it work organizationally—a systems perspective and systems skills.

Systems Skills.   Over a decade ago Bennis (1968, 19, 30) concluded that "the conditions of our modern industrial world will bring about the death of bureaucracy." He goes on to describe the organization of the future as "adaptive, problem-solving, temporary systems of diverse specialists, linked together by coordinating and task-evaluating executive specialists in an organic flux."

The integration of instrumental, interpersonal, and imaginal skills leads to systems awareness—sensitivity to how the whole organization relates to its individual parts. Systems skills involve the capacity to see and manage all the parts of a system or organization. It is also the ability to plan and design change in a system so as to maximally enhance its growth and development. In other words, systems skills require the integration of all the other skills. Peter Senge (1990) puts is this way:

> The systems perspective tells us that we must look beyond individual mistakes or bad luck to understand important problems. We must look beyond personalities and events. We must look into the underlying structures which shape individual actions and create the conditions where types of events become likely. (p. 41)

Something else also happens. *With a systems perspective comes simplicity.* When we begin to see the whole first and the parts second, we have experienced simplicity—something that carries over into all the parts of our lives. An example of this is found in the life of Ghandi, whose lifestyle became simpler the more powerful he became.

Leadership and the System

The high-tech, high-touch revolution appears to be causing a trend away from large, corporate, centrally controlled organizations to smaller, interdependent units. In this more diffuse setting, leadership must place a high priority on human relations. Two-dimensional theories of management have humanized leadership by focusing attention on the people factor as well as the production factor, but they have failed to take into account the environment—the organizational structure—in which people are organized to perform specific tasks. That is, the systems perspective is not integrated into two-dimensional management approaches.

A healthy, moral systems perspective occurs only when leadership has a minimal level of instrumental, interpersonal, and imaginal skills. Without instrumental skills, the leader is incompetent; without interpersonal skills, the leader is insensitive; and without imaginal skills, the leader lacks vision.

The values of the group determine or demand a leadership style that reflects the values of the group. Not only that, but the leader's values must transcend the values that are the common denominators of the group's priorities, or his or her leadership is going to be ineffective. *Beginning at Cycle 4 the group and its values become the central reinforcing factor for the exceptional growth of an individual or leader in the last four cycles of development.*

Cycles of Development, Leadership, and Organizational Structures

Each cycle of development has specific values that demand or impose a particular leadership style and organizational structure. Organizational structures can take many forms. Leadership styles fall into seven general styles, depending on the values in each cycle of development. Figure 9-2 illustrates the relationship between the seven cycles and leadership style, the effect on co-workers, and the form the organization takes.

The First Three Cycles. Every level of leadership is appropriate when the environment does in fact reflect the values of that cycle. The first three organizational styles are all hierarchy-driven as follows:

Cycle 1. The leadership style is dictatorial, with the experience of power as top-down. The institutional model will also be dictatorial, operating

FIGURE 9-2. Seven Cycles of Leadership and Organizational Development

Cycle 1	Cycle 2	Cycle 3	Cycle 4	Cycle 5	Cycle 6	Cycle 7
Safety/ Security	Security/ Family	Family/ Institution	Institution/ Vocation	Vocation/ New Order	New Order/ Wisdom	Wisdom/ World Order
Alien Mystery: I am vulnerable.	Protected: I am safe; I belong at my job at my home.	Civil Order: I work hard to succeed and achieve.	Relational: I am who I am and you are who you are.	Creative Project: I create a new order.	Cooperative Venture: We create a new order.	Global: We care for & co-create.
Style of Leader Dictator	Benevolent	Manager	Enabler as Mentor	Collaborator	Servant	Visionary
Coworker Character Oppressed	Preserver	Loyal Subordinate	Interpersonal & Searching	Creative & Independent	Wise & Inter- dependent	Prophetic
Organizational Character Dictatorial System	Benevolent Hierarchical System	Complex Heirarchical System	Laissez-Faire Enabling System	Collaborative System	Inter- dependent Network System	Global Convivial System

on a strict hierarchy with clear roles and lines of command at each level in the organization. An example would be a traditional military model under combat conditions. The co-worker experiences the situation as necessarily oppressive and constricting. An example would be the experience of a patient in a intensive-care ward.

Cycle 2. The leadership style is benevolent. The leader is autocratic and paternal or maternal. This is a standard style for a start-up family business. The institutional model is that of a top-down hierarchy, where the leadership is kind to the co-workers, but insists that all major decisions be from the top.

Cycle 3. The leadership style is that of the efficient executive or manager within a large corporate institution. The organization is a complex bureaucratic hierarchy. Bureaucracy here is a positive word, implying layered management systems with carefully described roles and qualifications for each position in the company. This will be typical of 90 percent of institutions having more than 200 employees. The co-worker lives in a carefully prescribed system with rules that need to be followed and rewards that can be anticipated for selective performance.

Bridging the Values Gap. In Figure 9-2 Cycle 4 is highlighted because of its special place in the growth cycle: it is the bridge to the new paradigm, with values that reflect an inner authority and vision, rather than an externally driven one as was the case in the first three cycles.

The last four cycles have increasing levels of collaborative management. Cycle 4 is the transitional cycle, and is reminiscent of what is going on in Russia and many other countries where power is brokered at the leadership level or the head of state. Within corporations, Cycles 5 through 7 are indicative of the "learning organization," an organization that sets its values objectively and learns to design a unique management structure that will exercise those values within the organization.

The critical skills at these stages are what Robert Carkhuff (1989) calls human and information capital.

> Most organizations develop their strategies in the area of marketing, distribution, production, and finance. Usually, most decisions are made predominantly on the basis of short-term financial considerations. Unfortunately for most American corporations, in the Age of Information, 85 percent of economic productivity growth is due to the synergistic interaction of human capital and information capital. (foreword)

Carkhuff is suggesting that the corporate world needs to put more of its financial resources into training its executives in interpersonal and systems skills, what he terms "human capital," and in complex information processing, which is the equivalent of imaginal skills. Information capital implies that complex information for shared decision making must be available to everyone collaborating at a peer level.

The leader is not a single person anymore. Rather computers and personnel are used to simplify information and make it available to decision makers in a way that allows it to be processed. This means that decision makers must learn new skills. They then become the new executors of information capital.

The Four Integrations

In order for leadership to maintain the level of functioning required at the later cycles, their growth must be supported and reinforced by the organization. The minimal conditions for this growth are what we call the four integrations: knowledge integration, intimacy integration, management team integration, and peer integration or professional peer support.

Knowledge Integration. This implies internal programs in leadership that keep personnel updated in knowledge and skill in the four skill areas just addressed. Personnel must develop minimal values and the skills required at each of the cycles, and must be competent in their fields of endeavor. In addition, they must begin to have an adequate balance between work and play.

Owning things and owning a role are both components of the doing side of life. We live in an age where the stress of working, of doing, causes people to be obsessed with their roles. Maintaining the role of executive, chief of police, or rock star can be more stressful than maintaining property. Doing has an essential maintenance dimension, which is a negative drain of energy. Doing something physical like repairing your house or your car is physically draining, but this does not compare to the loss of energy that is involved in maintaining other people.

When you maintain a role, what you are really doing is living up to others' expectations; this can prevent you from "being" yourself. When you listen to other people's problems—dealing with an irritable employee or someone you are counseling, or even visiting a sick friend—you are being drained of emotional energy. This is a necessary consequence of "doing" responsibly.

Play, on the other hand, enables us to exercise the "being" component of our lives. Play comes in two forms: recreation and leisure. Play is an activity without obligation or duty; there is no particular productive outcome planned. Creativity is often very productive, but what is created is often a surprise.

Work is the opposite of play, and is characterized by duty, obligation, and specific productive outcomes.

Detachment occurs as one balances the play or being areas with the stress of work or doing. When the play balances the work, you become detached, and being and becoming are set in motion. This causes an alteration in your consciousness that is critical to the growth that begins at Cycle 4.

When a person's values priorities do not reflect a sound work/play balance, life is predictably stressful. The balance is different for each of us, but there are limits for everyone. Our research found that when the percentage of values that people chose and prioritized in the work and maintenance area exceeded their play values by more than 20 percent, they usually complained of stress.

Values Technology created an instrument called "Time Out" that measures the hours of time spent in work and play areas over a ten-day period. We found that when people have less than an average of 2.5 hours of play a day over ten days, they were not only stressed, but their leisure area became inactive. This in turn affected their ability to be creative at work or at home.

We also discovered that the experience of leisure does not occur until adulthood. Once adulthood is reached, we find that when a people have less than 3.5 hours of play and leisure a day, their ability for intimacy, creativity, and meaning is significantly diminished. In other words, the detachment that results from balancing time for work and play in a harmonious manner enhances the structure of one's being and becoming.

Intimacy Integration. For leaders to have intimacy integrated into their lives, organizational policies must ensure that they have the correct balance between work and play so that their private lives are nurtured and they are able to creatively interact in the organization. Leaders need a sound support system at home. It is our contention that at Cycles 4 through 7 people's personal intimacy needs must be met if they are to grow. Intimacy is not necessarily a physical relationship; more importantly, it is a deep mutual sharing on a regular basis with a person you can trust with all your fears, stresses, and joys. This is a necessary integration, and it must take place outside the work environment.

When the work-play balance in the first integration is not achieved, intimacy becomes very difficult and can shift inappropriately to the work setting. This is inevitably destructive, since it confuses power and authority issues. Intimacy integration comes out of play activity, and it is a part of achieving the detachment we spoke of earlier. It prevents stress in the work environment, and prevents life decisions from becoming too overwhelming.

Management Team Integration. To achieve management team integration, organizational policies must ensure that it is possible to fully delegate a leader's work. This is an essential part of the strategic planning process. Leaders at Cycles 4 through 7 must be able to delegate anything they do. The work function of an individual and the team must always be designed so that in a crisis what any person does can be completely delegated. This is a detachment device to prevent the interruption of a person's life by the stress that emerges in these later cycles.

Peer Integration or Professional Peer Support. Organizational policies must be designed to ensure peer group consultation. A peer acts as friend and consultant for your total experience—a third-party observer of both your work and your family. At the higher echelons, leaders experience more pressure. This creates higher maintenance needs. The professional peer network provides the company executive with personal support and with the awareness that leadership is in fact a plural and cooperative venture.

David Richards pioneered the use of peer consultation with executives for a number of years. He writes:

> Planned role-reversing—consulting dyads of peers—offers a type of supportive interaction. It is worth consideration because of the easy access it provides to the securing of professional help with one's task and the very low—even nonexistent—monetary cost that is involved. . . . Life is so constituted that we need reservoirs of every kind of excellence; of intelligence, of knowledge, of practical ability, of morality. No man is sufficient for himself. At every turn, he must borrow and he must lend.

> Peer dyadic consultation is a process of borrowing and lending. From this process of interchange of ideas, abilities, knowledge, conceptualizing skills and workable schemes comes a mutual enrichment which enables both parties to face their respective tasks with increased enthusiasm, optimism and confidence. (Caplan & Killilea, 1972, p. 270)

It has been our experience that when an executive experiences a breakdown in more than one of these four integrations, he or she will regress to an earlier form of leadership style.

Institutions in Cycles 5 through 7 are born out of Phase III and IV values, where collaboration means intergroup collaboration of designated leadership. This does not mean that every team and group in such a company is at these higher levels, since an individual group must function at the level of the values of the group.

Collaborative management structures imply that each group will function at its own values level, with its required leadership style and structure. But within each group will be people who are designated as leaders and who are able to function at a value level that reflects the corporate structure; they will collaborate with other groups in the system to make systemwide decisions.

Leadership Styles in the Last Four Cycles

Each of the last four cycles has a distinctive leadership style. Like leaders, organizations also go through similar development cycles. Let's take a look at the characteristics of leaders and organizations in the last four cycles.

Cycle 4.   The leadership style is that of an enabling mentor, and such a leader is often in danger of becoming laissez-faire. It is a stage of leadership at which the leader needs to learn interpersonal skills through group dynamics, and to develop systems awareness and skills. The organizational structure is transitional and must contain support structures for the leadership, built in by the system, that include learning to value the people in the organization—the human capital.

Cycle 5.   The leadership style is collaborator, and the leader is in a process of discovering his or her special qualities and gifts. It is the full emergence of the imaginal and systems skills. The organization is a learning, collaborative system like the ones discussed above. The critical task is to ensure that all leadership personnel are trained in human and information capital skills. In the corporate setting, management information systems are very important to this stage of development.

Cycle 6.   The leadership style is a servant style whereby wise leaders quietly enable others to lead collaboratively, through delegation and assessment of resources, as they enhance the declared values of the system. The institution is based on an interdependent network of teams, divisions, or groups that are designed and held together by a common consensus value system.

The value system at this level is concerned about the corporation's positive impact on its personnel, local communities, and the environment.

Cycle 7. The leadership style is prophetic, with wise and internationally prophetic leaders enabling others to lead globally and collaboratively, enhancing the declared values of the system. The institution is based on global interdependent teams or institutions that are designed and held together by a common consensus value system. The value system at this level is concerned about its positive global impact on people, societies, and the environment.

The Effects of Leadership Style. Recent management literature often divides leadership styles into two camps: autocratic/authoritarian and participative/collaborative. The first person to address this distinction was McGregor with his description of Theories X and Y. McGregor recognized that each leadership style has its own consequence, and affects the experience of everyone in the organization. This is due primarily to the fact that a leadership style is based on selected values and a world view that dictates a particular view of the worker or a group's membership.

The concept that co-workers are "followers" is a judgment that occurs in the first three cycles. This concept permeates the perception by the leadership of the membership of an institution and the view of leadership by the institution's members. Each perceives and behaves toward the other through their understanding of reality—their world view. The leadership and membership are bound together symbiotically as a whole; they are dependent on each other, not separate.

In our schema the first three cycles are various forms of autocratic leadership and are all characterized by a leader-follower format, with management governing through carefully designed hierarchical structures in order to achieve efficient institutional functioning. Cycles 5, 6, and 7, on the other hand, can be considered to be participative or collaborative styles. Cycle 4 is a transitional cycle that is moving toward the collaborative model.

It is important not to oversimplify our understanding of leadership, because we may fail to recognize its developmental nature. To begin with, autocratic and collaborative modes are general descriptions of several styles of leadership—it is not just a matter of one or the other. Secondly, the reason that some organizations are run autocratically and others collaboratively is because the values in the environment and the situation demand it, not because someone just decides to do things that way.

Each style of leadership suits a particular set of circumstances that make that style the necessary style for that given set of circumstances. *Any style of leadership is the consequence of the values of the individual leader in relationship to the corporate setting and its membership.* These values can be described as belonging to a particular cycle of development; it is not the other way around. Therefore, if an organization wants to be participative in style, it must have leaders with a compatible values orientation. It is not just a matter of designing a different management style.

A Leadership Case Example

Jordan was the chief executive officer and founder of a small international marketing business. He asked to speak to me on the recommendation of the chairman of his board. The chairman pointed out that Jordan was a good, well-meaning man who had developed the company from nothing, and who had a vision of international collaboration that had inspired all the executives at one time or another. Looking deeply worried, he went on to say, "The president is a person who talks about trust and collaboration to our executives and international partners, but he runs the business in a authoritarian, top-down way!"

I met with Jordan a week later. After talking and listening to him for several hours, he agreed to fill out a values inventory. When we analyzed his responses, we found that his values showed that he was trusting and collaborative. But his day-to-day reality was that he was authoritarian. How could this be, I asked myself. His leadership style was more reflective of his foundation values, which were Security and Control/Order/ Discipline, rather than of his focus or vision values.

He noted that he wanted to be collaborative most of the time, but that the pressure of the job made him react like a survivor, as if the world were attacking him. His vision related to building an international organization that was sensitive to cross-cultural and human needs. But his vision was not believable to his co-workers because of the dictatorial way he treated employees.

At the point he spoke to me he was very aware of this discrepancy. He felt very guilty and had no explanation for his behavior. He said, "I want to be collaborative and delegate responsibility, then something stressful will happen here in the office or even at home, and I get very uptight, and everybody complains that I am super-controlling. The crazy thing is that most of the time I'm not even aware of it!"

I asked him to tell me what images he had that related to the values of Security and Control/Order/Discipline. At first he drew a blank. Then I asked him if he could remember any dreams that might indicate such a values orientation. He said that he did but that they had occurred when he was growing up as a child. He grew up in London and was only five years old when World War II broke out, and he told me that for five years during the war he had the same dream every night.

In the dream he was running across a white mud plain pursued by huge prehistoric birds called pterodactyls. He remembered with enthusiasm that he had seen a model of one in a museum. It was a long-beaked creature with a wing span of up to 40 feet. In the dream he eventually sank in the mud and was continually attacked by the monsters. Finally he broke out of the mud and ran across the white plain, tripped over a log, and fell over a cliff. He said, "Each night I fell over the cliff, but I never died, and I never hit bottom, I just woke up screaming." He noted that he had been to several psychoanalysts to try to figure out what the dream meant, but he got a lot of interpretations that made no sense to him.

A month later I was with Jordan at an executive leadership conference in a town in central Germany that had been heavily bombed by the Allies in World War II. One morning I was to meet Jordan for breakfast at 8:00 o'clock in the hotel restaurant. When I walked in, Jordan was standing by a table staring at several pictures on the wall with an agitated excitement. I asked him what was going on. "Look at the pictures," he exclaimed.

On the wall were pictures of German World War II bombers—the type that flew over London. He pointed to one in particular, a Stuker dive bomber—the single-engine, one-pilot plane that plagued London in the first year of the war because of the deadly accuracy with which it dropped incendiary bombs. Its wings were a V shape, reminding one of a huge bird. "For heaven's sake," shouted Jordan, "that's my pterodactyl!" He said that when he saw the picture, he had vivid flashes of the pterodactyls in his dreams.

It is true that most of the images we have in our dreams are metaphors of reality. Like many children, the child Jordan had been interested in dinosaurs, and had probably seen a drawing of a pterodactyl in a book or magazine. He had also seen at first-hand the Stuker dive bombers. They lasted for only a year before they were driven from the skies by the British Spitfire fighter planes. It became evident that the terrifying experience for Jordan was not as much seeing the airplanes in the skies over London as seeing his mother frightened at the sight of the enemy planes. This terrified him. The feelings were expressed each night through his dreams of being harassed and attacked by this prehistoric monster.

He went on to tell the story in the leadership seminar, explaining that any time an employee or client panicked or expressed anxiety about something, he got the same fear and tightness in the chest that he had as a child. Others in the group reported to him that when he was under pressure he always saw the dark side of things, whereas when there was no pressure he was very optimistic. Jordan was able to laugh at himself, but more importantly, he was able to change his behavior and attitude during times of stress and maintain his regular optimism.

A closer look revealed that the dream was filled with his foundation values of Control/Order/Discipline and Security. When he was more optimistic, he exercised his values of Empathy and Collaboration. His behavior as founder and chief executive officer of the company profoundly affected all those he was working with and their performance. This is the Genesis Effect: images that we have of reality are projected into our behavior through our leadership style, which in turn affects the organization and its performance.

Jordan's Vision. This example illustrates that when our foundation values dominate we see the world through the images that they generate. For Jordan it was unconscious images from his childhood that were caused by the London blitz—German warplanes transformed into prehistoric birds. When the foundation dominates, so will its images of reality.

After Jordan had described his dream and his insight to the other executives in the leadership seminar, someone noticed that the end of the dream had not been explained. In that part of the dream he was running away from pterodactyls, and he came to the precipice at the end of the plain. Backing toward it he fell over a tree branch and over the precipice.

Examining the dream more closely, Jordan remembered that he used to wake up screaming. He reflected that after he had had the same dream several times and never did die, "I really felt I was invincible." Tears came into his eyes. "I wanted to create a better world for people to live in." This better world was a world of empathy for human beings, where people collaborated rather that controlled by fear. This was the world described by his future and vision values. When he said this, the group clapped!

One of the factors that caused this consciousness shift in Jordan was that he was able to see his foundation and vision values simultaneously, and this allowed him to meditate on the different images and views of the world they projected. This caused a mind shift that enabled him to put his foundation in perspective and concentrate on his vision as a leader.

Conclusions

In the example of Jordan we see that what he was wanting to accomplish was a Cycle 5 to 6 organization, based on interpersonal collaboration. But any organization in its initial stages of development is going to be stressed; in his case, these stressors touched off his foundation values rather than his vision values, causing him to run the organization in the style of Cycles 2 to 3.

Jordan's world view was dominated in times of crisis by past images and their values. Whenever there was a crisis he acted like the five-year-old in London in World War II. Some mentoring helped him separate his past from the present reality, and he was able to operationalize his vision by acting out a leadership style at Cycle 5. He worked collaboratively with his executive team as they began to put a Cycle 5 collaborative system into place.

Although it is true that we each have foundation, focus, and future or visionary life and leadership styles, it is our internal image of reality that determines which of these will dominate in times of stress. It is important to build the skills that enable us to resist falling into the foundation area as our predominant style. We do this by building all the skills we need and making sure the organization has the four integrations built in at Cycle 4. This is precisely what Jordan's organization did.

The shift in Jordan's consciousness was a shift from a narrow world view of the leader as one person at the top of a pyramid governing a hierarchical organization, to a systems or holistic perspective, where leadership is plural and collaborative, functioning interdependently rather than independently. As this occurs in more and more organizations, the effect on western civilization is likely to be radical; it could transform our society into something quite different than is presently experienced. Why? The consequence for healthy organizations and leaders would be to create:

■ Leaders and organizations whose management design follows from their values rather than from other external purposes. They would become learning organizations, discovering new and creative ways to fulfill their missions.

■ Leaders and organizations whose management design would bring about efficient development of the corporation's product goals, while maximizing the possibility of the quality of life for its members through creative management design.

■ Leaders and organizations that in the future would move toward a concern about the overall societal and natural global environment, and that would approach issues of human justice in a nonjudgmental manner when dealing with cultures and groups that have significantly different ideological orientations.

■ Leaders and organizations that would begin to view the world through the eyes of simplicity. No matter what the viewpoint of such people, this could constitute a major global spiritual revolution.

Another factor in the development of an organization is the recognition that the organization is a live organism with a life of its own. What enabled Jordan to grow was not only his values and skills, but the support of his staff—the organization itself.

This chapter has been a foundation for understanding the last four cycles of development. In the next chapter we will examine Cycles 4 through 7 in more detail.

10

The Later Cycles
of Development

Each life state offers new growth resources and possibilities as well as new problems and losses. Wholeness is a lifelong journey of becoming. The gift of growth is received when we choose to develop our options intentionally. The process of growth, although deeply fulfilling, often involves pain and struggle.

Howard Clinebell, *Contemporary Growth Therapies*

The last chapter looked at the shift from Cycle 3 to Cycle 5, which we called the Mind Shift. In the first three cycles, our lives are characterized by a world view in which we see what happens as externally controlled by others. On the other side of the Values Gap, the last four cycles are characterized by an internal, self-initiating view of the world. Cycle 4 is the bridge between these two entirely different views of the world. In the later cycles even something as personal as one's religious beliefs shifts from an external orientation in which beliefs are accessed through the family and church toward an internal reality that is accessed by contemplation.

We also saw that leadership and organizational styles follow the cycles, and that institutional reinforcement is important for our growth and development through the cycles.

This chapter will look at the later four cycles—at their values, world view, ethical choices, discernment questions, and skill and leadership requirements.

171

Cycle 4: Institutional/Vocational

The Cycle 4 world view stands between the institutional values of Phase II-B and the personal values of Phase III-A, with the individual feeling uncertain in the area of decision making. For the first time, values appear to be relative, so you must search to find your own place and meaning in the scheme of things. In whatever institutional framework you find yourself, your task is to try to assess your successes in relationship to the new revelations and doubts you have about yourself, your gifts, and your vocation.

On the one hand, you see a world driven by rules and the expectations of those in authority who guarantee law and order in society. On the other hand, the world begins to offer an opportunity to make choices and to experience personal freedom that is human, dignifying, self-directed, and determined by your own special gifts and contributions.

For example, in August of 1991 Mikhail Gorbachev was toppled by the hard-line communists in Russia, who were attempting to curb the reforms that were initiated in 1988 and 1989. In the unstable times that followed, Russia was caught in the Values Gap between the old centrally controlled, rules-oriented society and the evolving pressure for personal freedom. The discomfort and unrest that results from this shift can also be seen in the progress of the civil rights movement in the United States and in women's liberation movements all over the globe. Each of these movements is an expression of a change in consciousness from a Phase II to a Phase III—the shift that is the Cycle 4 experience.

Figure 10-1 lists the goals and means values for Cycle 4.

Ethical Choices.   In Cycle 4, ethical issues no longer seem black and white and you try to reason your way to appropriate decisions. It is often not easy to make commitments without reservations. Growth is dependent upon learning to establish a balance between a need for independence and a predilection for reasoning on the one hand, and giving appropriate expression to interpersonal, emotional, and intuitive needs on the other hand. You most often find yourself in a state of ethical relativism where you support others' points of view but are unsure about your own.

Relativism holds that many points of view and decisions are possible on a given ethical issue, and that all are equal in importance. The trouble with this view is that there is no way to choose a personal course of action and feel that it is the right one. What is needed in this cycle is attention and commitment to a particular life-sustaining value system, such as the study of justice issues. In this cycle we move in the direction of significant personal growth during which we must integrate the institutional demands with which we are faced.

Discernment Questions. The discernment questions for Cycle 4 (Figure 10-2) are from the values of Stage III-A. The questions for Stage II-B were presented in Chapter 8 for Cycle 3.

FIGURE 10-1. Cycle 4 Goals and Means Values

STAGE II-B	STAGE III-A
Goals Values	**Goals Values**
Belief/Philosophy	Equality/Liberation
Competence/Confidence	Integration/Wholeness
Play/Recreation	Self-Actualization
Work/Labor	Service/Vocation
Means Values	**Means Values**
Achievement/Success	Adaptability/Flexibility
Administration/Control	Authority/Honesty
Communication/Information	Congruence
Competition	Decision/Initiation
Design/Pattern/Order	Empathy
Duty/Obligation	Equity/Rights
Economics/Success	Expressiveness/Joy
Education/Certification	Generosity/Compassion
Efficiency/Planning	Health/Healing
Hierarchy/Order	Independence
Honor	Law/Guide
Law/Rule	Limitation/Acceptance
Loyalty/Fidelity	Mutual Obedience
Management	Quality/Evaluation
Membership/Institution	Relaxation
Ownership	Search for Meaning/Hope
Patriotism/Esteem	Self-Assertion
Productivity	Sharing/Listening/Trust
Reason	

FIGURE 10-2. Cycle 4 Sample Discernment Questions

Equality/Liberation
- Is the question of personal equality important to you in the way you act?

Independence
- Are you sufficiently your own person?
- Is being assertive or initiating your own course of action difficult for you?

Search for Meaning/Hope
- Do you have a set of principles by which you live and that make life an adventure for you, or do you have pressing unanswered questions?

FIGURE 10-3. Examples of Cycle 4 Skills/Values Clusters

INTERPERSONAL SKILLS

Empathy

Skills: The ability to look at the world through another's eyes, recognizing the
differences between you, and to allow the other person to reflect in more
depth on who they are, and to feel accepted by you, not judged.

Congruence

Skills: The ability to communicate your feelings objectively to work associates in
a manner that is congruent with your actions and intentions. This skill is
essential to your emotional and spiritual development.

IMAGINAL SKILLS

Adaptability/Flexibility

Skills: To be willing to adjust your perceptions and reactions to be appropriate
for each situation and relationship, so that you are able to develop your
physical, emotional, and imaginal potential.

Expressiveness/Joy

Skills: The ability to express yourself openly in order to engender cooperation
and stimulate the thoughts and imaginations of other people.

Cycle 4 Skills. At Cycle 4 we are working on the high end of interpersonal skills and are beginning to develop imaginal skills. We learn to
separate our personal issues from group issues. It is at this point in life
that we learn to manage our emotions and to separate them from reason,
so that both functions are heightened. Examples of Cycle 4 skills and values clusters are given in Figure 10-3.

At the level of search and personal development, Cycle 4 people have
a new awareness of other people, but they may have insufficient systems
skills, which can be a source of stress. The dark side of this cycle is that it
is possible to use group and interpersonal skills to manipulate other
people. This can occur when we do not integrate all the skills into our
lives. For example, you might develop your imagination and have a vision of what you want, but if your interpersonal skills are not well developed, you could resort to using people for your own vision without
reference to their needs or visions.

At the leadership level, this becomes translated into a need to learn
group dynamics and human relations skills. Leaders need to be competent in facilitating small groups and processing feelings. Some leaders
may have difficulty with accountability in this cycle if they confuse
equality of people (Human Dignity) with equality of skills. Such a leader
is a good community builder but may have difficulty in delegating
responsibility. To avoid stress and distortion in this cycle, leaders need

strong support systems. The issues of support and the four integrations covered in the last chapter are very important.

Cycle 4 Leadership Style: Enablement.   The leadership style at Cycle 4 is that of enabler. Because of the conflict experienced by Cycle 4 leaders, this style should be regarded as temporary. At this cycle, leaders are caught between adherence to what the institution demands and a new view of human dignity and sense of self. The leader-follower distinction is not clear, because the leader now sees the human dignity dimension as equal to the work itself. The style is basically that of enabling human interaction in an institution, with heavy reliance on the traditional skills of management. A laissez-faire form of leadership can develop, with the leader unable to make critical decisions. This is particularly likely to happen to people who have had poor experiences of Cycle 3 institutions.

It is critical to growth at this level to learn planning skills. Cycle 4 leaders begin to plan much farther into the future—for the next five to ten years. This is an important change from the previous three cycles, in which a person's planning cycle is no more than a year into the future.

Cycle 4 Institutional Style.   The institution often ceases to exist for the Cycle 4 person. He or she may simply be running on old scripts, doing what is necessary in a management setting. At this level, the leader needs to function and gain expertise in small groups or teams.

Cycle 5: Vocation/New Order

At Cycle 5 the world is viewed as a project in which we need to participate and to which we have something unique to offer. Cycle 5 people find that they have suddenly become acutely aware of their gifts and of the ways in which they may be used productively. They see that they must discover new ways to integrate their gifts with the demands of society. They have also become intensely aware of the importance of making institutions more humane, and are motivated to alter society through the improvement of institutional life. Figure 10-4 lists Cycle 5 goals and means values.

Ethical Choices.   Ethical choices at Cycle 5 are based on a personally meaningful center of values to which you are clearly committed and which you can articulate. Actions are therefore guided by personal conscience. Rules and lawful guidelines are important, but you modify them if necessary, based on personal conscience. Growth at this stage is strongly dependent upon establishing a balance between time devoted to work and to leisure. You need to get personal affirmation from peer groups in order to counterbalance the ever-present possibility of disillusionment as your choices and vision of reality expand.

FIGURE 10-4. Cycle 5 Goals and Means Values

STAGE III-A	STAGE III-B
Goals Values	**Goals Values**
Equality/Liberation	Art/Beauty
Integration/Wholeness	Being Self
Self-Actualization	Construction/New Order
Service/Vocation	Contemplation
	Faith/Risk/Vision
	Human Dignity
	Justice/Social Order
	Knowledge/Insight
	Presence/Dwelling
	Ritual/Communication
Means Values	**Means Values**
Adaptability/Flexibility	Accountability/Ethics
Authority/Honesty	Collaboration
Congruence	Community/Supportive
Decision/Initiation	Complementarity
Empathy	Corporation/New Order
Equity/Rights	Creativity
Expressiveness/Joy	Detachment/Solitude
Generosity/Service	Discernment
Health/Healing	Education/Knowledge
Independence	Growth/Expansion
Law/Guide	Intimacy
Limitation/Acceptance	Leisure
Mutual Obedience	Limitation/Celebration
Quality/Evaluation	Mission/Objectives
Relaxation	Mutual Accountability
Search for Meaning/Hope	Pioneerism/Innovation
Self-Assertion	Research
Sharing/Listening/Trust	Simplicity/Play
	Unity/Diversity

Discernment Questions. Figure 10-5 provides examples of discernment questions for Stage III-B of this cycle.

Cycle 5 Skills. The positive skills at this level are those that allow you to move from an interpersonal approach to collaborative problem solving and group interaction. You see the parts in perspective as they relate to the whole. The examples of skills from Phase III-B means values shown in Figure 10-6 illustrate this.

FIGURE 10-5. Cycle 5 Sample Discernment Questions (Stage III-B)

Human Dignity
- In your work, do you place a high priority on the dignity of others, including in the way you treat the opposite sex and in your understanding of people who are of different cultural origins or financial or class status?

Art/Beauty as Pure Value
- How actively do you appreciate art and beauty?

Mutual Accountability
- Is mutual accountability important among your employees and peers?

Community/Supportive
- Do you have a community of peers who are supportive?

Complementarity
- Are you able to fully delegate anything you do at this time?

Intimacy
- Do you have all the skills of interpersonal intimacy that you need, or is this a difficult area for you?

FIGURE 10-6. Examples of Cycle 5 Skills/Values Clusters (Stage III-B)

Community/Supportive
Skills: Skills in group dynamics, with the ability to distinguish personal issues from group issues and to manage group conflict, for the purpose of developing the group to a level at which it becomes supportive of each of its members and promotes the efficient functioning of the organization.

Collaboration
Skills: The ability to cooperate interdependently with all levels of management and to ensure that all responsibility can be fully and appropriately delegated so that the organization can move forward to fulfill its goals and vision.

Limitation/Celebration
Skills: Recognizing that your limitations are the other side of what constitutes life-giving values for you. The ability to celebrate this and laugh at your mistakes and errors and grow from the experience, and to help others to do the same.

Leisure
Skills: Managing your time in a way that allows you to concentrate on leisure activities such as studying, sports, or gardening that require the same concentration of skills as your profession, and that leave you totally detached from daily stress.

Cycle 5 Leadership Style: Collaborative. The leadership style at Cycle 5 is democratic but is often overtly independent. At this point in life the leader's value focus is clearer and his or her imaginal and systems skills are releasing new energy. A person at this cycle often has difficulty in the area of time management, resulting in stress. The being/doing, work/play balance discussed in the last chapter is essential. As at other cycles, support systems are critical for personal growth. To function well, this leadership style must be built on the internalized skills in efficient management that were acquired at Cycle 3.

Leaders at this level have the ability to enable others to strategically plan 10 to 20 years into the future.

Cycle 5 leaders are enthusiastic and visionary and possess the skills of empathy and confrontation. They take peer authority seriously, and want to bring others' comments to bear on decisions, but may be so independent that they often fail to do so. The style is genuinely facilitative and democratic, when the leader is available! The Cycle 5 leader may be the school superintendent who is so creatively busy that she always arrives halfway through a planning meeting, or the local executive director who is so needed by the executive council in New York or London that he is frequently not at home directing his own organization. In other words, team support, collaboration, and time management are critical skills if this person is to succeed.

The Cycle 5 Institutional Style. The values at this cycle support and demand the creation of institutions that are built from a values orientation, and that give equal weight to efficiency and human dignity in the organization. It is an organization that takes human and information capital seriously (see Chapter 9).

Cycle 6: New Order/Wisdom

At Cycle 6, you now see all of humanity and the physical, material world as a sacred gift in which you must be responsibly involved. It is critically important at this cycle to find a suitable balance between time devoted to work and time set aside for intimacy and quality solitude. Figure 10-7 lists the Cycle 6 goals and means values.

Ethical Choices. Ethical choices are now informed by awareness of the rights of all human beings. You find yourself compelled to be more actively critical of unjust organizations in society—especially the injustices found in those organizations in which you are personally participating. Growth at this stage requires careful attention to finding a balance between involvement in organizational development based on

FIGURE 10-7. Cycle 6 Goals and Means Values

STAGE III-B	STAGE IV-A
Goals Values	**Goals Values**
Art/Beauty	Intimacy/Solitude
Being Self	Truth/Wisdom
Construction/New Order	
Contemplation	
Human Dignity	
Justice/Social Order	
Knowledge/Insight	
Presence/Dwelling	
Ritual/Communication	
Faith/Risk/Vision	
Means Values	**Means Values**
Accountability/Ethics	Community/Personalist
Collaboration	Interdependence
Community/Supportive	Prophet/Vision
Complementarity	Synergy
Corporation/New Order	Transcendence/Solitude
Creativity	
Detachment/Solitude	
Discernment	
Education/Knowledge	
Growth/Expansion	
Intimacy	
Leisure	
Limitation/Celebration	
Mission/Objectives	
Mutual Accountability	
Pioneerism/Innovation	
Research	
Simplicity/Play	
Unity/Diversity	

humane values, and time devoted to intimacy and solitude, which are truly energizing.

Growth is also dependent upon having several different life projects so that you don't become overly absorbed in any one particular project, and also to facilitate the development of a global world view. Such people need to able to envision future mission goals 25 to 50 years into the future. In fact, it is a test of their ability to function at this level.

The Cycle 6 person finds that he or she has a new perspective on the created order.

FIGURE 10-8. Cycle 6 Sample Discernment Questions

Wisdom/Truth
- Are you gaining more insight through a balance of quality solitude and knowledge?

Prophet/Vision
- Do others see you as prophetic and global in what you have to say? Do you have the human support systems you need?

Community/Personalist
- Does your living situation enhance your creativity and sense of interdependence with the others in the group?
- Are you convinced that the wisdom of two minds can always yield more than is possible by one, and do you act sufficiently on this?

Discernment Questions. The discernment questions for Stage IV-A of this cycle are given in Figure 10-8.

Cycle 6 Skills. For the positive expression of skills, you must have a healthy work/leisure balance already in operation, as well as peer support groups in the intimate, professional, and work areas. The stance of the leader is that of wise enabler who governs with a team on the basis of values-related goals, objectives, and norms. Skills in developing such norms at a total system level are therefore required, plus constant attention to both physical and emotional health.

In this cycle people are living with one foot in Phase IV, and integration is not guaranteed. Power can be an easy persuader for some, with the result that instead of enabling harmony in society, the individual has a tendency to make the society be like him or her. Hitler was an example of this.

A century ago Cycle 6 was a level of development accessible to only a few exceptional individuals. At one time such people—Gandhi or Churchill— were known only through a study of history. But now, because of global communication and enormous advances in education, there are many such individuals in the world. The values clusters in this cycle are once again moving to the personal level (Figure 10-9). The person tends to be primarily institutional in orientation but moving to the highest point of human and spiritual development—that of a fully integrated individual.

Cycle 6 Leadership Style: Servant Leadership. Servant leadership involves interdependent governance by a peer team, which manages a system on the basis of pre-chosen value clusters. This cycle relies on a

FIGURE 10-9. Cycle 6 Skills/Values Clusters

Education/Knowledge

Skills: Practice of ongoing learning that promotes knowledge and the pursuit of truth. It is also a dedication to helping others to be learners or to be involved in teaching.

Interdependence

Skills: Enabling and managing a group of peers committed to global promotion of knowledge, justice, and truth, and acting on the awareness that personal and inter-institutional cooperation are always preferable to individual decision making.

Detachment/Solitude

Skills: The ability to separate oneself from the stresses of daily life as a way of understanding and pursuing knowledge and truth.

---

minimal global perspective and an ability to see how the parts of one's institution are supported and affirmed through the values each individual person in the institution.

Servant leadership is different than all the earlier forms in that it not only moves beyond any form of autocracy, but it also transforms the value of independence into interdependence. It recognizes that when peers interact professionally at high levels of trust and appropriate intimacy, there is a synergistic creativity that cannot be obtained by any one individual. In other words, leadership at and beyond this cycle is always plural in form.

The most negative possibility at this cycle is the misuse of power, and governance by values that are detrimental to individuals and to society as a whole.

Leaders at this stage must acquire clarity about their values so that they can transcend institutional pressures.

The Cycle 6 Institutional Style. The Cycle 6 executive uses the concept of limited design criteria in planning for the organization, creating a management design that maximizes the development of all individuals in the system, guards the efficiency of the organization, and attends to the good of society as a whole. The servant leader is interested not only in what is produced by the organization, but also in the quality of interaction within the organization and the impact of the organization on the quality of life in society.

The key is that leadership is always a team operation that enables the institution to grow through a sytems perspective to become a "learning organization." Such a system is always heuristic—that is, it is a system of learners where leadership learns how to continually recreate the organization. Some components of the learning organization are:

- Layered mentoring of leaders, where leaders at higher cycles mentor people at earlier cycles.
- Leadership that has a common vision based on a core set of values arrived at by consensus.
- An organizational system that is laced with quality cross-disciplinary teams that are connected through a collaborative communications network.

The Phase IV vision of the world underlies the activities of the servant leader as he or she seeks to give life to a global world.

Cycle 7: Wisdom/World Order

The person now views the world as a mystery for which we must all care. Cycle 7 people are acutely aware that their vocation is global, requiring nothing less than the collaboration of all concerned institutions. They find themselves continually challenged to match a prophetic vision with practical applications, and to put a global vision into action at the local level. Figure 10-10 lists the Cycle 7 goals and means values.

Ethical Choices. Ethical choices involve activities that are designed to create an improved balance between the material and the human world. Global distribution of goods to meet human needs is a high priority. Critical to human growth in this cycle is an awareness of the whole field of consciousness.

The peculiar nature of this cycle is that it circles all the way around to the first cycle. The person who is fully integrated transcends this cycle and reaches people at all the other levels. Cycle 7 organizations are led by people who are conscious of using layered mentoring, with leaders at

FIGURE 10-10. Cycle 7 Goals and Means Values

STAGE IV-A	STAGE IV-B
Goals Values	**Goals Values**
Intimacy/Solitude	Ecority
Truth/Wisdom	Global Harmony
	Word
Means Values	**Means Values**
Community/Personalist	Convivial Technology
Interdependence	Human Rights
Prophet/Vision	Justice/Social Order
Synergy	Macroeconomics
Transcendence/Solitude	Minessence

higher cycles mentoring leaders at earlier cycles. On the other hand, since this cycle also engages Phase I, there is the danger of radical misuse of power. This is the most difficult cycle to be in.

Discernment Questions. Figure 10-11 gives examples of Cycle 7 discernment questions.

Cycle 7 Skills. The skills at Cycle 7 are high-end systems skills that have a global effect. At a healthy and integrated level, this world view connects the needs that any of us have had in our lives at the early cycles and translates them into global concerns through technology and human compassion. Figure 10-12 gives examples of Cycle 7 skills/values clusters.

FIGURE 10-11. Cycle 7 Sample Discernment Questions

Ecority
- Do you spend much of your life working on ecological issues?
- Do you have sufficient knowledge of technology and its ethical and ecological consequences globally?

Convivial Technology
- Is the technology you are developing simple enough for the uneducated to be able to use it in third-world countries?
- Have you considered the long-term effects of your work on other societies?

Human Rights
- Are you part of an international peer group that enables you to address human rights issues objectively with minimal stress?

FIGURE 10-12. Examples of Cycle 7 Skills/Values Clusters

Convivial Technology
Skills: The ability to creatively apply technology and to mobilize its use organizationally and internationally to improve social and ecological conditions in the world.

Macroeconomics
Skills: The ability to manage, plan, organize, and direct the use of financial resources at an institutional and interinstitutional level in order to create a more ecologically stable and equitable world economic order.

Minessence
Skills: The ability to miniaturize and simplify complex ideas into concrete and practical objectifications such as practical theory, art, or technology in a way that creatively alters the consciousness of the user, and impacts the natural environment and the quality of human life positively at a global level.

Healthy Cycle 7 leaders have the role of wise and prophetic enablers who govern with a team on the basis of value-related goals, objectives, and norms. They need skills in developing such norms in international institutions, and in coping with multicultural and language issues. They must be clear about complex value systems and their ethical consequences to the planet.

These leaders must be in touch with and well educated in the sociological, political, religious, and philosophical norms that stand behind global ethical issues. More than at any other cycle, they must have clarity about their own value centers, and they need a support group that insists that they have intimacy and solitude in their lives for a creative balance.

Cycle 7 Leadership Style: Prophetic.   The leadership expression at this cycle is visionary or prophet. Cycle 7 leaders use interdependent governance by a peer team of people who manage a system on the basis of prechosen value clusters. This cycle relies on a global perspective and an ability to see how one institution relates to other institutions in global society. Leaders at this level are able to plan at least 50 years into the future.

As a part of his own own spiritual discipline, Gandhi lived in a simple communal ashram of supportive peers, including his wife. This process led to the emancipation of millions from British rule. It was his vision of human equality (Global Harmony) that allowed him to fight for Indian rights in South Africa and in his own country of India, well beyond his own lifetime (Human Rights).

The most negative possibility at this cycle is the misuse of power, and governance by values that are detrimental to the individual working internationally and to society as a whole. Cycle 7 leaders must be clear about particular values so that they can be translated into institutional policy; and this policy must be amended and creatively criticized at every level in an institution to ensure an integrated perspective.

The Cycle 7 Institutional Style.   The Cycle 7 person now views the world as a mystery for which we must care. Such people are acutely aware that their vocation is a global one, requiring nothing less than the collaboration of all international institutions. The institutional style is one of international interinstitutional collaboration.

The skills of the integrated leader at this level are primarily characterized by the ability to integrate Phase IV with Phases I and II. The whole person at this cycle therefore integrates the values of Safety/Survival, Security, and Self-Preservation as they are experienced by others at a global level. They are always concerned about global world order at the human and environmental levels. Issues of harmony in the environment, world peace, and human equality are major action concerns.

Summary

Chapters 7 through 10 have reviewed the Seven Cycles of Development, revealing some of the conditions for personal transformation and growth. An integral part of this transformation is the relationship we have to institutions at each cycle, so we now need to look at the nature of organizations themselves. How do organizations develop? How do we go about measuring corporate culture and its effect on human transformation? Can we shape organizational life so that it enhances human transformation? We will explore the answers to these questions in Chapter 11.

11

Transforming Organizational Culture

In total over a period of about six months, we developed profiles of nearly eighty companies. Here's what we found: Of all the companies surveyed, only about one-third (twenty-five to be precise) had clearly articulated beliefs. Of this third, a surprising two-thirds had qualitative beliefs or values, such as "IBM means service." The other third had financially oriented goals that were widely understood. Of the eighteen companies with qualitative beliefs, all were uniformly outstanding performers. . . . We characterized the consistently high performers as strong cultures.

Terrence Deal *and* Allan Kennedy, *Corporate Cultures*

Deal and Kennedy (1982) demonstrated the connection between the beliefs or core values of an organization and the organization's culture. Lawrence Miller (1984, p. xiii) puts it this way: "The acceptance of new values has the power to create new cultures. . . . If we are to create new cultures

187

within our corporations, we must determine upon which values we will build those cultures."

In the last three chapters we have seen that there is an essential link between the development of exceptional human beings—the nitty-gritty of transforming people into integrated, creative, and self-initiating dynamic individuals—and the values that are reinforced in them by the institutions within which they live. We have already addressed the importance of the quality of family life in the chapters on the cycles of development. Equally important is the place where we work. Business culture is important even to family life—in most families there is at least one person who works in a company or corporation.

Values are the underpinning of corporate culture, and the success of any corporation rests upon the nature, integrative or disintegrative, of its culture. If a corporation is to develop or manage its culture to achieve its mission, it is absolutely essential to know what values it currently has. In the last two chapters we have mentioned some of the characteristics of the developmental cycles that organizations, like people, go through.

We have done a great deal of values research and consulting with corporations and other institutions. The questions that we have addressed are: How does one collect values-based information on individuals and groups? And how can we get results that are are specific enough to lead to an understanding of the institution's unique corporate culture, so that the corporation can effectively manage the process of strategic planning? We know that individuals and organizations are symbiotically linked and that both are motivated by their values. We wanted to measure the values of both the individuals and their institutions, and to be able to interpret the results in a way that contributed to the transformation of both.

All institutions have a value core out of which come all their behaviors, rules, and management structures—or what we call their corporate cultures. This value core is developed through the history of the organization and the popularly held images of the founder. In this chapter we will look at what the organizational life cycle looks like and the relationship of that life cycle to leadership. We will also examine how to measure and interpret values in people and organizations, and what the implications of this research are.

Institutional Life Cycles

There has been significant research on the development of organizations in one surprising area—that of western monastic organizations. These organizations are very old and their history is well documented.[1]

A team of religious sociologists wrote a book called *Shaping the Coming Age of Religious Life* (Cada et al., 1979), in which they studied the life

FIGURE 11-1. The Vitality Curve: The Life Cycle of an Organization

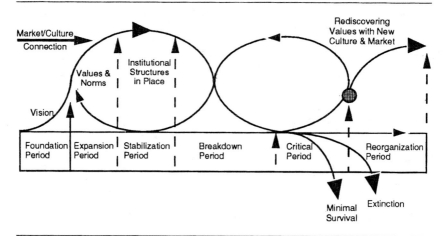

cycles of several religious congregations over a long period of history. They discovered that the religious groups that survived went through predictable cycles of development, and that different forms of religious life appeared in times of major societal transition.

They called this series of life cycles the "Vitality Curve"—the natural rise and fall of an institution in its usefulness and success in society through history. They also noticed that each institution went through a series of predictable stages, changes, and crises. Our research is consistent with their findings: this life-cycle phenomenon is true of any institutional form, no matter what its purpose. Figure 11-1 illustrates the Vitality Curve as a description of the life cycle of an organization.

Let's take a look at the six organizational stages described by Cada and his associates.

The Foundation Period.   Initially, the founder of the institution is its sole leader, and this period is characterized by the founder's vision and personal values, and it is these values that must meet the needs of the times and engender the support of the initial group. This period usually lasts no longer than the lifetime of the founder. The central crises in the Foundation Period are those common to any start-up company—they relate to capitalization, product development, and leadership direction. Very often the person who founds the institution is not the right person to manage it and give it continuity.

The Expansion Period.   The second stage, the Expansion Period, is that time when society discovers a need for the product, and the vision of the founder becomes a sign of hope for others. For example, Apple Computer's Steve Jobs pioneered in personal computers with the initiation of the Macintosh operating system; he had a vision of making computers friendly to anyone who wanted to use them to write, draw, or manage a business. The young Apple Computer, Inc. grew rapidly because this vision was enthusiastically shared by the internal staff, and the product met the needs of many people who had not expected to be able to learn to use a computer.

During the Expansion Period, the values of the founder become the norms of the organization. It is a time of excitement and geographical expansion. It is also a time when the values of the founder are interpreted and institutionalized, and very often documented. It is also a time when very often the expanding infrastructure of the company outgrows the management skills of the founders; delegation can become very important to the future of the organization.

The Stabilization Period. The third stage marks the high point of service in the form of successful initial product development and resulting financial stability and profitability. What causes this success is that the founder's values have been transformed into a product that meets a need of the wider culture, and the initial popularity of the product has settled into long-term demand. Today this period can last from ten to fifty years. This is the time for maximizing organizational structures and identity. It is the institutional parallel to Cycle 3 of the Seven Cycles of Development with its emphasis on conformity, unity, and loyalty, and putting a stable organizational structure in place.

The Breakdown Period. Inevitably there comes the Breakdown Period, marked by some natural shift in societal and cultural values and needs. People usually change when they have to, but institutions do not naturally change quickly, even when the demand for their products or services declines. The breakdown triggers a crisis of belief or a confusion of values, marked by denial that anything is really changing. Loss of creativity, loyalty, and personnel is a natural consequence. This leads within a short period of time to the Critical Period.

The Critical Period. The Critical Period is a time of crisis that challenges the very viability of the institution—whether it should close down, continue on a minimal basis, or try to renew itself. The critical factor is courageous leadership that tolerates the discomfort of making very difficult decisions.

The Reorganization Period. The Reorganization Period marks the critical decision point. For an organization to renew, the leadership has to return to and re-examine its founding values, articulate them, and redefine them so that they and the new, revised products are in line with the present values and needs of society.

In order for a system to be revitalized, its values must be re-examined and translated into permanent documents that reflect the new policies and structures of the organization. Revitalization involves a return to the founder's initial value base so that these original values can be re-envisioned but made relevant to the changed needs of the times. When this occurs succesfully, the cycle starts all over again.

Corporations and the Vitality Curve. Although this research was first conducted on religious organizations, the author's experience shows that all institutions go through the same cycles: A product is developed and becomes successful through the founding vision of some inventive entrepreneur; as it is marketed, a founding corporation is put in place. This is a danger point—many highly successful corporations fail in the Expansion Period because the founder has insufficient management skills. Once the system has stabilized, the product will sustain the system until the cultural and product needs of society change.

Revitalization may mean a return to the original inspiration of the founder, or it may mean starting all over in a new direction. But either way, starting over means having a new, exciting, innovative product—one capable of creating the enthusiastic support engendered by the product that initiated the system in the first place.

The new ideas that eventually revitalize an organization will only be present if the organization has values that sponsor, encourage, and support new ideas in the first place. In other words, the values in the culture of any organization determine whether or not that organization has longevity or not. This takes us back to the values that initiated the organization in the first place. So what is the relationship between an organization's leadership, how the organization develops, and the organization's values?

Boundaries

All organizations arise out of a central value system. Like people, they all go through predictable developmental life cycles. In Chapter 4 we saw that each individual is pulled into the future by a set of values we called future or vision values. This happens more easily when the individual's foundation values are taken care of so that they can focus on the present. The same is true for institutions.

Figure 11-2 illustrates the relationship of an organization's values to the simple components of that organization. The outer perimeter represents the boundaries of the organization: all the values held by the

FIGURE 11-2.   The Organization and Its Boundaries

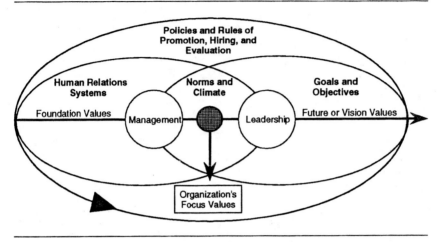

organization. The arrows illustrate that this is a dynamic relationship; the values of the system are changing and being integrated all the time as people come and go in the organization. Initially these values and the values of the founder or leadership group that started the organization would be the same. As the organization grows through its life cycle, these values are diluted by the values of other people.

The leadership must be in touch with the organization's future and vision values; this is what gets an organization started in the first place. At the same time, the leadership must be in touch with the employees—the management and human relations systems shown in Figure 11-2. Leadership is always difficult!

An organization's foundation values hold the social dimension of the institution together; they involve group loyalty, and include bottom-line issues such as salaries, benefits, management, and leadership education. It is the job of management to make sure that all these elements are in place and running efficiently. Because management must be concerned with these foundation issues, it functions on the border between focus issues and foundation values.

As Figure 11-2 shows, the focus area is really the space between the foundation and the future. In reality it exists only as a condition of these two, and has no meaning on its own; this is true with both an individual and an organization. However, the focus values are important because they give rise to the corporate atmosphere, which is a product of spoken and unspoken norms, which are in turn an expression of the priority values of the system.

Leadership, then, must be on the growing edge, with one foot in the day-to-day reality of the focus area, but very much in touch with the organization's overall goals and objectives, which are the basic organizing factors—the vision as it is reflected in future and vision values.

As the organization grows and becomes more complex, more structures are put in place and expanded geographical markets increase complexity in terms of language, communications, and cultural differences. The original leadership either changes its role or becomes obsolete, and professional corporate managers with a different set of skills are hired to run the organization. This always happens as the organization moves from the Foundation Period to the Expansion and Stabilization Periods.

The following four conclusions summarize what we have noted so far about organizational development and the Vitality Curve:

1. Every organization runs on a central value system that was initiated by the founder or founding group. Peters and Waterman (1982, p. 279) put it this way: "Let us suppose that we are asked for one all-purpose bit of advice for management, one truth that we were able to distill from the excellent companies' research. We might be tempted to reply, 'Figure out your value system. Decide what your company stands for. What does your enterprise do that gives everyone the most pride? Put yourself out ten or twenty years into the future: what would you look back to with the greatest satisfaction?'"

2. Every organization that is not founded on at least minimally adequate value centers will not survive the Vitality Curve, or natural organizational life cycle. In the same way that an individual and family need a minimally adequate value system, so does a large corporate entity.

3. The growth and development of the individual members of an organization are interconnected with the organization's structure and growth. The organization that is derived from human effort is in fact a projection of the founder's or founding group's internal images of reality. When those images are inadequate and are not repeatedly addressed and updated, the system will eventually fail.

4. Since values are at the heart of the organizational structure, it follows that there is a direct relationship between the cycles of development and the development of an institution. Most institutions that reach the Stabilization Period will have experienced the first three periods, much as an individual does in the process of growing up. When an institution is in a start-up mode, it is in a Survival Period, much like an individual's first cycle of development; the values experienced by the organization are going to be related to survival and security. As the founding group tries to get things started, the initial personnel are bound to be dependent upon them—this is the period of benevolent

leadership as in Cycle 2. In the Stabilization Period, the institution usually moves to a formal organizational structure as in Cycle 3. Rules and structures are more closed and more individually controlled in the first three cycles. The opposite occurs in Cycle 4 and after.

In the Breakdown Period some institutional leaders revert to Cycle 1 because their value center is inadequate to the challenge. A few transcend this inevitable breakdown and enable the institution to renew itself.

In the Reorganization Period it is necessary for leadership to review organizational values and re-envision the future, which in a modern industrial environment is going to draw the organization toward collaborative management systems (Cycles 5 to 7). A unique quality of the Cycle 5 to 7 institution is that it is a learning organization with a management design based on consensus and prechosen values. This has an integrative effect on the organization as these values are passed down through different levels and internal systems such as the management information systems, human resources, or marketing and distribution.

It is clear that it is essential to measure an organization's values if we are going to be able to create its future so that it has a positive effect on its membership and on society as a whole.

Measuring Corporate Values

Values—even corporate values—are measurable. Work on values measurement began in 1979 when the author and associates at Santa Clara University in California, in collaboration with Benjamin Tonna and associates at the University of Malta, began to research the possibility of developing instrumentation that would measure the 125 values in individuals and institutions. Our first inroad to this process was not assessing the values of individuals; our first measurement project was to analyze corporate documents to determine the values on which corporate culture is based.

Earlier we discussed the Genesis Effect, and the relationship between our inner images and the external expressions of those images through the management design or corporate culture of the institution. The mediator of the Genesis Effect is the values that are inherent in human communication as spoken and written language. This powerful relationship between language and values is the basis for determining an organization's culture and values by analyzing its documents.

In 1978 the author with Ronald Carignan, an internal consultant to the Oblates of Mary Immaculate, developed a formal method for document analysis. The Oblates, an international missionary organization in Rome, gave us our first opportunity to use this technology when it asked us to analyze its newly released (1982) management documents, which are called their Constitution and Rule.

Our analysis was done with people who represented three language groups: French, English, and Spanish, and our assignment included a cross-cultural historical study that compared the new draft document with the original 1826 Constitution and Rule, as well as the 1926 and 1961 versions.

The technology for analyzing documents has become much more sophisticated since that time. In brief, document analysis involves the following steps:

1. The documents are first analyzed to make sure that they truly represent the organization's overall operations. The documents must minimally be representative of the foundation, focus, and vision components of the organization's life. The documents that are chosen must be in present use in the institution.

2. The documents are scanned into a computer. A thesaurus program recognizes and counts occurrences of each of the 125 values or any of 6000 synonyms. The computer program outputs profiles that are based on the number of values by repetition in each paragraph of the document. Sets of paragraphs are then grouped for comparison. For example, separate chapters, books, or documents may be compared. Sections on executive leadership may be compared with sections on supervision, hiring, or promotional practices.

   Over the years we have found that the number of useful comparisons is innumerable and varies with the the purposes of the organization. For example, the information one wants to retrieve from the management document of an electronics company may be radically different from those derived from documents of a health-care system or a university.

   When the organization is international, the process is carried out in all the languages that are represented in the organization, because an organization's values transcend the language and make this possible. As we have incorporated more computerization of this process, it has become possible to do rapid processing of a lot of data, and we have been able to standardize the values and their definitions in several languages.

3. Once the paragraphs to be compared are established, the values we have derived from those sections are fed into the computer, and profiles are created that give the cycles of development, skills, time quality dimensions, leadership levels, and ethical orientation for each section that was analyzed. The profiles are then compared and analyzed.

Document Analysis Assumptions.   Document analysis is based on a set of assumptions about how an organization's values should be represented in its documents. They are outlined here because they are in reality a summary of assumptions about values and values analysis in general, including our own personal values. These assumptions are based on the belief that the major philosophical and management documents of an institution should contain a coherent value system. Documents should reflect an organization's values in these ways:

1. There is a balance between goal and means values.
2. There is an appropriate balance and relationship between foundation, focus, and future or vision values.
3. Foundation values are clearly represented as bottom-line values while also being open to development and new expression.
4. Focus-area values are appropriate and complete enough to promote integral human development and growth.
5. Future values are sufficient and suitable enough to give direction and motivation to the development of the focus-area values.
6. The overall values system is broad enough to integrate members at different stages of value development.
7. The document reflects and is consistent with historical changes in society, within the historical period it was written.
8. There are minimal values necessary for the integration of the institution into an international setting when this is appropriate.
9. The document favors values that grow out of and reflect the original philosophy and vision of the organization.
10. The values reflect sensitivity to a male or a female setting; there is an appropriate balance of male and female values.
11. A comparative analysis of historical documents shows that a new revision reflects continuity of the basic values in the foundation, focus, and future areas.
12. In organizations where legal prescriptions are a part of the document they should, by and large, relate to the foundation-area values; for example, boilerplate corporate legal documents should reflect foundation values.
13. The documents reflect values priorities consonant with the goals and ethical convictions and life style of the organization. This is more self-evident in some organizations than others; for example, a university should include values related to education.

Since 1978 we have analyzed many corporate documents. We have discovered that they are an invaluable resource for understanding corporate culture in any organization. Document analysis is a very important step in the overall quality assessment of institutions. On its own it is a very limited venture, but combined with other processes it becomes a critical piece of a larger picture.

The most important question in any document analysis is whether the results actually reflect the day-to-day experience of the organization's membership.

Individual and Group Assessment. In order to find our whether an organization's documents reflect the experience and values of the people in that organization, we next measure the values in the group. The measurement tools, the HT-Inventory and HT-Insight, took about eight years to develop. They are in the form of questionnaires designed to be filled out by individuals. Computer analysis of the answers results in a printout that analyzes the value patterns of an individual based on the 125 values. As our research continued, we discovered that we could take a composite of the individual value inventories and come up with group profiles of an institution or administrative group.

Our long-term goal was to provide a quality, values-based information service that would enable institutions to be more philosophically integrated so that they could make a conscious and positive contribution to the world.

Philosophy and Business

We now know that the longevity of any institution—even of society itself—is based on the continuity of its values. History informs us that this continuity occurs through important documents. For example, when the Roman Empire collapsed, beginning in the fifth century, many of the libraries of the ancient world were burned or destroyed in the chaos of change. They carried centuries of wisdom, and had they all been destroyed, the knowledge of science, mathematics, and an endless array of subjects would have been lost. A thousand wheels would have had to be reinvented. A reading from the Cambridge Medieval History notes:

> Through the Dark Ages which proceeded from the barbarization of Western Europe, it was the Church and its monks who preserved the remnants of ancient civilization and Christianity itself with its systematic thought and its ethics. The remedy was supplied by St. Benedict, the father of the later Western monasticism, in two ways. His rule was an ordered and practical code of laws for the working of a monastery, and it adapted monasticism to Western ideas and Western needs. (Previte-Orton, 1953, p. 283)

It was the Benedictine Rule—a basic but essential management document on how monasteries should be run, what their purpose was, and how the membership should conduct itself that provided continuity for civilization as the old Roman Empire in the west collapsed and a new order emerged. The monks were intelligent, dedicated, values-driven people who discovered new farming techniques, invented the first clock and new devices for clothmaking, and attracted thousands to settle in and around their property. The consequence was that many large European cities are the direct descendants of these early monastic settlements, which not only farmed and made cloth, but also planted the conceptual seeds of many of the institutions that we take for granted today, such as the textile industry, education, and medicine.

We now know that the longevity of any institution, whether it is the Benedictines or IBM, occurs only when it has documents that hold its values and describes its management processes and philosophy. Why? Because people die and change jobs, but the documents remain and provide continuity. William Ouchi (1981) reinforces this point of view, relating it to the modern business enterprise:

> The thought of mixing practical business matters with pie-in-the-sky concerns may seem strange, but popular beliefs aside, philosophy and business are the most compatible of bedfellows. A philosophy can help an organization to maintain its sense of uniqueness by stating explicitly what is and isn't important. It also offers efficiency in planning and coordination between people who share in this common culture. But more than a vague notion of company right-and-wrong there needs to be a carefully thought-out philosophy, preferably one available to all employees in booklet form. (p. 131)

Beyond the importance of documents is the reality of day-to-day organizational life: values are important in all aspects of the institution's existence. In their best-selling book *In Search of Excellence: Lessons from America's Best-Run Companies* (1982), Peters and Waterman conclude their study by saying:

> Every excellent company we studied is clear on what it stands for, and takes the process of value shaping seriously. In fact, we wonder whether it is possible to be an excellent company without clarity on values and without having the right sorts of values. (p. 280)

This is not a new idea even in business, but its general level of acceptance is new. In February of 1924 Thomas Watson, Sr., got the board of the Computing-Tabulating Recording Company to rename itself International Business Machines (IBM). He became the renamed company's first chief executive, and he built IBM on a set of workable and specific values that were very well documented in management literature. The central values were service and loyalty; these were supported by the value of creativity through research, cooperation, and teamwork.

The values of service and loyalty were a commitment to both employees and customers. IBM until this day will move employees laterally rather than fire them if they did not work out in a given job or project. The value of research ensured ongoing flexibility, and cooperation built

FIGURE 11-3. The Organizational Mind (Hierarchical Organizations)

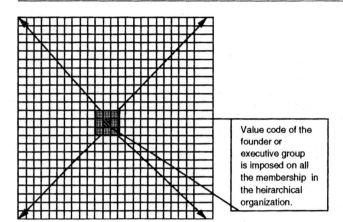

Value code of the founder or executive group is imposed on all the membership in the heirarchical organization.

community and placed loyalty to the company before the success of any individual. This was later partly codified in a book by Thomas Watson, Jr., entitled *A Business and Its Beliefs*, which described the company's values and philosophy.

We know from the history of all these organizations that they were efficient and productive to the extent that everyone in the organization had the same values system—both the Benedictines and IBM illustrate this. In both cases, success was a result of the mutually held values of Loyalty/Fidelity and Obedience/Duty, which produced a single mind: the organizational mind. Figure 11-3 illustrates this idea.

In this diagram of the hierarchical organizational mind, as in all traditional hierarchical organizations (Cycles 1 to 3), the values of the founder—Saint Benedict or Watson—are passed down through the organization to every employee through their commitment to the company.

Today there are new values emerging in corporate cultures, especially in North America, that are making the old hierarchical methods difficult if not impossible. These critical new values, such as Human Dignity, Independence, and Creativity, are changing the corporate and societal world view. Obedience is no longer a priority and the old way of value coding the organization is not workable. This new, confused version of the organizational mind is illustrated in Figure 11-4.

This is a very common experience today as organizations try to compete in the global market and find themselves outpaced by the competition—especially when the competition is the large Japanese giants that still run on a system that has a superior method of value coding and

FIGURE 11-4. The Organizational Mind (Hierarchical Imposed on New Values)

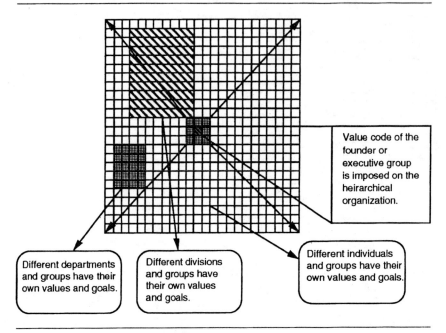

Value code of the founder or executive group is imposed on the heirarchical organization.

Different departments and groups have their own values and goals.

Different divisions and groups have their own values and goals.

Different individuals and groups have their own values and goals.

processing a single-minded efficient organization. What is the answer to this dilemma? A beginning point is to measure the values reality by assessing the corporate culture.

Analyzing the Corporate Culture to Initiate Change

The high point of our developmental work came about through our consulting with several international organizations. In the late 1980s we were asked to do a total system assessment on an international organization that had offices in eight countries covering five different language groups. The organization ran health-care facilities internationally. The countries involved were: Spain, Italy, and Germany in Europe, the United States and Canada, Brazil, and two Central American countries. The purpose was to retrieve information specific enough that they could discern what changes they needed to make in order to survive the next half-century.

The international executive board, based in Rome, wanted the assessment because there was a perceived lack of direction, collaboration, and cooperation from the five international regions: United States, Europe, Brazil, Canada, and Central America. In our initial interview, the board stated several times that they had lost their vision, which was to provide quality health care for the disadvantaged as well as the more affluent that they served.

Through their own internal resources they had already collected all the hard data available—statistical data such as the number of new personnel, number of employees leaving, number of people in particular job or language groups, and so on. The difficulty they were having was that this information did not lead with sufficient clarity to management planning—it simply described the problem.

This opportunity allowed us to compare the values of individuals with group profiles and document analysis in order to describe the corporate culture. We designed opinion surveys and interview formats to get at the actual day-to-day experience of the membership of the organization. The questions were directed at specific issues related to the quality of an employee's day-to-day experience; each question was coded to the 125 values.

We interviewed 700 people in the organization in five languages over a two-year period. Our analysis was particularly effective because the results from individual profiles, group profiles, the interview formats, and the document analysis were all based on the same 125 values and were therefore directly comparable.

We were amazed to find that interviews with 700 management and executive leaders in the organization, in five different languages, revealed that the values priorities in our document analysis was paralleled in the group analysis. The priorities were not always duplicated in the same order, but they were present in some form. This information gave us invaluable data for strategic planning.

Results of the Organizational Assessment.   The data that were collected gave us information about discrepancies in the organization. For example:

1. The management documents that were still in use were 50 years old and therefore outdated in some of their management attitudes. The highest level of management, an international executive council, was described in Cycle 3 language and values, and was expected to run the organization efficiently and hierarchically. The dominant number of people on the council were from Germany, where the cultural norms stress efficiency and obedience (see Chapter 3).

2. The next level of management leadership, often people who were CEOs of major institutions or general managers of a given region such as the United States, was described in the documents in terms of Cycle 5 values, reflecting a collaborative, empathetic, sharing, listening, and trust orientation.

3. When we looked at the values by region and compared the values with their history and experience, it became evident that geographically the organization was at widely varying stages of the institutional life cycle. Brazil and Central America were early in the institutional life cycle, with priority values in Cycle 2; they were experiencing problems of the Foundation Period and were far from stable. On the other hand, the United States was leaving the Stabilization Period, with values in Cycle 3 and 4, and feeling very uncomfortable about the future. Finally, the European countries were in the Breakdown Period and were experiencing a crisis of meaning and direction and alternated from Cycle 1 to Cycle 4, depending on what week you were talking to them.

When we compared the values analysis with the document analysis and examined the differences between regional groups, we found similar discrepancies, and we finally confirmed the same information at the grass-roots levels through the value-coded interviews. This information enabled the executive council to clearly see three problems:

1. The majority of the leadership, which was from the United States and Europe, was experiencing so much turmoil that their vision values were not evident. The consequence was that the groups in Brazil and Central America experienced a radical lack of support.

2. When personnel from the executive council visited the third-world countries, they tended to be experienced as authoritarian, widening the communication gap and feeling of lack of support by personnel in Brazil and Central America, and the values represented in the documents reinforced this.

3. Those in the second tier of leadership experienced the council as authoritarian, but this was exaggerated by the fact that they themselves were supposed to share their problems collaboratively. This made life so uncertain and threatening that it was difficult to get the leadership at the second level to come to meetings or cooperate at a meaningful level.

This analysis motivated the council to work cooperatively with all the leadership to change their experience of the organization. The executive council took a number of steps to correct the problems:

■ They updated their documents to describe the role of the executive council in terms of the same values and with the same expectations as those stated for all other levels of leadership in order to enhance cooperation and increase member countries' support of one another.

■ They readdressed their vision statement to make it operational for the whole organization.

- They set up a system of multicultural education and awareness. Executives for one country had to work for a short time in other countries in order to appreciate and experience their problems. This became an integral part of an ongoing leadership development program that included language education.

- They changed their strategic planning process so that it was truly international in order to compensate for the fact that each region was in a different part of the life cycle. They did this by revising the vision every three years, so that each region's plan was based on the international and not simply the local picture.

Since the data collection processes are all based on a common set of values, the assessment process itself begins to change an organization's reality. Assessment is not simply a matter of measuring values and then decoding the information in order to figure out what strategic planning is needed. When individuals understand their own values, they always see their realities reflected in the corporate culture (values-based document analysis), which in turn motivates them to move and act. This occurs as they connect their future values with the future reflected in the corporate reality. This is another example of what we referred to in an earlier chapter as a mind shift.

We also found that document analysis can be applied in opposite directions: to define the organization's values and culture, or to redirect its values and culture. Document analysis can lead to revision of documents in order to direct the corporate culture to new or revitalized values, and the revised documents can in turn be analyzed to verify that they do in fact reflect these new directions. We found that this reverse process is really necessary for all organizations—no matter how far along the road of efficiency and success they are—to ensure that their value centers are really what they intend them to be. Let us review another, less complex case in which we also measured a company's values.

Case Example: Bill's Family Business

Bill was the president of a small family real estate development business that his father had started some 30 years earlier. I was called in by Bill's partner to help with what appeared to be a leadership crisis in which Bill was identified as the problem.

When I first saw Bill, he was very stressed. He spoke most of the time about the bottom line and the monthly profit-and-loss statement. The business was not going well and he was blaming most of his problems on his partner and three of the management staff. He even blamed his

FIGURE 11-5.   Bill's Goals and Means Values

Goals Values	Stage	Means Values	Stage
Self-Interest/Control	I-A	Safety/Survival	I-A
Security	I-B	Economics/Profit	I-B
Self-Worth	II-A	Support/Peer	II-A
Service/Vocation	III-A	Limitation/Acceptance	III-A
Human Dignity	III-B	Search for Meaning/Hope	III-A
Being Self	III-B	Limitation/Celebration	III-B

wife for not supporting him enough in what he was trying to accomplish. When I first met him, his wife had left their house and said she was not going to return. Additionally, a number of long-term, trusted employees threatened to leave the firm if he did not learn to relax and listen to their opinions. I asked Bill to fill out an individual values questionnaire.

Bill's profile had most of his values in Cycle 4, the cycle that crosses over between a bureaucratic management view to a more collaborative style. His first six values in the goals and means areas, shown in developmental order, are listed in Figure 11-5.

Initially, the problem did appear to be Bill. After all, he was the president of the firm and made most of the decisions. Of the values listed in Figure 11-5, Bill's highest priorities were:

G1. Self-Interest/Control	G2. Security	G3. Self-Worth
M1. Economics/Profit	M2. Support/Peer	

His priority values are primarily out of the first two cycles of development and illustrate a very narcissistic orientation. He was very authoritarian in the way he related to his employees, his wife, and their two teenagers. One source of stress for him was that he felt that he was not living the values he believed in. The consequence was guilt and anxiety, leading to constant tiredness and irritability. He felt that he had no power over his life. Everything appeared to be controlled from the outside through the pressure of his business. Basically, he reflected the Cycle 1 to 2 world view that his values indicated.

Three months later Bill had made radical lifestyle changes that included delegating tasks at work and listening to his partner. His wife had returned and they were going to marriage counseling. But why the shift in Bill's attitude? Bill had re-evaluated his values. The same values showed up that were there before, but his priorities were different:

G1. Service/Vocation	G2. Human Dignity	G3. Being Self
M1. Limitation/Acceptance	M2. Search for Meaning/Hope Growth/Expansion	

These values were originally at the bottom of his list, but they have now moved to the top, beginning with Service/Vocation and Limitation/Acceptance, which are both from Stage III-A in Cycle 4 or 5. The values from Bill's original priorities were at Cycle 2. He had re-evaluated his life, his spending habits, and how he was running the business—the consequence was a new sense of the value Human Dignity. What caused the shift?

Group Insight: Transcending Time. Bill appears to have gone through a time warp. He moved through several cycles of development without going through years of gradual change! Time was transcended and normal development processes were accelerated. When we analyze Bill's values by looking at his future or vision values as they relate to his foundation and focus values, we see that before the confrontation with his wife and business associates, he had one value, Support/Peer, that is outside of himself. This second means value leads in turn to the goal value of Self-Worth. In my first interview with him, Bill said with tears in his eyes, "Even although I am very autocratic and difficult to live with, my peers at work supported me and gave me the only sense of worth that I have."

With Bill's permission, a document analysis was carried out on the management documents of his company, including such things as the annual reports for the last two years, mission statements, and boilerplate incorporation papers. The company's foundation values as indicated by these documents were as follows:

G1. Security	G2. Self-Worth
M1. Support/Peer	

These were all the same values that Bill was living his life by! Next we did a group analysis on the management group by giving a values inventory to each of the ten managers that worked with and under Bill.

The foundation values of this group were very similar:

G1. Family/Belonging	G2. Self-Worth
M1. Support/Peer	

The only difference between the document and group analysis values was the value of Family/Belonging, which for this group meant that they wanted to be a happy and loyal work family. Putting all this together, we were eventually able to state the company's foundation values as follows:

G1. Family/Belonging Security	G2. Self-Worth
M1. Support/Peer	

A second look at the situation made it clear that Bill's ability to transcend time and operate at an entirely new cycle of development was possible because of the shared values of the group, particularly the value of Support/Peer. After my initial interview with Bill and after we had looked at his earlier value priorities, Bill spoke apologetically to his wife and his associates, and asked for support and collaboration.

At a company retreat a month later, his partner said, "Bill has changed. He used to shout and yell and give orders without listening to anyone. Now he is much more open to the group's suggestions, and that has made all the difference." During the consultation we were able to point out to Bill and his associates that the values under which he was operating when he was under stress had not been taken away from him, but had been placed in perspective as a part of his foundation values.

A definition of hell is when one's future is the same as one's foundation. When Bill's foundation values were put into perspective, the future opened up to him and the group. Figure 11-6 demonstrates this point.

Circle A is Bill before his confrontation with his wife and business associates. His values are in Cycle 2 moving to alienation and survival in Cycle 1. The same values become the foundation of his support group at

FIGURE 11-6.   Transforming Consciousness

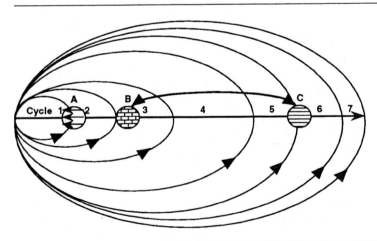

work, in circle B with the bricks in it to symbolize the foundation. The incredible thing is that this caused him to jump from Cycle 2 and function at Cycle 5 moving to 6! What sense can we make out of this?

The Pull of Future Values

After seeing this phenomena so many times, it is no longer strange to me. The reason for the alteration in Bill's profiles is that an individual's cycle of personal development can be transcended and upgraded by two or three cycles when the values of the group in which that individual functions are consciously chosen and acted upon by the group. A wrong mix of values can also reverse the effect.

However, there are two conditions that we have found must be in place for this transformation to occur:

1. The leadership of the group must be at the same cycle or one cycle ahead of the group for the effect to take place. This was true in Bill's case after he made the shift in consciousness.

2. If the leader is more than one cycle ahead of where the group is, then that person needs a strong support person within or outside the group to confer with. This is the same as the peer support frameworks we talked about in Chapter 7.

G1. Human Dignity	G2. Construction/New Order
M1. Growth/Expansion	

On the company retreat, the management team explained these values as the need to grow and expand the business, and doing this in such a way that the clients' human dignity would be improved and enhanced. They also added that they wanted the type of work environment that would enhance their own dignity. Bill bought into this—not only because he was a part of the group, but also because his values reflected many of the same concerns. Bill's personal future values were as follows:

G1. Service/Vocation	G2. Human Dignity	G3. Being Self
M1. Limitation/Acceptance Growth/Expansion	M2. Search for Meaning/Hope	

Starting with Bill's second goal (G2), the values he had were really his vision values, which he was able to share with the group. He was able to say that Search for Meaning/Hope and Being Self were personal goals, and that his goal for the company with them was Construction/New Order. This implied a new and successful form of the company. The group with Bill's agreement opted for wider stock ownership distribution and a more collaborative way of functioning based on the reality of a Cycle 5 vision.

The management group now had to deal with their focus values. They were moving from Cycle 3 in their foundation values to a Cycle 5 vision; what did they need to do to bridge the gap? The document and group analysis, along with Bill's own values, gave some direction. The focus values that bridged the gap were:

G1. Competence/ Confidence	G2. Service/Vocation	G3. Construction/New Order
M1. Efficiency/Planning	M2. Search for Meaning/Hope Decision/Initiation	

Once Bill and the group had come to a consensus on their focus values, they were able to convert the values into skills just as we did in Chapters 5 and 6. Their list was tailored and unique to them, because it came from their unique values. After looking at the skills derived from the goals and means combinations in their focus value cluster, the group decided that it needed the skills listed in Figure 11-7.

This example shows what can happen when there is administrative alignment. When a group of people who have a mixture of value priorities is able to define its priorities and live out these values, the group can transcend linear time and actually function at a higher cycle. The reverse is also possible when they fail to align. The value priorities of individuals in a group can greatly enhance the group's development rather than retard it.

The Holographic Organization of the Future

The company we just described lived out their earlier administrative reality at Cycle 1 and 2, dominated by their foundation values, which were reinforced by their CEO. But when the values were defined and brought into their awareness, they were able to provide support to one another that enabled them to live at Cycle 5, where their focus and vision values were.

FIGURE 11-7. Example of Tailored Management Skills

- Ability to do efficient strategic planning in order to accomplish our goals.

- Ability to initiate choices and decisions and act on them as a way of exercising authority in the workplace in a manner that brings personal acceptance and respect from clients and coworkers. This includes having management learn minimal interpersonal and group processing skills.

- Ability to evaluate the present management structure and to examine other models more in line with a collaborative structure.

The same sort of thing occurred in the international organization that we described earlier. These experiences of growth and integration are what we call a mind shift, and are in part a consequence of the group's larger field of consciousness. But more than awareness is required; the group must also experience interaction in the form of support and commitment to vision values. This is the heart of the human transformation process: growing in personal values and skills with the appropriate support from primary institutions of influence.

In Bill's company the same value coding is occurring as we saw in the efficient traditional hierarchical organization like the Benedictines of old: The values of the founder are being moved through the organization to make it a single mind. But in the new organization of the future, this an experience of consensus. We call this the holographic organization. Figure 11-8 demonstrates this concept.

Contemporary organizations are at their most efficient and effective when they operate on a clear consensus of values, agreed to by the membership, coded in their documents, and reinforced by a quality information database such as the one available in the first example of the international health-care organization. This higher level of operation will have longevity only when the organization ensures the transference of values through an ongoing program of leadership and personnel development.

FIGURE 11-8. The Organizational Mind: Holographic Organization

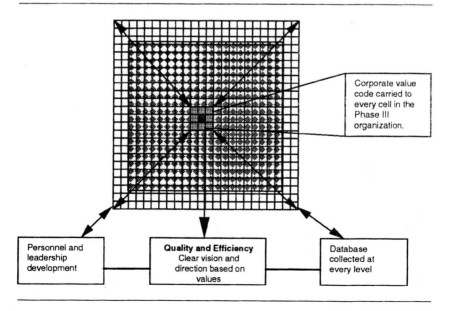

Corporate value code carried to every cell in the Phase III organization.

Personnel and leadership development

Quality and Efficiency Clear vision and direction based on values

Database collected at every level

The process of carrying out a values management program is not the subject matter of this book, but these two examples tell us that it is not only possible to do, but that it is the future of organizational development. Appendix C describes the process steps used to apply values management to bring about corporate change; it also provides two real-world examples of the process.

The holographic organization, based on sound values that dignify its personnel and enhance the quality of life for all the social groups it affects will be the successful corporation of the future. The success of Japan is admirable, but since those systems live their reality out of Cycle 3 values as did the traditional western organizations of the 1880s, they will inevitably move into the Breakdown Period in the next few years as their local population becomes internationalized.

The holographic organization promises a better and more humane world. In the final chapter we will look at this future in a little more depth.

12

Values and the Knowledge Explosion: The Future Is Calling

> *But what about the knowledge-value society to which we are moving? In the end, the most important means of production for creating knowledge-value is the individual mind, and those charged with generating it must strive to bring to bear as much knowledge, experience, and perception as they can. Creating knowledge-value is a pursuit in which labor and the means of production have become inseparably wedded; the worker is the means of production.*
>
> Taichi Sakaiya, *The Knowledge Value Revolution*

In 1988 in Bilbao, Spain, I made a presentation to the Second World Basque Congress on values measurement and its implications for business and education. Six months later, I sat with Dr. Benjamin Tonna in front of 20 scholars in philosophy, aesthetics, ethics, psychology,

211

education, theology, and business at the University of Deusto, Spain, for ten days, to answer all their questions about values theory, instrumentation, and validity studies.

Development in Spain moved quickly after that: within another six months teams had been assembled and all the values programs had been translated with manuals into Spanish. They are now used extensively in Spain in business and in public and private education. The person who promoted values technology in Spain was Dr. Roberto Pasqual of Deusto University. I asked him recently why there was so much more interest in values in Spain than I had experienced in the United States.

He replied that in Spain they knew what a dictatorship is like, having experienced it under Franco. They know what he did with Hitler to the Basques, and they know what World War II was like. Even more than these things, he said, it was the future that was getting most of their attention. "What do you mean?" I asked.

Roberto reminded me that in 1993 the borders to all the common market countries in Europe opened for the first time in centuries, and a free-market economy flowed with almost all trade barriers removed. Even the entrance requirement for universities in all these countries has become standardized, he pointed out. He went on to say that if we are not clear about *our* values, we will be swallowed up in the values of other countries!

Dr. Shirley McCune of MCREL (Mid-Continent Region Educational Laboratories) in Denver uses values technology in strategic planning for school administrators in the United States. In talking to her about values assessment and modern education, she says:

"Education, like most other sectors of society, is under intense pressure to change and restructure its institutions and programs. The degree of change necessary is far beyond improvement efforts or simply fixing up around the edges. It calls for a transformation of educational leaders and organizations."

Strategic planning is one of the organizational change tools used frequently in working with educational organizations. Work with local districts, state agencies, and national education organizations has demonstrated the value of strategic planning techniques for helping educators gain a new perspective on societal and educational changes and the need for change. Yet action has not followed from this knowledge.

An analysis of the reasons for limited action follow-up helped us understand that the strategic plans that were being developed were often beyond the skills and values of individuals and organizations. Although educators intellectually accepted the need for change, they had not been able to link their rational perspectives with their values. The result was that their overall vision of what was possible, individually and organizationally, lacked clarity and commitment.

In 1988, with the encouragement of MCREL's McCune, values technology was incorporated into the strategic planning process of the National Education Association (NEA) as a part of their internal scanning process to determine the strengths of the organization. The inventory was given to key members of the organization, who were then brought together to learn about their personal values, the dominant organizational values (through group profiles), and how value patterns assisted or inhibited the work of the organization. Techniques were developed to help educators translate their future values into an organizational vision of the future.

Dr. McCune now says, "The impact of this process on individuals and the NEA was truly amazing. A relatively resistant staff member gained a sense of renewal and an improved capability for working with the organization. Staff members who had frequently been passive receivers of information now demonstrated a new enthusiasm for learning about values technology and increasing the understanding of their affiliates. The energy demonstrated by the staff was contagious in the member leaders and staff not involved in the training."

On a hot summer's day in July in 1991 I sat in the office of the president of a new Japanese company in Silicon Valley in California. The parent company was in Japan and was owned by the father of the president of the U.S. affiliate. We had been summoned there by a vice president who wanted to consider doing some values analysis work in the company. The issue appeared to be differences in cultures: conflicts over attitudinal differences between the Japanese who ran the company and local Americans working in management. At one point the Japanese president said, "I wonder if the Americans are lazy?"

Further discussion revealed that what he was concerned about was loyalty and longevity. At one point he said with polite exasperation, "For us from Japan, planning means strategizing carefully relative to product development and marketing over the next ten years. But when I talk to my American managers, they talk about long-term planning as preparing for the next three months!" He went on to note that they had no competition in the field where their products were because of the superior quality of what they were producing. An ominous future seemed to be confronting the American managers if they failed to listen to the values of their Japanese partners.

Global Need for Future Values

Recent changes in the Soviet Union, the Middle East, and Eastern Bloc countries are all related to ideology, and ideologies are all based on values. With the former Soviet Union and the United States cooperating where before they were uneasy enemies, we can see the possibility of the decline of global conflict. But the thriving global village pictured by some futurists has not yet emerged because we find cultural misunderstandings when we try to work together across cultures. Never before in history has there been such a pressing need for the leadership of societies and organizations to be clear about what their values are and ought to be.

At the same time that we have seen a rapid decline of global conflict, an increasing number of people—many millions around the world— have been short of food because of poor management of distribution, ideological conflicts, fears of environmental disasters, and agricultural production diverted to supply the tons of cocaine available on the streets of every major city in the United States and Europe. These realities tell us that we will need to educate our worldwide population on values that promote human welfare on a global scale. For example, selling arms is not okay, and company policies that ignore human dignity in the work-place, education·without values, and ignoring the global environment are not okay. These are all concepts that are value laden and that are call-ing us to action from our own future values.

Global Trends

Taichi Sakaiya (1991) says about moving into our future:

> But what about the knowledge-value society to which we are moving? In the end, the most important means of production for creating knowledge-value is the individual mind, and those charged with generating it must strive to bring to bear as much knowledge, experience, and perception as they can. (pp. 68-69)

Sakaiya is suggesting that global society is moving into an entirely new era, that this is not simply an extension of our present technological age, but something new altogether.

His thesis is that human organizations in world society have always been related to the most prominent, least expensive, and most available resources for production. And those societies that were best able to use those resources were the ones that prospered. In ancient Rome, slavery was a major resource and something that was managed and utilized fully by the Roman state. In the industrial period, it was steel and tech-nology that was most fully developed; the consequence was the ascendence of the West and eventually of the United States.

Sakaiya points out that in the post-World War II period it was the dis-covery and utilization of petroleum that eventually placed Japan as num-ber one in the global economy. Why and how? Japan has limited space and natural resources, but by being able to develop plastics and other petroleum by-products that were very much in demand by leading con-sumer nations like the U.S., they became the new successful and wealthy nation on the block.

Japan was also able to develop the most efficient management system known to society since the development of the Roman Catholic hierarchy in the early 1900s. It is popular for psychologists, Circle Q experts, and those who speak of quality management to say that these things were borrowed from American psychology by the Japanese. In reality, this is far from the truth.

The present Japanese management system has its roots in Japanese history for at least the last two hundred years, and stems from ancient family systems that demanded loyalty from all who worked under their care. In many modern Japanese companies, to be hired as an employee is to be hired for life as a member of a family. The manager who hires a single young man may expect that young man to get married at some point. The employing manager may also expect to advise the young man on whom he should marry, and grant the permission for him to marry at a given time. The first loyalty of an employee in Japan, then, is to his company and his manager. This radical form of loyalty is very strange to a person born in the United States or Canada.

This is a limited example of what the Japanese management system implies. First of all, it is not scientific management, and it cannot be duplicated in the United States or in the West because it is basically a very tight and coherent value system that is culturally supported by that society. Japanese business values are Unity/Uniformity, Loyalty, Self-Worth, and Family/Belonging. It is this reality, along with the Japanese ability to creatively develop products from petroleum derivatives, that has made them world leaders who are respected for service and quality.

Power Shift

Alvin Toffler (1990) believes that we are moving into a new global era. Toffler states that our current era of tremendous change is caused by a shift in power. Historically, until the nineteenth century all power was held by those who wielded the largest and most efficient sword. But all that is changing. In the 1800s and until recently, the power began to shift to those who controlled wealth. Toffler asserts that in the emerging era, power will be held by those who control knowledge:

> Today, in the fast-changing, affluent nations despite all inequities of income and wealth, the coming struggle for power will increasingly turn into a struggle for the distribution and access to knowledge. . . . The control of knowledge is the crux of tomorrow's worldwide struggle for power in every human institution. (p. 20)

Experiencing the 21st Century

In a wonderful book called *Civilization*, Kenneth Clarke points out that the French Revolution took place in part because of the writing and publishing of the first French dictionary. Once the dictionary had been printed, language became standardized and the aristocracy could not use it for their own ends only.

Dictionaries provide minimal standardized understanding of everyday written language, and social revolution results. We now have a universal set of standardized meanings for 125 values, giving us access to whole new levels of communication that transcends language and culture. Values are at the heart of the knowledge revolution that Toffler and Sakaiya are talking about.

In 1987 I was at a meeting in central Brazil where a group of 15 executives discussed their ownership and acceptance of the foundation, focus, and future values of their organization as derived from their management documents. The document analysis had taken a year and involved 300 pages of material.

The difficulty was that the session had to be conducted in five languages: Italian, Portuguese, German, English, and Spanish. Practically none of the executives spoke more than one language. But the values had been translated with their meanings into each language and given to them in a written form to study. The depth of the discussion was amazing, even with constant translation, because 90 percent of the conversation was around a common set of values, commonly understood, and experienced by each person within the context of their own particular culture. These values and their meanings transcended the language and culture barriers. *They were experiencing a taste of things to come: they were experiencing the knowledge values of the 21st century.*

Values as Special Knowledge

The strength of the Japanese management system is that it has a coherent value system. It is a value system that comes out of a long history of survival and loyalty to one's emperor, to one's manager, and to one's family. Their success derives not so much from their values and methodology, but from a management system based on a philosophy of life, entrenched with a consensus value system, that is unique and different in each Japanese company. The value code of the founders and leaders of their corporations is translated through loyalty to every employee in the system. This is what makes their companies so efficient, productive, and quality driven.

A new generation of Japanese young people is tasting the independent attitudes inherent in global experience, along with new attitudes toward women and people of other ethnic origins. It is unlikely that their current methods of management will last beyond another 25 years in spite of its effectiveness in the last quarter-century. There is nevertheless an important lesson to be learned: that values underpin unity of purpose and action.

For American companies to be equally successful, they must have an equally powerful values system based on their own values and a creative approach to life. The new corporation and the new society of the 21st century will be holographic, or consensus oriented.

In the knowledge-value revolution, knowledge will be encapsulated in value priorities identified in common by the group—whole societies, international organizations, educational or health care systems, or national or local businesses. Organizations will be successful if they do consensus-based long-term planning (for 50 years and more) based on a set of values in which they have confidence—values that work and that can stand the ethical test of the new international environment of the 21st century.

Chapter Notes

Chapter 2

1. This process in turn has developed the human imagination and given rise to new ideas and technology. Bronowski (1974) puts it this way:

> The notion of discovering an underlying order in matter is man's basic concept for exploring nature. The architecture of things reveals a structure below the surface, a hidden grain which, when it is laid bare, makes it possible to take natural formations apart and assemble them into new arrangements. For me this is the step in the ascent of man at which theoretical science begins. And it is as native to the way he conceives his own communities as it is to his conception of nature. (p. 95)

2. A recent work by Hunter Lewis (1990) exemplifies the problem. He defines values as follows: "Although the term *values* is often used loosely, it should be synonymous with personal beliefs, especially personal beliefs about the 'good,' the 'just,' and the 'beautiful,' personal beliefs that propel us to action, to a particular kind of behavior and life."

Lewis goes on to say that since values are beliefs, the critical issue is how we come to a knowledge of those beliefs. He concludes there are six ways of knowing what our values are: authority such as the Bible, logic, sensory experience, emotions, intuition, and science. When you put these things together, he appears to be saying that values either come from authority and emotions, as in religious fundamentalism, or from the logical and observable, as in science. The book reflects the present misunderstanding and confusion that most people have about values.

Chapter 3

1. Denis and John Carmody (1990, p. 41) say about the nature of a world view: "World view should connote not only one's orientation in the realm of space and time, geography and history, but also the values one spontaneously attributes to air and land, tribe and city, the self that is artistic and the self that is afflicted by what the philosopher Martin Neidegger caller 'everydayness.'"

2. Sue and Sue (1990, p. 151) see a Phase I influence for African-Americans: "Slavery was one of the most important factors shaping the social-psychological functioning of black Americans. Interpersonal relations between whites and blacks were highly structured, placing blacks in a subservient and inferior role."

3. For Erik Erikson (1980, pp. 94–95), Phase II is the final stage before adulthood, a stage he terms *identity*.

> "The sense of ego identity, then, is the accrued confidence that one's ability to maintain inner sameness and continuity is matched by the sameness and continuity of one's meaning for others. Thus, self-esteem, confirmed at the end of each major crisis, grows to be a conviction that one is learning effective steps toward a tangible future, that one is developing a defined personality within a social reality which one understands."

4. Eileen Cantin (1974, pp. 76–77), writing about the thoughts of the French philosopher Mounier, describes two levels of transcendence:

> "The most basic mode of transcendence and the one which paves the way for higher modes is production. By modifying the world around him and making it more and more an objectification of himself, the person extends his physical and, through it, his personal being. He gives himself a new and more extensive body and he gives something of his own humanity to impersonal reality. Transformation of matter implies not only its personalization, but also provides new opportunities for the emergence of the human spirit. As the condition of matter is transformed so are the conditions for the expression and emergence of the human spirit heightened. The second level of transcendence is that which is achieved through interpersonal relations. The person is called to surpass himself by sharing himself with another person . . . A community of persons finds its cohesion within a We which is itself a Person. The We emerges from the community in much the same fashion as the I emerges from its material conditions, i.e., in response to a call."

Chapter 4

1. Carol Gilligan (1982) studied the play habits of male and female children. Her research showed that women have a different way of being in the world than men do. Women are relational in their approach to the world, even in how they make moral decisions; whereas men tend to come from a bias of competition and separateness. She says that this affects our perceptions of everything:

> Conceptions of the human life cycle represent different attempts to order and make coherent the unfolding experiences and perceptions, the changes, wishes, and realities of everyday life. But the nature of such conceptions depends in part on the position of the observer. . . . When the observer is a woman, the perception may be of a different sort. Different judgments of the images of a man imply different ideas about human

development, different ways of imagining the human condition, different notions of what is of value in life. (p. 5)

Chapter 5

1. Most developmental theorists like Kohlberg and Erickson or Levinson assume that the development of the human being is always tied to the aging process. The concept is that time is linear. That is to say, the future is in a place in time, perhaps several years away. The past is seen as something you did at another time. Within the existential framework, the assumptions about the critical factors for human integration are different.

2. Anton Boison (1936, pp. 147–148) noted that the failure to act is the key to all human and spiritual growth. He notes that for him the term *personal failure* denoted a "sense of inner disharmony which extends from the 'divine discontent' which is a precondition of effort and of growth, to enable the person to compensate for the possibility of the loss of that which makes life worth living to the individual."

Chapter 6

1. The French psychologist Jean Piaget did definitive work in establishing the stages by which a child acquires rational knowledge. He described a child's imagination or use of the imagination as developing in stages from rudimentary fantasy, to the ability to differentiate between quantity and quality, to the ability through language to categorize and order data, and finally to think abstractly as in mathematics and philosophy. For Piaget, developmental skills were primarily those related to cognitive reasoning, a part of what we call instrumental skills. However, he saw that the imagination is what makes reasoning skills possible.

In his book *Stages of Faith*, James Fowler (1981) suggests that the imaginal capacity of a person can mean more than this:

Our use of the word *image* requires some explanation. I maintain that virtually all our knowing begins with images and most of what we know is stored in images. Several points must be developed here. First, evidence from a variety of sources suggests that our knowing registers the impact of our experiences in a far more comprehensive way than our own consciousness can monitor. (p. 25)

This is close to what Jung refers to as the intuitive side of the personality, which is more developed in some people than in others. Basically, this is an unconscious process of reading external data and making insightful, intuitive, or unconscious conclusions about what the information means. For Jung, the logical connections are actually made unconsciously by the psyche. Further, for Jung the imagination has a transcendent dimension; it not only synthesizes information in new ways, but does it by adding additional archetypal information. What we have done in our work is to make a composite of all these dimensions, and have additionally suggested that the imagination is enhanced as a skill through the developmental processes.

2. In his book *The Ascent of Man*, Bronowski (1973) documents that the initiation of human social organization as we now know it occurred between 8000 and 6000 B.C., when nomadic tribes of primitive humans stopped wandering and became settled agricultural communities.

> The largest single step in the ascent of man is the change from nomad to village agriculture. . . . The turning point in the spread of agriculture in the Old World was almost certainly the occurrence of two forms of wheat with a large, full head of seeds. Before 8000 B.C. wheat was not the luxuriant plant it is today; it was merely one of many wild grasses spread throughout the Middle East. . . . By some genetic accident, the wild wheat crossed with the goat grass and formed a fertile hybrid . . . and produced Emmer with twenty-eight chromosomes. That is what makes the Emmer so much more plump. The hybrid was able to spread naturally, because its seeds are attached to the husk in such a way that they scatter in the wind. (pp. 64–65)

Bronowski goes on to point out that another incredible genetic accident occurred when the Emmer cross-fertilized again with the goat grass to produce a very heavy forty-two chromosome derivative that we call bread wheat. Bronowski describes a strange ecological event that happened then:

> Yet there is something even stranger. Now we have a beautiful ear of wheat, but one which will never spread in the wind because the ear is too tight to break up. . . . Suddenly man and plant have come together. Man has a wheat that he lives by, but the wheat also thinks that man was made for him only so it can be propagated. For the bread wheats can only multiply with help, man must harvest and scatter the seeds; and the life of each, man and the plant, depends on the other. (p. 68)

This strange historical act of interdependence created agricultural communities, which in turn created the need of men and women to live and stay in one place. From this grew the city, the social organization of human beings, and the direct consequence of interpersonal interaction, whose high point is intimacy. It was the creation of this environment that made the feeling, emotional side of civilization a possibility.

Chapter 7

1. Underhill (1955) notes why it is that the study of the mystics is so important:

> The most highly developed branches of the human family have in common one peculiar characteristic. They tend to to produce—sporadically it is true, and often in the teeth of adverse external circumstances—a curious and definite type of personality. . . . We meet these persons in the east and the west; in the ancient, medieval, and modern worlds. Their one passion appears to be the prosecution of a certain spiritual and intangible quest: the finding of a "way out" or a "way back" to some desirable state in which alone they can satisfy their craving for absolute truth. (p. 4)

Chapter 11

1. The early Christian communities began full of optimism and idealism; they envisioned themselves as symbolic of a new Kingdom of Hope on earth. It was from the very beginning a network of smaller communities that was international, but a single corporate system. The concept was that the individual was symbiotically linked and nurtured by the group; and that the group, rather than the individual, was the primary unit of development.

Many of these institutions—for example, the Order of Friars Minor (the Franciscans), the Benedictines, the Jesuits, and the Ursulines—have been in existence for centuries. The Benedictines have been around for nearly 1500 years. Obviously they are different from the modern industrial organization like IBM, not only in purpose but in longevity.

Appendix A

Values Definitions

1. **Accountability/Ethics.** The ability that flows from awareness of one's personal system of moral principles to enrich others by addressing their conduct in relationship to their value system. This assumes the capacity to understand another's level of ethical maturity.

2. **Achievement/Success.** Accomplishing something noteworthy and admirable in the world of work or education.

3. **Adaptability/Flexibility.** The ability to adjust oneself readily to changing conditions and to remain pliable during ongoing processes.

4. **Administration/Control.** Having the authority to be in command, to exercise specific management functions and tasks in a business or institution.

5. **Affection/Physical.** Physical touching that expresses fondness or devotion.

6. **Art/Beauty.** Experiencing and/or providing intense pleasure through that which is aesthetically appealing in both natural and person-made creations simply for the mental and emotional stimulation and pleasure it provides.

7. **Authority/Honesty.** The freedom to experience and express the full range of personal feelings and thoughts in a straight forward,

forward, objective manner. This ability comes from a personal integration of thoughts and feelings and results in experiencing personal integrity and power.

8. **Being Liked.**   The ability to experience friendly feelings from one's peers.

9. **Being Self.**   The capacity to own one's truth about oneself and the world with objective awareness of personal strengths and limitations plus the ability to act both independently and cooperatively when appropriate.

10. **Belief/Philosophy.**   Adherence to a belief system, set of principles, or established philosophy that is based on universally accepted authoritative documents such as the Bible, Koran, or Upanishads, which espouse the concept of reverence for the universal order.

11. **Care/Nurture.**   The ability to be physically and emotionally supported by family and friends throughout one's life from childhood through aging, and to value doing the same for others.

12. **Collaboration.**   The ability of an organizational leader to cooperate interdependently with all levels of management to ensure full and appropriate delegation of responsibility.

13. **Communication/Information.**   Effective and efficient transmission and flow of ideas and factual data within and between persons, departments, and divisions of an organization.

14. **Community/Personalist.**   The ability to exercise sufficient depth and quality of commitment to a group, its members, and its purpose so that both independent creativity and interdependent cooperation are maximized simultaneously.

15. **Community/Supportive.**   The recognition and will to create a group of peers for the purpose of ongoing mutual support and creative enhancement of each individual. The additional awareness of the need for such a group in the work environment and with peer professionals, to enable one to detach from external pressures that deter one from acting with clarity on chosen values and ethical principles that might otherwise be compromised.

16. **Competence/Confidence.**   Realistic and objective confidence that one has the skill to achieve in the world of work and to feel that those skills are a positive contribution.

17. **Competition.**   The ability to be energized by a sense of rivalry, to be first or most respected in a given arena such as sports, education, or work.

18. **Complementarity.** The capacity to enable persons in a corporation or institution to work cooperatively with one another so that the unique skills and qualities of one individual supplement, support, and enhance the skills and qualities of the others in the group.

19. **Congruence.** The capacity to experience and express one's feelings and thoughts in such a way that what one experiences internally and communicates externally to others is the same.

20. **Construction/New Order.** The ability to develop and initiate a new institution for the purpose of creatively enhancing society. This assumes technological, interpersonal, and management skills.

21. **Contemplation.** Self-discipline and the art of meditation that prepares one for intimacy with others and unity with the universal order.

22. **Control/Order/Discipline.** Providing restraint and direction to achieve methodological arrangements of persons or things according to the prescribed rules.

23. **Convivial Technology.** The ability to creatively apply technology to improve distribution of the basic necessities of life so that social conditions throughout the world are improved.

24. **Corporation/New Order.** The skills, capacity, and will to create new organizational styles or to improve present institutional forms in order to enhance society.

25. **Courtesy/Hospitality.** Offering polite and respectful treatment to others as well as treating guests and strangers in a friendly and generous manner, and to value receiving the same treatment from others.

26. **Creativity.** The capacity for original thought and expression that brings new ideas and images into a practical and concrete reality in ways that did not previously exist.

27. **Decision/Initiation.** The ability to feel that it is one's responsibility to begin a creative course of action, or to act on one's conscience without external prompting.

28. **Design/Pattern/Order.** Awareness of the natural arrangement of things plus the ability to create new arrangements through the initiation of arts, ideas, or technology; for example, architecture.

29. **Detachment/Solitude.** The regular discipline of nonattachment that leads to quality relationships with others and with the universal order.

30. **Dexterity/Coordination.** Sufficient harmonious interaction of mental and physical functions to perform basic instrumental skills.

31. **Discernment.** The capacity or skill to enable a group or organization to come to consensus decisions relative to long-term planning through openness, reflection, and honest interaction.

32. **Duty/Obligation.** Closely following established customs and regulations out of dedication to one's peers and a sense of responsibility to institutional codes.

33. **Economics/Profit.** Accumulation of physical wealth as a means of being secure and respected.

34. **Economics/Success.** Exercising the ability to attain favorable and prosperous financial results in business through effective control and efficient management of resources.

35. **Ecority.** The capacity, skills, and personal, organizational, or conceptual influence to enable persons to take authority for the created order of the world and to enhance its beauty and balance through creative technology in ways that have worldwide influence.

36. **Education/Certification.** Completing a formally prescribed process of learning and receiving documentation of that process.

37. **Education/Knowledge.** The experience of ongoing learning as a means of gaining new facts, truths, and principles. One is motivated by the occasional reward of new understanding that is gained intuitively.

38. **Efficiency/Planning.** Thinking about and designing acts and purposes in the best possible and least wasteful manner before implementing them.

39. **Empathy.** Reflecting and experiencing other people's feelings and states of being through a quality of presence that has the consequence of their seeing themselves with more clarity, even without any words being spoken.

40. **Endurance/Patience.** The ability to bear difficult and painful experiences, situations, or persons with calm stability and perseverance.

41. **Equality/Liberation.** Experiencing oneself as having the same value and rights as all other human beings in such a way that one is set free to be that self and to free others to be themselves. This is the critical consciousness of the value of being human.

42. **Equilibrium.** Maintaining a peaceful social environment by averting upsets and avoiding conflicts.

43. **Equity/Rights.** Awareness of the moral and ethical claim of all persons, including oneself, to legal, social, and economic equality and fairness plus a personal commitment to defend this claim.

44. **Expressiveness/Joy.** The ability to share personal feelings and fantasies so openly and spontaneously that others are free to do the same.

45. **Faith/Risk/Vision.** Behavioral commitment to values that are considered life-giving even at risk to one's livelihood or life.

46. **Family/Belonging.** The people to whom one feels primary bonds of relationship and acceptance; attachment to the place where one's parents live.

47. **Fantasy/Play.** The experience of personal worth through unrestrained imagination and personal amusement.

48. **Food/Warmth/Shelter.** Personal concern about having adequate physical nourishment, warmth, and comfort and a place of refuge from the elements.

49. **Friendship/Belonging.** The ability to have a group of people with whom to share on a day-to-day basis.

50. **Function/Physical.** Concern about the ability to perform minimal manipulations of the body to care for oneself and concern about the body's internal systems and their ability to function adequately.

51. **Generosity/Compassion.** The ability to share one's unique gifts and skills with others as a way of serving humanity without expecting reciprocation.

52. **Global Harmony.** Knowing the practical relationship between human oppression, freedom, and creative ecological balance so that one can influence changes that promote greater human equality.

53. **Global Justice.** Commitment to a world order in which all persons have equal value but different gifts and abilities to contribute to society, combined with the ability to elicit interinstitutional and governmental collaboration to provide the basic rights and life necessities for the poor in the world.

54. **Growth/Expansion.** The ability to enable an organization to develop and grow creatively. This assumes skills in management design and organizational development at a corporate level.

55. **Health/Healing.** Soundness of mind and body that flows from meeting one's emotional and physical needs through self-awareness and preventive discipline. This includes an understanding that commitment to maintaining a personal inner rhythm and balance relates to positive feelings and fantasy.

56. **Hierarchy/Order.** The methodical, harmonious arrangement of persons and things ranked above one another in conformity to established standards of what is good and proper within an organization.

57. **Honor.** High respect for the worth, merit, or rank of those in authority, such as parents, superiors, and national leaders.

58. **Human Dignity.** Consciousness of the basic right of all human beings to have respect and to have their basic needs met so that each person has the opportunity to develop to full potential.

59. **Human Rights.** Committing personal talent, education, training, and resources to creating the means for all people in the world to experience their basic right to such life-giving resources as food, habitat, employment, health, and minimal practical education.

60. **Independence.** Thinking and acting for oneself in matters of opinion and conduct without being subject to external constraint or authority.

61. **Integration/Wholeness.** The inner capacity to organize the personality (mind and body) into a coordinated, harmonious totality.

62. **Interdependence.** Seeing and acting on the awareness that personal and interinstitutional cooperation are always preferable to individual decision making.

63. **Intimacy.** Regularly and fully sharing one's thoughts, feelings, fantasies, and realities, mutually and freely, with another person.

64. **Intimacy/Solitude.** The experience of personal harmony that results from a combination of meditative practice and mutual openness and total acceptance of another person, which leads to new levels of meaning and awareness of truth in unity with the universal order.

65. **Justice/Social Order.** Taking a course of action that addresses, confronts, and helps correct conditions of human oppression in order to actualize the truth that every human being is of equal value.

66. **Knowledge/Insight.** The pursuit of truth through patterned investigation, motivated by increased intuition and unconsciously gained understanding of the wholeness of reality.

67. **Law/Guide.** Seeing authoritative principles and regulations as a means for creating personal criteria and moral conscience, and questioning those rules until they are clear and meaningful.

68. **Law/Rule.** Governing personal conduct, action, and procedures by the established legal system or code. Living life by the rules.

69. **Leisure.** Use of time in a way that requires as much skill and concentration as one's work but that totally detaches one from work in a spontaneous, playful way so that others are free to do the same.

70. **Limitation/Acceptance.** Giving positive mental assent to the reality that one has boundaries and inabilities, based on objective self-awareness of personal strengths and potential as well as weakness and inability. The capacity for self-criticism.

71. **Limitation/Celebration.** The recognition that personal limits are the framework for exercising one's talents. The ability to laugh at one's own imperfections.

72. **Loyalty/Fidelity.** Strict observance of promises and duties to those in authority and to those in close personal relationships.

73. **Macroeconomics.** The ability to manage and direct the use of financial resources at an institutional and interinstitutional level toward creating a more stable and equitable world economic order.

74. **Management.** The control and direction of personnel in a business or institution for the purpose of optimal productivity and efficiency.

75. **Membership/Institution.** The pride of belonging to and functioning as an integral part of an organization, foundation, establishment, etc.

76. **Minessence.** The capacity to miniaturize and simplify complex ideas or technological instruments (tools) into concrete and practical objectifications in a way that creatively alters the consciousness of the user.

77. **Mission/Objectives.** The ability to establish organizational goals and execute long-term planning that considers the needs of society and how the organization contributes to those needs.

78. **Mutual Accountability.** The skills to maintain a reciprocal balance of tasks and assignments with others so that all are answerable for their own areas of responsibility. This requires the ability to express and mobilize anger in creative and supportive ways in order to move relationships to increasing levels of cooperation.

79. **Mutual Obedience.** The mutual and equal responsibility of all members of a group to establish and adhere to a common set of rules and guidelines.

80. **Obedience/Duty.** Dutifully complying with moral and legal obligations established by parents and civic and religious authorities.

81. **Ownership.** Personal and legal possession of skills, decisions, and property from which one derives a sense of personal authority.

82. **Patriotism/Esteem.** Honor for one's country based on personal devotion, love, and support.

83. **Physical Delight.** The joy of experiencing all the senses of the body.

84. **Pioneerism/Innovation.** Introducing and originating creative ideas for positive change in organizations and providing the framework for actualizing them.

85. **Play/Recreation.** A pastime or diversion from the anxiety of day-to-day living for the purpose of undirected, spontaneous refreshment that can result in heightened awareness of oneself as separate from daily pressures.

86. **Presence.** The ability to be with another person that comes from inner self-knowledge that is so contagious that another person is able to ponder the depths of who he or she is with awareness and clarity.

87. **Prestige/Image.** Physical appearance that reflects success and achievement, gains the esteem of others, and promotes success.

88. **Productivity.** The energy that results from generating and completing tasks and activities and achieving externally established goals and expectations.

89. **Property/Control.** Accumulating property and exercising personal direction over it for security and for meeting basic personal physical and emotional needs.

90. **Prophet/Vision.** The ability to communicate the truth about global issues in such a lucid manner that those who hear are able to transcend their limited personal awareness and take action.

91. **Quality/Evaluation.** Appreciating objective self-appraisal and being open to what others reflect back about oneself as necessary for self-awareness and personal growth.

92. **Reason.** The trained capacity to think logically and reasonably based on a formal body of information. The capacity to exercise reason before emotion.

93. **Relaxation.** Diversion from physical or mental work that reduces stress and provides a balance of work and play as a means of realizing one's potential.

94. **Research.** Systematic investigation and contemplation of the nature of truths and principles about people and human experience for the purpose of creating new insights and awareness.

95. **Responsibility.** The ability to be personally accountable for and in charge of a specific area or course of action in an organization or group.

96. **Rights/Respect.** The moral principle of respecting the worth and property of another as I expect others to respect me and my property.

97. **Ritual/Communication.** Skills and use of ceremony and the arts as a communication medium for raising critical consciousness of such themes as world social conditions and awareness of the transcendent.

98. **Rule/Accountability.** The need to have each person openly explain or justify his/her behavior in relationship to established codes of conduct, procedures, etc.

99. **Safety/Survival.** Concern about the ability to avoid personal injury, danger, or loss, and to do what is necessary to be protected in adverse circumstances.

100. **Search for Meaning/Hope.** A personal exploration arising from an inner longing and curiosity to integrate personal feelings, imagination, and objective knowledge in order to discover one's unique place in the world.

101. **Security.** Finding a safe place or relationship where one is free from cares and anxieties and feels protected.

102. **Self-Actualization.** The inner drive toward experiencing and expressing the totality of one's being through spiritual, psychological, physical, and mental exercises that enhance the development of one's maximum potential.

103. **Self-Assertion.** The will to put oneself forward boldly regarding a personal line of thought or action.

104. **Self-Interest/Control.** Restraining one's feelings and controlling one's personal interests in order to survive physically in the world.

105. **Self-Preservation.** Doing what is necessary to protect oneself from physical harm or destruction in an alien world.

106. **Self-Worth.** The knowledge that when those one respects and esteems really know him/her, they will affirm that he/she is worthy of that respect.

107. **Sensory Pleasure.** Gratifying sensual desires and experiencing one's sexual identity.

108. **Service/Vocation.** The ability to be motivated to use personally unique gifts and skills to contribute to society through one's occupation, business, profession, or calling.

109. **Sharing/Listening/Trust.** The capacity to hear another's thoughts and feelings actively and accurately and to express personal thoughts and feelings in a climate of mutual confidence in one another's integrity.

110. **Simplicity/Play.** The capacity for deeply appreciating the world combined with a playful attitude toward organizations and systems that is energizing and positive. The ability to have a wholistic view of complexity, and to be detached from the world as primarily material in nature.

111. **Social Affirmation.** The personal respect and validation that comes from the support and respect of one's peers and that is necessary for personal growth and success.

112. **Support/Peer.** The ability to have people who are one's equals and who sustain one in both joyful and difficult times.

113. **Synergy.** Harmonious, energized relationships within a group that produce results that far surpass what might be predicted based on the collective abilities of its members.

114. **Technology/Science.** Systematic knowledge of the physical or natural world and practical applications of the knowledge through inventions and tools.

115. **Territory/Security.** Provision for physically defending property, a personal domain, or nation state.

116. **Tradition.** Recognizing the importance of ritualizing family history, religious history, and organizational and national history in one's life in order to enrich its meaning.

117. **Transcendence/Solitude.** Exercising spiritual discipline and detachment so that one experiences a global and visionary perspective as a result of a personal relationship to the universal order.

118. **Truth/Wisdom.** Intense pursuit and discovery of ultimate truth above all other activities. This results in intimate knowledge of objective and subjective realities, which converges into the capacity to clearly comprehend people and systems and their interrelationship.

119. **Unity/Diversity.** Recognizing and acting administratively on the belief that an organization is creatively enhanced by giving equal opportunity to people, both male and female, and from a variety of cultures, ethnic backgrounds, and with diverse training.

120. **Unity/Uniformity.** Harmony and agreement in an institution that is established to achieve efficiency, order, loyalty, and conformity to established norms.

121. **Wonder/Awe/Fate.** The ability to be filled with marvel, amazement, and fear when faced with the overwhelming grandeur and power of one's physical environment.

122. **Wonder/Curiosity.** A sense of marvel and amazement about the physical world coupled with a desire to learn about it and explore it personally.

123. **Word.** The ability to use the power of language to heal and transform the values and world views of the hearers. To communicate universal truths so effectively that hearers become conscious of their limitations, so that life and hope are renewed and the hearers recognize their place in the larger, universal order.

124. **Work/Labor.** The ability to have skills and rights that allow one to produce a minimal living for oneself and one's family.

125. **Workmanship/Art/Craft.** Skills requiring manual dexterity that produce artifacts and modify or beautify the person-made environment.

Appendix B

Values Instrumentation and Validity Studies

Values Technology is a dynamic research and development company focused on bringing values-based instrumentation and strategic planning into the business, education, and health-care sectors.

The company provides measurement supported by educational processes and consultation to organizations and individuals both domestically in the United States and internationally. Our goal is to assist major institutions in organizational transformation in order to accomplish organizational objectives through the identification and integration of core values.

Values Technology's goals are based on the belief that values are the key to the health of a society, its institutions, and individuals. More than twenty years of research by VT has identified 125 values. The critical issue becomes which of the values are essential for effective leaders and successful organizations—and for healthy individuals and family life.

237

When individuals and institutions set their goals and objectives based on a healthy set of mutually supportive values, the impact on the individual and the results of the organization are positive—and the benefits are realized throughout society.

In order for institutions to nurture their agreed-upon values, they need ways to assess the values currently in operation within their organizations, an approach for identifying discrepancies in desired values, and a vehicle for organizational change and values alignment. Values Technology offers multilingual tools and support to meet these needs. We provide a vehicle for assisting organizational leaders in effective planning for organizational growth and development, and for helping individuals and families to grow productively.

Our products and services include:

- **Tools for values management.** A range of computerized instruments for use in organizational assessment and strategic planning, including corporate and individual values analysis and document analysis.
- **Multilingual values technology.** These instruments are available in French, German, Spanish, and English.
- **Continuing research database.** Confidential databases are updated each time an instrument is utilized—either individually or at the corporate level. Databases that include minimal personnel information allow values data to be broken out in different ways and compared with multiple factors. For example, such a database would allow a corporation to track the values of personnel who are identified as successful.

Applications of these products and services include:

- **Strategic planning.** Information gained from the database and tools can then be used in designing a strategic plan.
- **Values-based systems design.** Implementation of the strategic plan can occur through values-based systems design—including leadership practices, policy changes, and personnel evaluations.
- **Consulting for organizational transformation.** Methods are recommended for implementing changes that will bring about organizational transformation.

Values Technology's intention is to encourage and support positive values changes in business, education, and health-care systems. Productive areas for the use of values-based data have been in conflict resolution, negotiation, and resource management. Our vision for future application of the instrumentation extends beyond the realm of these institutions—to providing a tool for conflict management and peace negotiations on a global level.

Specific Product Descriptions

1. **Values Management Inventory.** The Hall-Tonna Inventory is a questionnaire that an individual fills out either on a computer screen or on a scoring sheet. The results are provided on a multi-page printout and interpreted with the help of a manual. This analysis gives individuals information on their values health, leadership style, ethical orientation, and the skills they need to improve and develop. It is designed for use by personnel departments in industry and education in developing leaders and selecting personnel. There are supplemental reports available that go into more depth and further clarify skills needed to maximize leadership potential.

2. **Group Insight.** This instrument is a composite analysis of individual values profiles at the group level. It provides information on discrepancies in leadership levels and overall values of the group, and is used primarily by group managers or external consultants for helping small groups set goals and objectives.

3. **Corporate Report.** This report is a composite profile based on individual data throughout the organization; it provides critical information on the organization's values profile. The corporate report identifies areas of potential leadership conflict and gives suggestions for management design in order to improve effectiveness and reduce stress in the corporation. It also spells out the skills needed to meet the leadership requirements called for by the values of the organization, and is particularly helpful for team management and development. The overall purpose of the Corporate Report is to provide top-level leadership with valuable information for strategic planning.

4. **Document analysis.** This program identifies the underlying core values in an organization's documents. By comparing these values with the values in the Corporate Report, a clear perspective is gained on the discrepancies between the organization's image as it is written down and as it is experienced and practiced. This instrument is a critical tool for strategic planning.

5. **Discipleship.** This religious version of the Values Management Inventory codes an individual's values with scripture and is designed for people who are concerned about religious or spiritual growth from a Christian perspective. There is also a religious version of the Corporate Report.

6. **Couples.** This instrument is a tool for family life development that can be offered in and through educational and religious organizations. It is directed at giving families and couples a common understanding of the values needed for more positive relationships.

Product Validation

Validation is an empirical set of methods that meet APA standards and that are used to determine whether instrumentation measures what it claims to measure. The validation of the Hall-Tonna Inventory, which underpins all the instrumentation we have been describing, was conducted between 1985 and 1988. The validation studies were directed by Dr. Oren Harari of the University of San Francisco. A decision was made early in the planning stage to be more thorough than any other known validity studies on currently used instrumentation, such as the MBTI or the MMPI. The following studies were conducted:

1. **Standardization.** During the initial stages, the definitions of the 125 values were standardized. This took approximately three months and involved a formally conducted group session of multidisciplined and multilingual personnel to come to a consensus definition of each of the values within the context of a particular stage and phase, and agreement about whether each value was a goal or a means value. Additionally, each of the questions on the Hall-Tonna Inventory was rephrased to coincide with the definition it was intended to reflect.

   Following this exercise, the values were scrambled by a computer, and each test sheet listed ten definitions and thirteen separate sentences, each representing a question from the questionnaire (the HT Inventory). These were then mailed to several hundred people, who were asked to correlate the two groups. The results showed a correlation of more than 90 percent.

2. **Reliability.** This step involved sending more than 100 questionnaires to a population of people who were not familiar with the values inventory or the theories related to it. They filled out the questionnaires and returned them in a sealed envelope.

   The same population was given another questionnaire to fill out three weeks later, observing the same rules. The results were then correlated, showing an average reliability of more than 90 percent.

3. **Comparison with Other Similar Tests**. A separate group of people who were not familiar with the instrumentation was asked to simultaneously fill out the HT Inventory and two of the following three instruments: the *Personality Orientation Inventory*, the *Myers Briggs Type Indicator*, or the *AVL Scale of Values*. Comparative statistical analyses were run, showing how the instrument measured similar factors on the one hand and giving additional and different information on the other hand. The results of this and other analyses can be found in the *Manual for the Hall-Tonna Inventory of Values* by Brian P. Hall, Oren Harari, Barbara D. Ledig, and Murray Tondow (New York: Paulist Press, 1986).

4. Norm Studies. The HT Inventory was administered to groups of more than 30 people from common norm groups. Examples include genetic engineers, firemen, marriage and family therapists, and women executives in the computer industry. These studies identified and contrasted each group's highest and lowest ten values priorities. The results showed that the instrument did differentiate and measure different values in various populations. Studies were carried out on more than thirty norm groups.

In addition to the studies listed above, the process of validation is ongoing. Since 1986, multilingual standardization of definitions has been carried out in Spain, Italy, and Germany. In one study a client population of 700 people from five different language groups took the inventory and received individual interviews to confirm the results.

Acceptance by Major Institutions

The instrumentation has been accepted and is being used nationally in Spain in public and private education through the Universities of Madrid and Deusto. In the United States, the instrumentation has been adapted by the National Education Association for use in 51 states and terroritories and for an international strategic planning project.

Appendix C

Applications: The Corporate Change Process

This appendix describes the process used to bring about corporate change using values measurement. In addition to a step-by-step description of the process itself, we will also provide two example applications, both composites of a number of consulting experiences: (1) a corporate report prepared for a high-tech company, and (2) a description of the change process as it was applied to a health-care institution in crisis.

Organizational Values Assessment

The basis for values information about a corporation is the individual and group Values Management Inventories and the values-based document analysis of key corporate documents. The inventory is a questionnaire that each individual fills out. The resulting data are compiled and used to prepare individual, group, and corporate reports. The document analysis involves a process where the values are derived through the scanning of key management documents. Personnel information that is tailored to the organization can be added to this core data.

The Values Management Process in an Organization

The steps by which this information is managed to initiate corporate change in an organization are outlined below. This outline is a guideline: although this is the general process, it often happens that in customizing the process to an organization, not all the components are used, or they may be carried out in a different order. The paragraphs in italics add clarifying information about the process.

Step 1. Getting Started

■ Establish top-level leadership participation.

This is a process of simply talking to the client. It is basically an educational experience, in which the client talks about the organization and is educated about why and how values motivate and drive organizations and people. It is critical to share information about what values are, how they are measured, the vitality curve and its implications for organizations today, and the methodology outlined here.

■ Gather information about the organization and its needs.

This is a listening process in which the facilitator gathers information about the organization. This includes reviewing and studying key organizational documents such as mission and philosophy statements and the most recent annual report.

■ Prepare program and assessment plans with the leadership.

This involves strategizing around the collection of documents for document analysis, and getting the executive team to fill out questionnaires.

■ Select personnel to be trained.

Many organizations want to have not only management personnel but also a similar number of other people internal to the organization trained to understand values methodology. For some companies this includes a human resources or executive development director.

■ Develop and initiate the communications protocol for the beginning of the program.

Once the leadership has decided to carry out a values management process in the organization, it is very important to strategize about how this is to be communicated to the membership. As we have seen early in this book, the concept of values is confusing to many people. Therefore this part of the program involves a first level of education and communication with the overall membership. More than anything, they need to know that the executive team is participating and is supportive of the idea.

Step 2.   Unearthing the Organization's Values

- Conduct mentoring seminars for leadership and trainees using the individual values inventory (VMI).

  This involves a consultant going over each executive's individual values profile privately, giving them the space to learn and understand the values at their own levels, and to build confidence in the process. This involves having the executives review their vision values and definitions, and reflecting on where they would like to be and what they would like to accomplish by one year from the review.

- Collect data on the larger population.

  This is simply deciding what overall population should be involved in filling out questionnaires, and taking action to see that this occurs.

- Conduct a document analysis.

  A team comes to the company and reviews its documents and selects the documents for analysis. They are most concerned with all documents that reflect the culture, that are public, and that reflect a sound balance of the organization's foundation (boilerplate documents), focus (leadership training processes) and vision (mission statements and annual reports) values. These are then analyzed using the computerized thesaurus programs.

- Conduct values seminars and in-depth interviews with select management populations.

  This involves conducting an educational process using individual profiles for a wider management population. This often includes additional interviews to collect concrete data on the day-to-day reality as experienced by the rank and file.

Step 3.   Understanding the Organization's Values Through Analysis of the Data

- Present the corporate report to the leadership of the organization. The data analysis in the report provides leadership with information in seven categories:

  I.   Cycle of Development

  A description of the focus of the group's energy, its interactive process, and its management and leadership styles.

  II.   Organizational Structures

  An exploration of the organizational structures that are most feasible for the group.

III. Group Interactions

A description of the interactive processes that are likely to take place between the subgroups that form the group.

IV. Specific Value Clusters

A description of the value clusters chosen by the group and how these affect group behavior.

V. Skills, Time, Vocation

A discussion of the skills that the group is choosing through their value choices, time orientation, and vocational direction.

VI. Summary of Document Analysis

VII. Overall Summary

The summary is based on observations made in Parts I to VI.

Step 4. Reflecting on the Organization's Culture

- Understand what the values say about the organization by examining: goal-related value clusters, foundation values, vision values that drive and motivate the organization (its special gifts), and the skills that are necessary to make its chosen values operational.

  This is initially accomplished in a one-day seminar with the leadership. The group reviews the corporate report and its explanation of their foundation, focus, and vision values. The values at this point are modified by the executive team in order to create a set of consensus values for the organization.

- Prepare the organization's culture statement about values, ethics, and the uniqueness of the organization's philosophy of management and education.

  The organization's values are converted into a management philosophy document by expanding the standard definitions to include day-to-day experiences and concerns of the company. This then becomes a basic educational document for each division of the company.

- Leadership reviews the draft document and provides feedback for final revisions so that they gain ownership.

  This is another event where the leadership gives a final review of the document and any final modifications, before they vote to accept it and agree as a group to support and abide by its implications.

Step 5.   *Sharing the Organization's Culture and Values Statement*

- Build trust by sharing the cultural statement in values seminars that are conducted at each level, with evaluation and feedback throughout the organization.

- Rewrite the final document with feedback material and disseminate the final document.

- Develop with leadership the strategy of an overall values management program. This involves deciding who should be trained, what services will be utilized, and what priorities will be used.

  This is a minimal description of how the values process begins to continue through each level of the organization. The original documents remain the same but are modified and expressed a little differently in different divisions that have special needs; for example, Management Information Systems, the Human Resources Department, or Marketing may have somewhat customized documents.

Step 6.   *Implementation of a Values Management Program*

This step involves action in six areas:

- Values-based strategic planning
- Values-based human resource management
- Values-based policy and evaluation development
- Leadership consultation and decision management
- Values-based group development and conflict management
- Consultation on curriculum planning and development

Application Example 1: A Corporate Report

A substantial part of the methodology just outlined relies on data collection and analysis. This results in a corporate report, which is usually based on the executive management structure of an organization. An example of a corporate report follows.

Note that the process might also involve a systemic report, which would look at the whole system, comparing divisions, international units, and so on. An example of this level of report would be too extensive for our purposes here.

The corporate report example given here is a composite of a number of corporate consulting experiences. We'll call the hypothetical client the Computer Engineering Corporation.

About 80 percent of a corporate report is based on the analysis of a group report. The group report was the result, in this case, of the composite data from 25 individual reports, each filled out by a management executive. A document analysis report is included to confirm the values data collected on the management team. The paragraphs in italics are clarifying comments for the reader.

Corporate Report
The Computer Engineering Corporation

TABLE OF CONTENTS

Part I. Cycle of Development

Primary Group Leadership Style

About 79% of the group are at Cycle 4, the intrapersonal cycle. Another 12% are at Cycle 3, the institutional cycle, and 8% are at Cycle 5, the collaborative cycle. *This is a breakdown of the cycles from the group report. These cycles were covered in depth in Chapter 8.*

The orientation at this cycle is laissez-faire. The leadership style is that of the Enabler. The main characteristic of this cycle is the feeling experienced by leadership of being caught between the desire to enable the interpersonal processing of the group and supporting group members in their needs and personal aspirations and having to deal with strong institutional constraints.

This results in reluctance to take precise action. Enablers are good community builders but may have difficulty delegating responsibility. When there is a lack of interpersonal and group dynamic skills, the tendency may be to act autocratically when under pressure.

Of the 79% who are at Cycle 4, 42% are moving from the institutional cycle, a cycle at which there is resistance to change. These members will prefer to follow the rules and established ways of doing things. They are most comfortable with an autocratic leadership and followership style. *The computer program takes each of the seven cycles and further divides them into three components indicating whether a percentage of the group is in the middle of the cycle, or at the lower end, or at the higher end, anticipating the next cycle. This gives the report a range of seven cycles, presented as 21 possible steps.*

Of the 79% at the intrapersonal cycle, about 12% are moving to the communal/collaborative cycle, Cycle 5. At the communal/collaborative cycle, people tend to be highly independent and their orientation is toward change and development. They are most comfortable with a democratic leadership and followership style. However, they have skills to learn in the area of system management, small group facilitation, conflict management, and so on.

Other Leadership Styles

The 12% of the group who are at Cycle 3, the institutional cycle, are moving toward the intrapersonal cycle. While there will be some differences between these members, in general they will prefer to follow the rules and established ways of doing things. They will be most comfortable with an autocratic leadership and followership style.

The 8% of the group who are at the communal/collaborative cycle are the strongest leadership group. Their orientation will be to a participative form of management where collaboration rather than dependence or independence is stressed.

Implications

One implication is that 54% of the group will prefer to maintain the status quo. *This refers to the 42% who are in the lower end of Cycle 4 plus the 12% who are at Cycle 3, which has a standard institutional orientation. In a study done by Alfred Darmanin (1985), it was found that most people function one cycle below their expectation of themselves. Therefore, the lower percentage in a given cycle is added to the previous cycle to determine the system's resistance factor.*

A second implication is that the Enablers who are not moving to or from a cycle (25%) may fluctuate between the two groups. If this group is to work together effectively, they need skills in:

- system management, creating new structures

- goal-setting and climate development

- personal stress management

- diagnosing and confronting behavior that interferes with the healthy functioning of the group

- group dynamics, including the ability to manage conflict within a group in order to move it into creative goal-setting

- brainstorming techniques

Part II.   Organizational Structures

The majority of people in the group (79%) are in the intrapersonal cycle. The leadership style at this cycle is that of Enabler.

The range of leadership styles in the group indicates that some people in the group are probably very dependent on leadership (up to 54%), while others may be very independent. Strong lines of authority are needed to prevent open conflict and polarity from occurring.

If the group is one that works together in cooperative ventures and polarity is problematic, then people in leadership may find it helpful to make most of their decisions cooperatively, getting each person's opinion about a particular subject individually and making a decision based on the information obtained from each member. The decision would then be shared with the group as a whole. Decisions affecting only one person should be discussed and shared with the person individually and confidentially.

The leadership level required for this group is charismatic leadership backed by strong participative structures. Eight percent of the people in the group are at this stage of development, but there is an additional 15% that have the potential of operating this way if they have the opportunity for training and support. *This refers to the 15% who are at the highest end of the Cycle 4 scale.*

Since there is a gap between the world view of some people in the group, there is some potential for differences of opinion and conflict. The majority of the group (79%) has a strong interpersonal orientation, and will want decisions to be made through consensus. This will be very draining for leadership, because it requires considerable processing between members who hold very different world views. Interpersonal, group dynamics, and decision-making skills and processes are critical if leadership is to function effectively and avoid burnout.

The majority of members need a lot of personal affirmation and guidance in their life direction. This is true for 79% of the group. There are 23%—the 15% at the upper end of Cycle 4 and the 8% in Cycle 5—who will probably be more self-initiating and need some support in skill building, possibly from a source external to the group who can mentor them. It is important for leadership to be able to assess the skills of group members objectively, to take charge and give direction to the group. It is important for them not to confuse equality of people with equality of skills.

This group reflects a shift from hierarchy that is based on power and designated function to a more collaborative model. In such a situation, leadership is always vulnerable to gossip and to power plays. It is important for those who are in leadership positions to have the skills to remain objective, evaluate clearly, and make decisions based on their integrity and knowledge of the group and its needs.

Part III.   Group Interactions

The Enablers in the group (64%) may experience those in the institutional cycle (12%) as being too rigid and concerned with institutional laws and guidelines. The Enablers are more concerned with personal expression and relationships although most of them may be just as resistant to change as the first group. They will avoid change more indirectly and may talk about it and discuss it, but will have difficulty reaching clarity about what it should be and in actually bringing it about. They will need the guidance of leadership. Discussions regarding future direction can be a point of disagreement between these two groups.

The Enablers moving to communal/collaborative (15%) will be those most likely to be interested in change, but they will need skills they may not yet have in order to practically facilitate this. It will be important for them to put certain structures into place if they, as well as the rest of the group, are to move into the future in a positive and creative way.

The institutional cycle people (25%) will probably experience the majority of the group as being excessively independent. They will also be at odds or in disagreement with the 23% who are moving to or who are in Cycle 5. The Enablers may seem to thrive on confusion, or at least on inaction.

Implications

Communication will probably be a problem in this group because it is composed of two disparate world views. The institutional people and those moving toward the communal/collaborative style will not understand one another. Some of the more skilled people in the group can possibly bridge this gap but will probably also find communication between these world views difficult.

Cycle 4 members will want to process and discuss issues and group interactions at length. Cycle 3 members will tend to be very task-oriented and will become impatient with anything that holds up the task at hand. Decision-making between the Enablers and the institutional people will be difficult. Skills in clear, empathic communication and in managing conflict creatively will be helpful. The best solution may be to divide the group into two for decision-making processes.

Skills that are needed to improve group interaction are as follows:

Interpersonal Skills

- The ability to separate reason from emotion in individual interactions
- The ability to accurately identify other people's emotions and to be able to report them

- The ability to express anger and negative emotions creatively in a way that enhances cooperation rather than alienating individuals
- The ability to recognize the need for emotional as well as cognitive communication
- The ability to affirm others regularly and to give and receive emotional support *(The discussion of skills was in Chapter 6.)*

Group Dynamic Skills

- The ability to clarify and understand the difference between personal and group issues
- The ability to use interpersonal and group techniques required for the management of group conflict in a group setting
- The ability to enable a group to brainstorm and clarify complex information for the purpose of setting short- and long-term goals and objectives

Part IV.   Specific Value Clusters

The Focus Values

The highest priority values for this group are:

G1. Competence/ Confidence	G2. Service/Vocation	G3. Self-Actualization
M1. Management	M2. Productivity	

The values suggest that the group relates its goals of personal wholeness to competence and confidence to personal growth and wholeness through service. As the definitions that follow suggest, competence and work are for this group the foundation for personal development and growth.

Competence/Confidence: Realistic and objective confidence that one has the skill to achieve in the world of work and to feel that those skills are a positive contribution.

Service/Vocation: The ability to be motivated to use personally unique gifts and skills to contribute to society through one's occupation, business, profession, or calling.

Self-Actualization: The inner drive toward experiencing and expressing the totality of one's being through spiritual, psy-

chological, physical, and mental exercises that enhance the
development of one's maximum potential.

The means to do this are through the skills associated with the values of management and productivity, which are defined as follows:

Management: The control and direction of personnel in a business or institution for the purpose of optimal productivity and efficiency.

Productivity: The energy that results from generating and completing tasks and activities and achieving externally established goals and expectations.

These values suggest that leadership might confuse what a person does with who they are. Secondly, it might suggest that emotional affirmation, as well as affirmation for productivity, is not taken seriously enough in the group. Again, this raises the question of whether the members of the group have sufficient interpersonal skills. However, without emotional support systems this might not be possible.

Productivity probably reflects an emphasis on work as a means to approval and affirmation. It needs to be upgraded to a Phase III value such as Creativity or Mission/Objectives.

Foundation Values

The foundation values for this group are:

G1. Family/Belonging	**G2.** Self-Worth
M1. Support/Peer	

These values are the foundation of what everyone in the group needs in order to function at their best. This is the bottom line need of the group. The goal values are defined as follows:

Family/Belonging: The people to whom one feels primary bonds of relationship and acceptance; attachment to the place where one's parents live.

Self-Worth: The knowledge that when those one respects and esteems really know him/her, they will affirm that he/she is worthy of that respect.

For people in this group, time with their families and personal affirmation of who they are and what they do are critical. The means to do this reaffirms this point of view, as the value definition illustrates:

Support/Peer: The ability to have people who are one's equals and who sustain one in both joyful and difficult times.

This value cluster indicates that personal self-worth can be reinforced through being esteemed and respected by others and through a positive experience of family. Note that Family/Belonging has become a foundation value, indicating that its appropriate function is foundational rather than a primary focus of energy within the workings of the system. The organizational expression of family is camaraderie, and this is not possible when there is not an experience of mutual respect between members of the organization. Self-Worth is a natural precursor to Competence/Confidence, the first goal in the focus area above.

The foundational values must be in place if group members are to function at their best. The following questions are raised:

- Do members experience affirmation and respect in the workplace?

- Are members rewarded for work well done?

Communication skills that enhance cooperation and the ability to give positive feedback and to deal creatively with differences of opinion will help.

Vision Values

The vision values for this group are:

G1. Construction/New Order	G2. Faith/Risk/Vision
M1. Growth/Expansion	

The vision goal values are defined as follows:

Construction/New Order: The ability to develop and initiate a new institution for the purpose of creatively enhancing society. This assumes technological, interpersonal, and management skills.

Faith/Risk/Vision: Behavioral commitment to values that are considered life-giving even at risk to one's livelihood or life.

This is a promising fit when put together with the skills-related means value:

Growth/Expansion: The ability to enable an organization to develop and grow creatively. This assumes skills in management design and organizational development at a corporate level.

This vision is very healthy and productive for the group. It indicates that the group is motivated toward strategic planning as expressed through Growth/Expansion. The ability to risk appears to be present. The value of Construction/New Order indicates the need for a new management and organizational structure. The vision values indicate that this, in turn, can lead to the end goal of Faith/Risk/Vision, which is the highest level of commitment to one's values. In this group, that probably means providing a vision for the corporation based on assessment, planning, and leadership formation or development.

Summary of Value Clusters

There is strong congruency between the focus, foundation, and vision value clusters. In tracking the values through these areas we see that each member's Self-Worth, reinforced through mutual esteem and respect and leading to an experience of camaraderie in the system, will lead to professional Competence/Confidence. This in turn will enable the integrative process of personal actualization and wholeness, enhanced by members learning to trust one another and to share deeply, with the ultimate goal of Growth/Expansion becoming possible through the strategic planning of the organization.

Part V. Skills and Time

The value choices indicate a high level of interpersonal skills (47%), adequate system skills (30%), and instrumental skills at 41%. Imaginal skills are high (21%). The combination of Work and Maintenance is 79% and Play and Play-Freesence 68%.

The meanings of these terms are covered in Chapters 6 and 8. The percentages listed here are percentages of themselves. That is, when we say the imaginal skills are 21%, this means that of all the possible values whose primary skills are imaginal, this group chose 21% of them. In Chapter 6 we noted that a person or group needs an minimum of 9% of these to have a meaningful and creative life. Fourteen percent is a sound average; therefore 21% is high. These percentages are not indicative of the group's behavior but rather of their desired behavior.

Implications

When the level of interpersonal skills is this high and the instrumental skills are high (they are normally not over 16%) and the system skills are this low, it suggests that the group may have low interpersonal skills but a lot of creativity. The high level of imaginal skills suggests that the group has excellent leadership potential and potential for being a powerful planning group as long as the interpersonal and group dynamic skills of the membership are well developed.

Part VI: Document Analysis

An initial analysis of those documents titled Annual Report, Mission Statement, and Long- and Short-Term Objectives and Goals was done. To be helpful, a full document analysis would need to be done to determine the values in the corporate culture. However, this limited document analysis does converge with the above information in three ways:

- The analysis consistently shows a move from a hierarchical form of management to a participative form based on a human and information capital approach to organizational development.
- The leadership style is that of Enabler, or people caught between the demands of the system and the need to move things forward with an equal concern for the personnel involved.
- The overall analysis shows that the system comes from an institutional form of management, illustrating that the system is reinforcing traditional ways of doing things.

The foundation values in the documents were the same as those listed in the group analysis given earlier. The focus and vision values were the same, but had several additions that would enhance the group's functioning. These are here for the group to consider:

Focus Cluster in the Documents

G1. Competence/ Confidence	**G2.** Service/Vocation	**G3.** Self-Actualization
M1. Management Productivity Efficiency/Planning Economics/Success	**M2.** Sharing/Listening/ Trust Empathy Congruence	

Vision Cluster in the Documents

G1. Construction/New Order	**G2.** Faith/Risk/Vision
M1. Growth/Expansion Community/Supportive Mission/Objectives Collaboration	

Clearly, the documents add important information in that all the value additions are means- or skill-related values. The fact of their presence would end up as a recommendation in the summary.

Part VII.   Summary

This group's configuration makes healthy group functioning difficult, especially in the areas of consensus decision making and general management. The group most likely experiences considerable frustration at its inability to move forward with its vision smoothly and productively. It is possible that they work very hard and yet don't see the rewards of their efforts.

Leadership of this group will tend to be draining. It is important for leadership to have adequate skills to move the group through its tendency to process and discuss, to concrete and creative planning and decision making. The imaginal skills level and wide range of value mixes indicates that the group probably does have the skills to move ahead if the appropriate support structures and training are provided.

Skills that are needed by the leadership to improve group interaction are not present in the group's values but are very present in the additional values evident from the document analysis. The additional values from the documents are from Cycle 3 and 5. It is the Cycle 5 values and their skills that need to be learned and emphasized by the leadership.

Cycle 3	**Cycle 5**
Productivity	Sharing/Listening/Trust
Efficiency/Planning	Mission/Objectives
Economics/Success	Collaboration
	Empathy
	Congruence

Skill Recommendation from the Values:

Interpersonal Skills

- The ability to separate reason from emotions in individual interactions.

- The ability to identify accurately other people's emotions and be able to report them.

- The ability to express anger and negative emotions creatively in order to enhance cooperation rather than alienation between individuals.

- The ability to recognize the need for emotional as well as cognitive communication.

- The ability to affirm others regularly and to give and receive emotional support.

Group Dynamic Skills

- The ability to clarify and understand the difference between personal and group issues.
- The ability to use the interpersonal and group techniques required for the management of group conflict in a group setting.
- The ability to enable a group to brainstorm and clarify complex information for the purpose of setting short- and long-term goals and objectives.
- The ability to assess organizational climate, simplify complex information, and do strategic planning based on climate, values, and skills analysis relative to the quality of human interaction in the leadership group.

What the Organization Can Do to Enable Value Integration

- Set organizational norms and policies to enhance the behavioral experience of the values that have been identified.
- Develop the appropriate interpersonal and group dynamic skills in the leadership of the group.
- Ensure that the appropriate support structures are in place as the group moves forward in the planning process.

Application Example 2: A Sponsored Health-Care System

The second case is an example of what can occur in a values-based consultation. As with the first example, this is a composite case using clients we have worked with over a period of years, and does not reference any one client system.

A sponsored health-care system is a network of health-care facilities supported and managed by a central executive team office with centralized financial and computer services. Such a venture is necessary for the survival of health care today. The example we are using here is a Catholic health-care system. Many religious congregations founded hospitals in the United States a hundred years ago as an expression of their mission to care for the poor and disadvantaged. We are using this example because of its complex value implications, implications that are common to most organizations and are therefore of concern to the organizational specialist.

Background Information

In this composite example, we acted as consultants to a health-care system consisting of 15 general hospitals on the eastern seaboard of the United States. The sponsoring, or founding, institution is a religious community of women that began running hospitals in 1880. At their peak, their congregation was composed of 1500 sisters. At present they number 953, and the average age is over 64 years. They have had no new members for five years.

Up until 1950, all the hospitals were run by their own sisters at the administrative and direct-care level. Now the hospitals are largely run by professional lay administrators and staff. The sisters are still working in nursing and pastoral care, but comprise less than 10 percent of the staffing. They continue to have strong board representation at the local level.

Stated Concern and Reason for the Consultation

The consultation was requested by the chief executive officer of the health-care system after a board meeting at which the provincial—the sister who had the most authority in the sponsoring congregation— voiced considerable concern. She raised the question of how their sponsorship could work more satisfactorily, since it was becoming increasingly evident to many that the values (what the sisters call charism or gift) of the sponsoring body were not being carried over operationally into the health-care system in a manner that was understood either by the public or the sisters. This had been felt or expressed in a number of ways:

- Declining support on the part of the sisters both in board presence and representation.
- Increased gossip and criticism of local CEOs by the sisters.
- Declining public support and criticism that the system does not have its priorities "straight"—that it is more concerned with business ethics and survival than it is with the poor and disadvantaged as it once was.
- Severe criticism of several CEOs and system executives whom the sisters say do not represent their values anymore; they were calling for their resignation.
- Declining sense of worth and trust among the CEOs themselves.
- Increased competition among facilities in the system rather than increased cooperation.

Assumptions Leading to the Consultation

Thirty years ago when religious systems were very autocratic, values for the group were centralized in one person who would make most of the decisions. In recent years, with the tendency to shared and delegated team leadership, the values have become more a function of the group rather than of one person. Consequently, when a group does not have minimal operational norms, behaviors, and policies that are held in common and that flow from a common value center (or faith center in religious terminology) that they are all aware of, then each person will naturally function out of his or her own individual value center. The consequence is the drifting away from the center.

The same phenomenon occurs in a health-care system such as the one we are describing, but even more dramatically. When the central value core of the sponsoring institution and the health-care system are not minimally congruent and clearly understood, then each part of the system will gravitate toward its own value orientation through its policies and local operational behavioral norms.

Depending on a number of stress factors, the symptoms that generally flow from a lack of clarity about the shared core value clusters are:

- Growing independence, often perceived as a lack of cooperation.
- Lack of clarity about the system's goals. Since goals flow from our value core, it follows that this will be a natural outcome.
- If this becomes a serious problem, then there will be personnel dissatisfaction and a loss of meaning and support, as well as low-quality service and an increase in internal conflict.

Our work with this client was based on a number of assumptions:

1. Society, the church, and health-care systems are at the epicenter of transition. This transition implies movement from a familiar to an unfamiliar place. But more that anything, this transition implies that major value shifts are taking place in societal and institutional life.

2. When a system is unaware of what its central value core is, the values naturally shift in the transition period, often causing polarity and conflict. Further, since the pressures and life styles of two systems (the religious congregation and the health-care system) are different, the rate of value change is also different, causing even more discrepancies. Such a process is normal but is happening more rapidly at this point in history due to the advent of technology and information systems.

3. It is the core values of a system reflected through its day-to-day operational behavior and policies that reflect its image to the public.

4. It is the core values of a system reflected through its day-to-day operational behavior and policies that enable the organization to move forward and bring its vision to fruition more efficiently.

5. Historical as well as recent organizational literature has confirmed the fact that it is sound management documents in a system that carry its values into the future in a consistent manner. In fact, they embody the corporate expression of the culture of a given institution. However, when the values are not clearly known and understood, changes in society, which always tend to change the nature of institutions, will change the internal operating values of the system. Until recently, this was a larger problem because we did not have the technological means by which to identify core values inherent in our management documents.

6. A final assumption is that in complex value systems it is important to integrate the values of each part of the system into the representative parts of the whole in order to ensure congruency and cooperation throughout the system.

Strategies from the Assumptions

Strategy 1: A value analysis of all relevant documents using the document analysis program. In this case, it would include analysis of documents in both the religious congregation and health-care system.

Strategy 2: Discovering the core values in the documents and enabling the executives of the system to decide what that core ought to be and whether anything needs to be added or subtracted.

Strategy 3: Looking at the values in the central administrative groups to enable them to see more clearly where they are from a values perspective. This would be a team development process, not an evaluative procedure.

Strategy 4: Developing behavioral norms and translating them into operational management behavior through the establishment of new policies, leadership formation programs at different levels (such as CEOs and board members), and establishing additional personnel policies and procedures for hiring and evaluation.

Processes to Enable the Strategies

Process 1: An initial one-day in-house seminar with the system executives, a number of CEOs from the health-care system, and several board representatives. The seminar would explore values-based management theory and some of the assumptions listed above. This would be followed by the development of an agreement to complete the strategies with costs and time-lines defined.

Process 2: A four-day, in-house, focused seminar for health-care system executives, based on the individual and group values reports.

The Goals of the Seminar:

- Enhanced value awareness at the team and system level.

- Enhanced awareness of the group's needs and values-based management design for the purpose of increasing cooperation within the team. This would also be a pilot for future in-house leadership formation programs at different levels in the system.

The Contents of the Seminar:

- Values and management theory including an understanding of document analysis and its relationship to societal and institutional change and management.

- Use of the Insight Values Inventory (now the Values Management Inventory) to enable members of the team to understand and develop their vision of where they would like to be in the health-care system in one year.

- Use of the Corporate Report to examine the team's central value core and group needs. The team members can also compare their personal values to those of the group at this time.

Process 3: Process 3 has two parts:

- Value analysis of the primary documents of the religious congregation. Three months would be allowed for this process. Two days of consultation would be held with two or three members of the congregation who would advise about value cluster complexes particular to their system.
- Value analysis of representative documents from the health-care system. This would include an initial one-day consultation to decide on the documents to be analyzed and an additional two-day consultation with two or three executives of the health-care system to check value cluster complexes particular to their system.

Process 4: A brief would now be prepared to explain the results of the analysis of both sets of documents with suggestions for new documents, rewrites, and strategic management processes arising from the document analysis.

Process 5: A second four-day in-house workshop for the same executives would encompass the following:

- Review of the analysis results of the two sets of documents analyzed.
- Examination of the core values in both sets of documents in order to derive through group consensus a new or modified value center for the health-care system that minimally integrates the values of the religious congregation.
- Initiation of a process in which core values are defined out of the experience of the representatives of the health-care system in order to compare them with the executive values elicited in Process 2.
- Engagement in a process of developing behavioral norms for the executive group from the core-defined values. This could also serve as an example in a wider leadership formation process.

Process 6: Formation of a Leadership Formation Team to work and examine in more detail the processes and data collected so far. Initiating the design of a systemwide leadership formation process and processes for executive development and evaluation.

Process 7: Formation of a Strategic Planning Team to work in examining in more detail the data so far collected. Initiation of a design for ways of collecting additional quality information for the development of a planning and decision-making database.

Process 8: Beginning process consultation relative to:

- Development of educational materials and processes
- Development of hiring and evaluation procedures based on the core values
- Development of quality information databases and methods for consulting to that information and updating the databases

The methodology of process is subject to individual institutional needs, resources, and time-lines.

Bibliography

Albizuri, Itziar, Micaela Portilla, Juan Calzon Alvarez, Luis Torralba, Mercedes Izaguirre, and Javier Lopez. *Los Valores En La Ley Organica de Ordenacion General del Sistema Educativo: Un Analisis de Documentos a Traves de La Metodologia de Hall-Tonna.* Bilbao, Spain: I.C.E., Universida De Deausto, 1993.

Allen, M. J., and W. M. Yen. *Introduction to Measurement Theory.* Monterey, Calif.: Brooks/Cole, 1979.

American Psychological Association. *Standards for Educational and Psychological Tests.* Washington, D.C.: American Psychological Association, 1974.

Anastasi, A. *Psychological Testing.* 4th ed. New York: Macmillan, 1976.

Argyris, Chris. *Integrating the Individual and the Organization.* New York: Transaction Publications, 1990.

_____. *Overcoming Organizational Defenses.* Boston: Allyn and Bacon, 1990.

Aristotle. *The Nicomachean Ethics, Book II.* Great Books of the Western World. New York: Encyclopaedia Britannica, 1952.

Aschenbrenner, George A. "Consciousness Examined." *Review for Religious,* 1972, 31, 14.

Ashley, Benedict M., and Kevin D. O'Rourke. *Health Care Ethics: A Theological Analysis.* St. Louis: Catholic Health Association, 1982.

Assigioli, R. *Psychosynthesis.* New York: Viking Press, 1971.

Bandler, Richard, and John Grinder. *Frogs into Princes: Neuro Linguistic Programming.* Moab, Utah: Real People Press, 1979.

_____. *The Structure of Magic: A Book About Language and Therapy.* Palo Alto, Calif: Science & Behavior Books, 1975.

Bardwick, Judith M. *Psychology of Women.* New York: Harper & Row, 1971.

Bateson, Gregory. *Steps to an Ecology of Mind.* New York: Ballantine Books, 1972.

Bellah, Robert N., Richard Madsen, William Sullivan, Ann Swidler, and Steven Tipton. *The Good Society.* New York: Knopf, 1991.

Bennis, W. G. *Organizational Development: Its Nature, Origins, and Prospects.* Reading, Mass: Addison-Wesley, 1969.

Bennis, W. G., and P. E. Slater. *The Temporary Society.* New York: Harper and Row, 1968.

Bentov, Itzhak. *Stalking the Wild Pendulum: On the Mechanics of Consciousness.* New York: E. P. Dutton, 1977.

Blake, Robert F., and Jane Mouton. *Consultation: A Comprehensive Approach to Organizational Development.* Reading, Mass.: Addison-Wesley, 1983.

Blekinsopp, Joseph. *The Men Who Spoke Out.* London: Dalton, 1969.

Boison, Anton T. *The Exploration of the Inner World: A Study of Mental Disorder and Religious Experience.* Philadelphia: University of Pennsylvania Press, 1936.

Bolen, Jean S., M.D. *Goddesses in Everywoman: A New Psychology of Women.* San Francisco: Harper & Row, 1984.

Bradford, Leland P. *Group Development.* La Jolla, Calif.: University Associates, 1978.

Bronowski, J. *The Ascent of Man.* Boston: Little, Brown, 1973.

Brownlie, Ian (ed.). *Basic Documents on Human Rights.* Oxford: Clarendon Press, 1981.

Brueggemann, Walter A. *In Man We Trust: The Neglected Side of Biblical Faith.* Atlanta: John Knox, 1972.

Buckley, Michael. "Rules for Discernment of Spirits." *The Way,* 1973, 20.

_____. *The Search for Authenticity.* New York: Holt, Rinehart & Winston, 1965.

Bugental, James F. T. *The Search for Existential Identity.* San Francisco: Jossey-Bass, 1976.

Bullock, Alan. *Hitler: A Study in Tyranny.* New York: Harper & Row, 1971.

Burke, James. *Connections.* Boston: Little, Brown, 1978.

_____. *The Day the Universe Changed.* Boston: Little Brown, 1985.

Burke, W. Warner, and Leonard D. Goodstein (eds.). *Trends and Issues in OD: Current Theory and Practice.* San Diego, Calif.: University Associates, 1980.

Burns, James M. *Leadership.* New York: Harper Colon, 1978.

Cada, Lawrence, et al. *Shaping the Coming Age of Religious Life.* New York: Seabury Press, 1979.

Campbell, D. T., and D. W. Fiske. "Convergent and Discriminant Validation by the Multitrait-Multimethod Matrix." *Psychological Bulletin,* 1959, 56, 81–105.

Campbell, Joseph (ed.). *The Portable Jung.* New York: Penguin Books, 1971.

Cantin, Eileen. *Mounier: A Personalist View of History.* New York: Paulist Press, 1974

Caplan, G., and M. Killilea (eds.). *Support Systems and Mutual Help.* New York: Grune & Stratton, 1972.

Caplan, Ruth B., et al. *Helping the Helpers to Help: Mental Health Consultation to Aid Clergymen in Pastoral Work*. New York: Seabury Press, 1972.

Capra, Fritjof. *The Turning Point*. New York: Bantam Books, 1982.

Carkhuff, Robert R. *Empowering the Creative Leader in the Age of the New Capitalism*. Amherst, Mass.: Human Resource Development Press, 1989.

_____. *Human Processing and Human Productivity*. Amherst, Mass.: Human Resource Development Press, 1986.

Carmody, D. L., and J. T. Carmody. *Exploring American Religion*. Mountain View, Calif.: Mayfield, 1990.

Carretto, Carlo. *Letters from the Desert*. Maryknoll, N.Y.: Orbis Books, 1972.

Cassirer, Ernst. *The Philosophy of Symbolic Forms. Vol. 1, Language*. Translated by Ralph Manheim. New Haven, Conn.: Yale University Press, 1965.

Chodorow, Nancy. "Family Structure and Feminine Personality." In *Woman, Culture, and Society*, edited by M. Z. Rosaldo and L. Lamphere. Stanford, Calif.: Stanford University Press, 1974.

_____. *The Reproduction of Mothering*. Berkeley: University of California Press, 1978.

Claremont de Castillejo, Irene. *Knowing Woman*. New York: Harper & Row, 1973.

Clark, Kenneth. *Civilization*. New York: Harper & Row, 1969.

Clements, R. E. *Prophecy and Covenant*. Naperville, Ill.: Allenson, 1965.

Clinebell, Howard. *Contemporary Growth Therapies*. Nashville, Tenn.: Abingdon, 1981.

Corey, Gerald, Marianne S. Corey, and Patrick Callanan. *Issues and Ethics in the Helping Professions*. Monterey, Calif.: Brooks/Cole, 1984.

Covey, Stephen R.: *The Seven Habits of Highly Effective People*. New York: Simon and Schuster, 1990.

Cox, Sue. Female Psychology: *The Emerging Self*. Chicago: Science Research Associates, 1976.

Crenshaw, James L. (ed.). *Studies in Ancient Israelite Wisdom*. New York: Ktav, 1976.

Cronbach, L. J. "Coefficient Alpha and the Internal Structure of Tests." *Psychometrika*, 1951, 16, 297–334.

_____. *Essentials of Psychological Testing*. 3rd ed. New York: Harper & Row, 1970.

_____. "Validity on Parole: How Can We Go Straight?" *New Directions for Testing and Measurement*, 1980, 5, 99–108.

Cronbach, L. J., and P. E. Meehl. "Construct Validity in Psychological Tests." *Psychological Bulletin*, 1955, 52, 281–302.

Darmanin, Alfred. *The Skilled Leader*. Malta, Spain: The Media Centre, 1985.

Davies, Paul. *God and the New Physics.* New York: Simon & Schuster, 1983.

de Chardin, Pierre Teilhard. *Le Milieu Divin: An Essay on the Interior Life.* New York: Harper & Brothers, 1960.

de Guibert, Joseph. *Theology of the Spiritual Life.* New York: Sheed and Ward, 1954.

de Laszlo, Violet S. (ed.). *Psyche and Symbol: A Selection from the Writings of C. G. Jung.* Garden City, N.Y.: Doubleday, 1958.

DePree, Max. *Leadership Jazz.* New York: Dell, 1993.

de Saint-Exupery, Antoine. *The Wisdom of the Sands.* New York: Harcourt, Brace, 1950.

Deal, Terrence E., and Allan A. Kennedy. *Corporate Cultures: The Rites and Rituals of Corporate Life.* Reading, Mass.: Addison-Wesley, 1982.

Dinnerstein, Dorothy. *The Mermaid and the Minotaur: Sexual Arrangements and Human Malaise.* New York: Harper & Row, 1977.

Dix, Dom Gregory. *The Shape of the Liturgy.* London: Dacre Press, 1945.

Douglas, Ann. *The Feminization of American Culture.* New York: Avon Books, 1977.

Drucker, P. F. *The Age of Discontinuity: Guidelines to our Changing Society.* New York: Harper, 1969.

Dunnette, M. D., and W. C. Borman. "Personnel Selection and Classification Systems." *Annual Review of Psychology,* 1979, 30, 477–525.

Dyer, William G. *Contemporary Issues in Management and Organization Development.* Reading, Mass.: Addison-Wesley, 1983.

Edward, Joyce, and Turrini Ruskin. *Separation-Individuation: Theory and Application.* New York: Gardner Press, 1981.

Elgin, Duane. *Voluntary Simplicity: An Ecological Lifestyle That Promotes Personal and Social Renewal.* New York: Bantam Books, 1982.

Erikson, Erik H. (ed.). *Adulthood.* New York: W. W. Norton, 1978.

Erikson, Erik H. *Childhood and Society.* New York: W. W. Norton, 1963.

_____. *Gandhi's Truth.* New York: W. W. Norton, 1969.

_____. *Identity and the Life Cycle.* New York: W. W. Norton, 1980.

_____. *Identity: Youth and Crisis.* New York: W. W. Norton, 1968.

Fabry, Joseph B. *The Pursuit of Meaning: Logotherapy Applied to Life.* Boston: Beacon Press, 1968.

Fiedler, F. E. *A Theory of Leadership Effectiveness.* New York: McGraw-Hill, 1967.

First International Conference on Moral and Religious Development. *Toward Moral and Religious Maturity.* Morristown, N.J.: Silver Burdett, 1980.

Fleming, David L. *A Contemporary Reading of the Spiritual Exercises.* St. Louis: Institute of Jesuit Sources, 1976.

Fowler, James W. *Stages of Faith*. San Francisco: Harper & Row, 1981.

Frankl, Viktor E. *The Doctors and the Soul*. New York: Vintage Books, 1965.

_____. *Man's Search for Meaning*. New York: Simon & Schuster, 1959.

_____. *Psychotherapy and Existentialism*. New York: Simon & Schuster, 1967.

Freire, Paulo. *Pedagogy in Process*. New York: Seabury Press, 1978.

_____. *Pedagogy of the Oppressed*. New York: Herder & Herder, 1972.

French, Wendell L., and Cecil H. Bell, Jr. *Organizational Development*. Englewood Cliffs, N.J.: Prentice-Hall, 1978.

Friars Minor of the Franciscan Province of Saint Barbara (trans.). *Early Franciscan Classics*. Paterson, New Jersey: Saint Anthony Guild Press, 1962.

Friday, Nancy. *My Mother/My Self*. New York: Dell Books, 1978.

Friedman, H. S. "On Shutting One's Eyes to Face Validity." *Pychological Bulletin*, 1983, 94, 185–187.

Fromm, Erich. *The Anatomy of Human Destructiveness*. New York: Holt, Rinehart & Winston, 1973.

_____. *Escape from Freedom*. New York: Avon Books, 1941.

_____. *The Heart of Man*. New York: Perennial Library, 1964.

Gardner, Howard. *Frames of Mind: The Theory of Multiple Intelligences*. New York: Harper Basic Books, 1985.

_____. *The Unschooled Mind: How Children Think and How Schools Should Teach*. New York: Harper Basic Books, 1991.

Gerbault, Alain. *Firecrest: Round the World*. New York: David McKay, 1981.

Gerstein, Martin, and Pappen-Daniel. *Understanding Adulthood*. Fullerton, Calif.: California Personnel and Guidance Association, 1981.

Ghiselli, E. E. *Theory of Psychological Measurement*. New York: McGraw-Hill, 1964.

Gilligan, Carol. *In a Different Voice*. Cambridge, Mass.: Harvard University Press, 1982.

Gould, Roger L. *Transformations: Growth and Change in Adult Life*. New York: Simon & Schuster, 1978.

Green, Thomas H., S.J. *Weeds Among the Wheat Discernment: Where Prayer and Action Meet*. Notre Dame, Ind.: Ave Maria Press, 1984.

Hall, Brian P. *Developing Leadership by Stages: A Value-Based Approach to Executive Management*. London: Manohar Publications, 1979.

_____. *The Development of Consciousness: A Confluent Theory of Values*. New York: Paulist Press, 1976.

_____. *The Genesis Effect: Human and Organizational Transformation*. New York: Paulist Press, 1987.

_____. *The Personal Discernment Inventory.* New York: Paulist Press, 1980.

_____. *Shepherds and Lovers.* Ramsey, N.J.: Paulist Press, 1982.

_____. *Spiritual Connections.* Dayton, Ohio: Values Technology, 1991.

_____. *Value Clarification as Learning Process.* New York: Paulist Press, 1973.

Hall, Brian P., and Joseph Osburn. *Nog's Vision.* New York: Paulist Press, 1976.

Hall, Brian P., and Maury Smith. *Value Clarification as Learning Process: Handbook for Clergy and Christian Educators.* New York: Paulist Press, 1973.

Hall, Brian P., and Helen Thompson. *Leadership Through Values: An Approach to Personal and Organizational Development.* New York: Paulist Press, 1980.

Hall, Brian P., and Benjamin Tonna. *God's Plans for Us: A Practical Strategy for Discernment of Spirits.* New York: Paulist Press, 1980.

Hartman, Robert S. *The Structures of Values: Foundation of Scientific Axiology.* Southern Illinois University Press, 1967

Haught, John F. *The Cosmic Adventure.* New York: Paulist Press, 1984.

Hemphill, J. K. "Leader Behavior Descriptions," Columbus: Ohio State University Personnel Research Board, 1950.

Hersey, Paul, and Kenneth R. Blanchard. "Life-Cycle Theory of Leadership." *Training Development Journal,* 1969, 23 (5), 26–34.

_____. *Management of Organizational Behavior: Utilizing Human Resources.* Englewood Cliffs, N.J.: Prentice-Hall, 1972.

Heschel, A. *The Prophets.* New York: Harper & Row, 1963.

Hillman, James. *The Dream and the Underworld.* New York: Harper & Row, 1979.

Hofstede, Geert. *Cultures and Organizations: Intercultural Cooperation and Its Importance to Survival.* Glasgow: HarperCollins, 1991.

Howe, Ruel L. *Man's Need and God's Action.* Greenwich, Conn: Seabury Press, 1953.

Hudson, Frederic M. *The Adult Years: Mastering the Art of Self-Renewal.* San Francisco, Jossey-Bass, 1991.

Hutchins, Robert Maynard (ed.). *Great Books of the Western World.* Chicago: Encyclopaedia Britannica, 1952.

Ignatius of Loyola. *The Spiritual Exercises of St. Ignatius.* Translated by Louis J. Puhl. Westminster, Md.: Newman Press, no. 169.

Illich, Ivan. *Celebration of Awareness.* New York: Doubleday, 1969.

_____. *Deschooling Society.* New York: Harper & Row, 1971.

_____. *Gender.* New York: Pantheon Books, 1982.

_____. *Tools for Conviviality.* New York: Harper & Row, 1973.

_____. *Toward a History of Needs.* New York: Pantheon Books, 1978.

Jackson, Paul, S.J. (ed.). *Sharafuddin Maneri: The Hundred Letters.* New York: Paulist Press, 1980.

Jaynes, Julian. *The Origin of Consciousness in the Breakdown of the Bicameral Mind.* Boston: Houghton Mifflin, 1976.

Johnston, William. *Silent Music: The Science of Meditation.* New York: Harper & Row, 1974.

Jung, Carl G. *Collected Works.* Bollingen Series. New York: Pantheon Books, 1953–54.

_____. *Memories, Dreams, Reflections.* New York: Pantheon Books, 1963.

_____. *Psychological Types; or, The Psychology of Individuation.* Translated by H. Godwin Baynes. New York: Harcourt, Brace, 1923.

_____. *Tipi Psicologici.* Universale Scientifica. Translated by Cesare L. Musatti and Luigi Aurigemma. Torino: Editor Boringhieri, 1977.

Kaiser, Hellmuth. *Effective Psychotherapy.* Edited by Louis B. Fierman. New York: Free Press, 1965.

Kaplan, R. M., and D. P. Saccuzzo. *Psychological Testing: Principles, Applications, d Issues.* Monterey, Calif.: Brooks/Cole, 1982.

Katz, D., and R L. Kahn. *The Social Psychology of Organizations.* New York: Wiley, 1966.

Keirsey, D., and M. Bates. *Please Understand Me: An Essay on Temperament Styles.* Del Mar, Calif.: Prometheus Nemesis Books, 1978.

Kelsey, Morton T. *God, Dreams, and Revelation: A Christian Interpretation of Dreams.* Minneapolis: Augsburg Publishing House, 1974.

Kerlinger, F. N. *Behavioral Research: A Conceptual Approach.* New York: Holt, Rinehart, & Winston, 1978.

Kirschenbaum, Howard. *Advanced Value Clarification.* La Jolla, Calif.: University Associates, 1977.

_____. *On Becoming Carl Rogers.* New York: Delacorte Press, 1979.

Kluckholm, Clyde. "Values and Values Orientation in the Theory of Action," in *Toward a General Theory of Action,* by Talcott Parsons and Edward A. Shils. Boston: Harper Torchbooks, 1951.

Koestenbaum, Peter. *Existential Sexuality: Choosing to Love.* Englewood Cliffs. N.J.: Prentice Hall, 1974.

_____. *The New Image of the Person.* Westport, Conn: Greenwood Press, 1978.

Kohlberg, Lawrence. *Essays on Moral Development. Volume I: The Philosophy of Moral Development,* San Francisco: Harper & Row, 1981.

_____. *The Philosophy of Moral Development.* San Francisco: Harper & Row, 1981.

Kraeling, Emil. *The Prophets*. Chicago: Rand McNally, 1969.

Langer, Susanne K. *Philosophy in a New Key*. Cambridge: Harvard University Press, 1957.

Leech, Kenneth. *Soul Friend*. San Francisco: Harper & Row, 1977.

Leslie, Robert E. *Jesus and Logotherapy*. New York: Abingdon Press, 1965.

Lever, Janet. "Sex Differences in the Complexity of Children's Play and Games." *American Sociological Review*, 1978, 43, 471–483.

_____. "Sex Differences in the Games Children Play." *Social Problems*, 1976, 23, 418–487.

Levinson, Daniel. *The Seasons of a Man's Life*. New York: Alfred A. Knopf, 1978.

Lewis, Hunter. *A Question of Values*. New York: Harper & Row, 1990.

Likert, R. *The Human Organization*. New York: McGraw-Hill, 1967.

Likona, Thomas (ed.). *Moral Development and Behavior: Theory, Research, and Social Issues*. New York: Holt, Rinehart & Winston, 1976.

Lindblom, Johannes. *Prophecy in Ancient Israel*. Philadelphia: Fortress, 1965.

Lowen, Alexander. *Narcissism: Denial of the True Self*. New York: Macmillan, 1983.

Loye, David. *The Sphinx and the Rainbow: Brain, Mind, and Future Vision*. Boulder, Colo.: Shambhala Publications, 1983.

McCune, Shirley D. *Guide to Strategic Planning for Educators*. Alexandria, Va.: Association for Supervision and Curriculum Development, 1986.

McGregor, Douglas. *The Human Side of Enterprise*. New York: McGraw-Hill, 1960.

Maccoby, Eleanor (ed.). *The Development of Sex Differences*. Stanford. Calif.: Stanford University Press, 1966.

Mahler, Margaret. *Essays in Honor of Margaret S. Mahler: Separation-Individuation*. New York: International University Press, 1971.

_____. *On Human Symbiosis: The Vicissitudes of Individuation*. New York: Lane Medical Library, 1968.

_____. *The Psychological Birth of the Human Infant*. New York: Basic Books, 1975.

Malatesta, Edward (ed.). *Discernment of Spirits*. Collegeville, Minn.: Liturgical Press, 1970.

Maly, Eugene. *Prophets of Salvation*. New York: Herder, 1969.

Margolis, Maxine. *Mothers and Such: Views of American Women and Why They Changed*. Berkeley: University of California Press, 1984.

Maslow, Abraham. *Dominance, Self-Esteem, Self-Actualization: Germinal Papers of A. H. Maslow*. Edited by Richard J. Lowry. Monterey, Calif.: Brooks/Cole, 1973.

_____. *The Farther Reaches of Human Nature*. New York: Viking Press, 1971.

_____. *Motivation and Personality.* New York: Harper & Row, 1970.

_____ (ed.). *New Knowledge in Human Values.* New York: Penguin Books, 1959.

_____. *Religions, Values, and Peak-Experiences.* New York: Penguin Books, 1976.

_____. *Toward a Psychology of Being.* New York: D. Van Nostrand, 1968.

May, Herbert G., and Bruce M. Metzger (eds.). *The New Oxford Annotated Bible with the Apocrypha.* New York: Oxford University Press, 1962.

May, Rollo. *The Meaning of Anxiety.* New York: Pocket Books, 1977.

Messick, S. "Test Validity and the Ethics of Assessment." *American Psychologist,* 1980, 35, 1012–1027.

Miller, Jean Baker. *Toward a New Psychology of Women.* Boston: Beacon Press, 1976.

Miller, Lawrence M. *American Spirit: Visions of a New Corporate Culture.* New York: Warner Books, 1984.

Milne, A. A. *The House at Pooh Corner.* New York: E. P. Dutton, 1928.

Mische, Gerald, and Patricia Mische. *Toward a Human World Order.* New York: Paulist Press, 1977.

Mowvley, Harry. *Reading the Old Testament Prophets Today.* Atlanta: John Knox, 1979.

Murphy, J. M., and C. Gilligan. "Moral Development in Late Adolescence and Adulthood: A Critique and Reconstruction of Kohlberg's Theory." *Human Development,* 1980, 23, 77–104.

Murphy, Roland. *Seven Books of Wisdom.* Milwaukee: Bruce, 1960.

Myers, I. B. *Gifts Differing.* Palo Alto. Calif.: Consulting Psychologists Press, 1980.

Naisbitt, John. *Megatrends.* New York: Warner Books, 1982.

Nelson, Harry and Robert Jurmain. *Introduction to Physical Anthropology.* St. Paul, Minn.: West, 1987.

Neumann, Erich. *The Origins and History of Consciousness.* Translated by R.F.C. Hull. Princeton, N.J. : Princeton University Press, 1954.

Nicholls, J., R. A. Pearl, and B. G. Licht. "On the Validity of Inferences About Personality Constructs." *Psychological Bulletin,* 1983, 94, 188–190.

Oden, Thomas C. *The Structures of Awareness.* Nashville, Tenn.: Abingdon Press, 1969.

O'Leary, Virginia E. *Toward Understanding Women.* Monterey, Calif., Brooks/Cole, 1977.

Ornstein, R. *The Psychology of Consciousness.* San Francisco: W. H. Freeman, 1975.

Ornstein, Robert, and Paul Ehrlich. *New World, New Mind: Moving Toward Conscious Evolution.* New York: Doubleday, 1989.

Ouchi, William G. *The M-Form Society: How American Teamwork Can Capture the Competitive Edge.* Reading, Mass.: Addison-Wesley, 1984.

_____. *Theory Z: How American Business Can Meet the Japanese Challenge.* Reading, Mass.: Addison-Wesley, 1981.

Peck, M. S. *People of the Lie: The Hope for Healing Human Evil.* New York: Simon & Schuster, 1983.

_____. *The Road Less Traveled: A New Psychology of Love, Traditional Values, and Spiritual Growth.* New York: Simon & Schuster, 1978.

Peters, Thomas J., and Robert H. Waterman, Jr. *In Search of Excellence.* New York: Warner Books, 1982.

Petterson, James Allan. *Counseling and Values: A Philosophical Examination.* Cranston, R.I.: Carrol Press, 1976.

Pfeiffer, J. William, and Leonard D. Goodstein (eds.). *The 1984 Annual: Developing Human Resources.* San Diego, Calif.: University Associates, 1984.

Poulain, Augustin F. *The Graces of Interior Prayer.* Translated by Leonora L. Yorke Smith. Westminster, Vt.: Celtic Cross Books, 1978.

Previte-Orton, C. W. *The Shorter Cambridge Medieval History*, Volumes 1–11. Cambridge: Cambridge University Press, 1953.

Progoff, Ira. *The Practice of Process Meditation: The Intensive Journal Way to Spiritual Experience.* New York: Dialogue House Library, 1980.

_____. *The Symbolic and the Real: A New Psychological Approach to the Fuller Experience of Personal Existence.* New York: McGraw-Hill, 1973.

Rad, Gerhard. *The Message of the Prophets.* New York: Harpers, 1977.

_____. *Wisdom in Israel.* Translated by James Martin. Nashville, Tenn.: Abingdon, 1972.

Rahner, Hugo. *Ignatius the Theologian.* London: Chapman, 1968.

Raths, Louis E., Merrill Harmin, and Sidney B. Simon. *Values and Teaching: Working with Values in the Classroom.* Columbus, Ohio: Charles E. Merrill, 1966.

Rawls, John. *A Theory of Justice.* Cambridge: Harvard University Press, 1971.

Reeves, Clement. *The Psychology of Rollo May.* San Francisco: Jossey-Bass, 1977.

Reid, David P. *What Are They Saying About the Prophets?* New York: Paulist Press, 1980.

Restak, R. "The Hemispheres of the Brain Have Minds of Their Own." *New York Times,* January 25, 1976.

Richards, Sister Innocentia, Ph.D. *Discernment of Spirits.* Collegeville, Minn.: Liturgical Press, 1970.

Roberts, David E. *Psychotherapy and a Christian View of Man.* New York: Charles Scribner's Sons, 1950.

Rokeach, Milton. *Beliefs, Attitudes, and Values: A Theory of Organization and Change.* San Francisco: Jossey-Bass, 1968.

_____. The Nature of *Human Values.* New York: Free Press, 1973.

_____. *The Three Christs of Ypsilanti: A Psychological Study.* New York: Knopf, 1964.

_____ (ed.). *Understanding Human Values: Individual and Societal.* New York: Free Press, 1979.

Rokeach, Milton, Richard Bonier, et al. *The Open and Closed Mind: Investigations into the Nature of Belief Systems and Personality Systems.* New York: Basic Books, 1960.

Ross, Maggie. *The Fire of Your Life.* New York: Paulist Press, 1983

Rubin, Lillian. *Intimate Strangers: Men and Women Together.* New York: Harper & Row, 1983.

_____. *Worlds of Pain.* New York: Basic Books, 1976.

Ruch, Richard S., and Ronald Goodman. *Image at the Top.* New York: Free Press, 1983.

Ryckman, Richard M. *Theories of Personality.* New York: D. Van Nostrand, 1978.

Sakaiya, Taichi. *The Knowledge Value Revolution, or, a History of the Future.* Tokyo: Kodansha International, 1991.

Sartre, Jean-Paul. *Being and Nothingness: An Essay on Phenomonological Ontology.* New York: Washington Square Press, 1956.

Scarf, Maggie. *Unfinished Business.* New York: Doubleday, 1980.

Schein, Edgar R., *Organizational Culture and Leadership.* San Francisco: Jossey-Bass. 1992.

Schumacher, E. F. *A Guide for the Perplexed.* New York: Harper & Row, 1977.

_____. *Small Is Beautiful.* New York: Harper & Row, 1973.

Sebald, Hans. *Momism: The Silent Disease of America.* Chicago: Nelson Hall, 1976.

Selg, Ottfried. *Wege Zu Gelebten Werten,* Augsburg: OSA-Verlag, 1990.

Senge, Peter M. *The Fifth Discipline: The Art and Practice of the Learning Organization.* New York: Doubleday, 1990.

Sheehy, Gail. *Passages.* New York: Dutton, 1976.

Simon, Sidney B., Leland W. Howe, and Howard Kirschenbaum. *Values Clarification: A Handbook of Practical Strategies for Teachers and Students.* New York: Hart, 1972.

Sobel, Robert. *I.B.M.: Colossus in Transition.* New York: Bantam Books, 1983.

Soleri, Paolo. *Archeology: The City in the Image of Man.* Cambridge, Mass: MIT Press, 1969.

Sowa, J. F. *Conceptual Structures: Information Processing in Mind and Machine.* Palo Alto, Calif.: Addison-Wesley, 1984.

Spence, J. T., and R. L. Helmreich. "Beyond Face Validity: A Solution." *Psychological Bulletin,* 1983, 94, 181–184.

Spencer, Anih. *Mothers Are People Too: A Contemporary Analysis of Motherhood.* New York: Paulist Press, 1984.

_____. Seasons: *Women's Search for Self through Life's Stages.* New York: Paulist Press, 1984.

Springer, Sally P., and Geog Deutsch. *Left Brain, Right Brain.* San Francisco: W. H. Freeman, 1989.

Stack, Carol B. *All Our Kin: Strategies for Survival in a Black Community.* New York: HarperCollins, 1983.

Stevens, Anthony. *Archetypes: The Natural History of the Self.* New York: Quill, 1983.

Stevens, Edward. *Business Ethics.* New York: Paulist Press, 1979.

Stogdill, R. M. *Handbook of Leadership.* New York, Free Press, 1974.

Sue, Donald W. (ed.). *Counseling the Culturally Different: Theory and Practice.* New York: John Wiley, 1990.

Tenopyr, M. L. "Content-Construct Confusion." *Personnel Psychology,* 1977, 30, 47–54.

Tillich, Paul. *The Courage to Be.* New Haven: Yale University Press, 1952.

_____. Systematic *Theology:* Chicago: University of Chicago Press, 1963.

Toffler, Alvin. *Future Shock.* New York: Random House, 1970.

_____. Power Shift. New York: Bantam Books, 1990.

Toner, Jules, S.J. *A Commentary on St. Ignatius' Rules for the Discernment of Spirits.* St. Louis: Institute of Jesuit Sources, 1982.

Tonna, Benjamin. *Gospel for the Cities: A Socio-Theology of Urban Ministry.* Translated by William E. Jerman. Maryknoll, N.Y.: Orbis Books, 1982.

Tournier, Paul. *The Meaning of Persons.* New York: Harper & Row, 1957.

Underhill, Evelyn. *Mysticism.* New York: Meridian Books, 1955.

Van der Hoop, J. H. *Conscious Orientation.* New York: Harcourt Brace, 1939.

Vaughn, F. *Awakening Intuition.* New York: Anchor Books, 1979.

Villiant, George. *Adaptation to Life.* Boston: Little, Brown, 1977.

Vroom, V. H., and E. L. Deci. *Management and Motivation.* New York: Penguin, 1970.

Wadsworth, Barry J. *Piaget's Theory of Cognitive Development.* New York: David McKay, 1971.

Waterman, Robert H. *The Renewal Factor: How the Best Get and Keep the Competitive Edge*. New York: Bantam Books, 1988.

Weber, Max. *The Protestant Ethic and the Spirit of Capitalism*. Translated by Talcott Parsons. London: George Allen & Unwin, 1976.

Wheatley, Margaret J. *Leadership and the New Science*. San Francisco: Berrett-Koehler, 1992.

Wheeler, Daniel D., and Irving L. Janis. *A Practical Guide for Making Decisions*. New York: Free Press, 1980.

Wilber, Ken. *A Sociable God*. New York: New Press, 1983.

Wilson, Robert R. *Prophecy and Society in Ancient Israel*. Philadelphia: Fortress, 1980.

Wolf, Fred Alan. *Star Wave: Mind, Consciousness, and Quantum Physics*. New York: Macmillan, 1984.

Wright, John H. "Discernment of Spirits in the New Testament." *Communio*, 1974, 1, 2.

Wyssm, Dieter. *Depth Psychology: A Critical History*. New York: W. W. Norton, 1966.

Yalom, Irvin D. *Existential Psychotherapy*. New York: Basic Books, 1980.

_____. Inpatient *Group Psychotherapy*. New York: Basic Books, 1983.

_____. The Theory *and Practice of Group Psychotherapy*. New York: Basic Books, 1975.

Index

Hall-Tonna Values Map

Phases	Phase I SURVIVING "the world is a mystery over which I have no control" PRE-CONVENTIONAL		Phase II BELONGING "the world is a problem with which I must cope" CONVENTIONAL		Phase III SELF-INITIATING "the world is a creative project in which I want to participate" POST-CONVENTIONAL		Phase IV INTERDEPENDENT "the world is a mystery for which we care on a global scale" GLOBAL ETHIC & MORALITY	
Stages	1: SAFETY	2: SECURITY	3: FAMILY	4: INSTITUTION	5: VOCATION	6: NEW ORDER	7: WISDOM	8: WORLD ORDER
Goals Values	**Goals** Self-Interest/Control Self Preservation Wonder/Awe/Fate	**Goals** Physical Delight Security	**Goals** Family/Belonging Fantasy/Play Self Worth	**Goals** Belief/Philosophy/Values Competence/Confidence Play/Recreation Work/Wealth/Value	**Goals** Equality/Liberation Integration/Wholeness Self Actualization Service/Vocation	**Goals** Art/Beauty Being Self Construction/New Order Contemplation Faith/Risk/Vision Human Dignity Knowledge/Insight Presence	**Goals** Intimacy/Solitude Truth/Wisdom	**Goals** Ecority Global Harmony Word
Means Values	**Means** Food/Warmth/Shelter Function/Physical Safety/Survival	**Means** Affection/Physical Economics/Profit Property/Control Sensory Pleasure Territory/Security Wonder/Curiosity	**Means** Being Liked Care/Nurture Control/Order/Discipline Courtesy/Hospitality Dexterity/Co-ordination Endurance/Patience Equilibrium Friendship/Belonging Obedience/Duty Prestige/Image Rights/Respect Social Affirmation Support/Peer Tradition	**Means** Achievement/Success Administration/Control Communication/Info Competition Design/Pattern/Order Duty/Obligation Economics/Success Education/Certification Efficiency/Planning Hierarchy/Order Honor Law/Rule Loyalty/Fidelity Management Membership/Institution Ownership Patriotism/Esteem Productivity Reason Responsibility Rule/Accountability Technology/Science Unity/Uniformity Workmanship/Art/Craft	**Means** Adaptability/Flexibility Authority/Honesty Congruence Decision/Initiation Empathy Equity/Rights Expressiveness/Joy Generosity/Compassion Health/Healing Independence Law/Guide Limitation/Acceptance Mutual Obedience Quality/Evaluation Relaxation Search/Meaning/Hope Self Assertion Sharing/Listening/Trust	**Means** Accountability/Ethics Collaboration Community/Supportive Complementarity Corporation/Stewardship Creativity Detachment/Solitude Discernment Education/Knowledge Growth/Expansion Intimacy Justice/Social Order Leisure Limitation/Celebration Mission/Objectives Mutual Accountability Pioneerism/Innovation Research Ritual/Communication Simplicity/Play Unity/Diversity	**Means** Community/Personalist Interdependence Minessence Prophet/Vision Synergy Transcendence/Solitude	**Means** Convivial Technology Global Justice Human Rights Macroeconomics

Value Cluster	F O U N D A T I O N							F O C U S								V I S I O N				
Steps %	0	1	2	3	4	5	6	7	8	9	10	11	12	13	14	15	16	17	18	19	20/21

Cycles	CYCLE 1 AUTHORITARIAN	CYCLE 2 BENEVOLENT Transition 1 Locus Control: External Responsibility: Internal	CYCLE 3 MANAGER	CYCLE 4 FACILITATOR Transition 2 Locus Control: Internal Responsibility: Internal	CYCLE 5 COLLABORATOR	CYCLE 6 SERVANT-Transformational Transition 3 Locus Control: External WE Responsibility: Internal WE	CYCLE 7 VISIONARY

© 2004 Values Technology